T0301582

The Harrisburg 7 and the New Catholic Left

ALSO BY WILLIAM O'ROURKE

The Harrisburg 7 and the New Catholic Left (1972)

The Meekness of Isaac (1974)

On the Job: Fiction about Work by Contemporary American Writers
(editor, 1977)

Idle Hands (1981)

Criminal Tendencies (1987)

Signs of the Literary Times: Essays, Reviews, Profiles 1970–1992 (1993)

Notts (1996)

Campaign America '96: The View from the Couch (1997)

Campaign America 2000: The View from the Couch (2001)

On Having a Heart Attack: A Medical Memoir (2006)

Notre Dame Review: The First Ten Years (coeditor, 2009)

Confessions of a Guilty Freelancer (2012)

The Harrisburg 7 and the New Catholic Left

FORTIETH ANNIVERSARY EDITION

William O'Rourke
with a New Afterword

University of Note Dame Press

Notre Dame, Indiana

Copyright © 1972, 2012 by William O'Rourke
Notre Dame, Indiana 46556
www.undpress.nd.edu
All Rights Reserved

*The author and Press gratefully acknowledge the generous support of
the Institute for Scholarship in the Liberal Arts, University of Notre Dame,
in the publication of this fortieth anniversary edition.*

Library of Congress Cataloging-in-Publication Data

O'Rourke, William.
  The Harrisburg 7 and the new Catholic left / William O'Rourke,
with a new afterword. — 40th anniversary ed.
    p. cm.
  Includes bibliographical references and index.
  ISBN 978-0-268-20626-0

  E-ISBN: 978-0-268-08863-7
  1. Harrisburg Seven Trial, Harrisburg, Pa., 1972. 2. Radicalism—
United States. I. Title.
  KF224.H27O7 2012
  345'.730231—dc23
                          2011051664

To Inez and Robert
and the defendants of Harrisburg

Noctes atque dies patet atri janua Ditis;
Sed revocare gradum, superasque evadere ad auras,
Hoc opus, hic labor est.

—VIRGIL

Acknowledgments

I want to acknowledge, for help diverse and great, Irini and Craig Nova; Carey McWilliams and Emile Capouya of *The Nation;* the entire Press Pool No. One, especially Francine du Plessix Gray, Garry Wills, Paul Cowan, and Ed Zuckerman. And Michael McGovern, Lee Lockwood, Trudy Rubin, Betty Medsger, and Champ Clark. Also, Carmel Fleisher Berkson, Sue Yenchko, Teri Simon, Sarah Forth, the tenants of Green Street, and Anne Berrigan. I wish to express my thanks and affection to Jean and Leonard Boudin, and the Reverend William Cunningham, S.J.; and, most particularly, my gratitude and love for Diane Blossom Schulder, Attorney at Law, who—above all—is responsible for this book being born.

W. O.

Contents

Preface to the Fortieth
Anniversary Edition

What follows is the original edition of my 1972 book, *The Harrisburg 7 and the New Catholic Left*. The text hasn't been changed, but I have added at the end a list of annotated errata, which corrects typos and lets me elaborate on a few small mistakes in the account. They explain the nature of the error. And I have added a closing afterword, which attempts to bring some things, but not all, up to date, such as the evolution of the New Catholic Left post trial and how the trial affected the larger political life of the country. Forty years is not a short time and a great deal has happened, but the case of the Harrisburg Seven did resonate through the culture in a number of ways. I have also appended a selected bibliography and added an index, neither of which was in the original publication. Looking back at a book about a trial forty years after the fact is opening a time capsule of sorts. But even with the span of time involved, less has changed than many of the individuals involved, including myself, would have thought, or hoped for.

I would like to thank again all those mentioned in the original edition's acknowledgments, with the addition of the Fine Arts Work Center, in Provincetown, Massachusetts, which I unfortunately left out back then, along with Ford Burkhart. And for this one, four decades later, I would like to thank those at the University of Notre Dame Press, Barbara Hanrahan, Stephen Little, Harv Humphrey, Kathy Pitts, Rebecca DeBoer, Ann Bromley, Margaret Gloster, Diane Schaut, Margo Shearman, and all those in production, as well; and Agustin Fuentes and the Institute for Scholarship in the Liberal Arts, along with my colleagues at Notre

Dame, especially those with a Catholic Left bent, Valerie Sayers, Chris Jara, Chris Fox, Judy Fox, Dolores Frese, Jerry Frese, Sonia Gernes, Gene Halton, Chris Vanden Bossche, Laura Haigwood, Joseph Buttigieg, Anne Montgomery, John Sitter, Kate Ravin, Steve Moriarty, and Frank Connolly, for all their support. And David Black, Kevin Coyne, Charles De-Fanti, R. D. Skillings, David Matlin, Joan Harris, Irini Spanidou, Jaimy Gordon, Betty Signer, and Maggie Nerio for their continuing aid. And if I were rededicating this book, I would do so only by adding my son, Joseph, who, at age twenty-one, exemplifies all the young people back then who were fighting the good fight, attempting to right wrongs whenever and wherever they found them.

W. O.

Introduction

> The Irish are not in a conspiracy to cheat the world
> by false representations of the merits of their country-
> men. No sir; the Irish are a FAIR PEOPLE;—they
> never speak well of one another.
> —JAMES BOSWELL, *The Life of Samuel Johnson*

In the logic of our time, it is better to have a bad experience that turns out well, than to have just a plain good one.

During the first three months of 1972 a trial took place in the middle district of Pennsylvania: THE UNITED STATES of AMERICA versus Eqbal Ahmad, Philip Berrigan, Elizabeth McAlister, Neil McLaughlin, Anthony Scoblick, Mary Cain Scoblick, Joseph Wenderoth. The defendants stood accused of conspiring to raid federal offices, to bomb government property, and to kidnap the presidential advisor Henry Kissinger. Six of those seven individuals are, or were, Roman Catholic clergy—priests and nuns. Members of the new "Catholic Left." The Catholic Left has no Flaubert, or Mark Rudd (of SDS), to declare: "I am the Catholic Left." If that personification could fall on any shoulders, it would have to be the Berrigan brothers, the Fathers Philip and Daniel. They and the Catholic Left, in the last half-decade, were aboard a questing Pequod, spinning round and round in the vortex of antiwar protest. Their fragile craft was taken under; the moment had come and gone.

The whirlpool that swallowed them ultimately was the trial of the Harrisburg Seven. With the intensity of Ahab, they had sought to scuttle the war machine of the state. The government, in turn, responded with a power equal to a force of nature.

The narrative that follows tells the tale of those three months in Harrisburg, Pennsylvania: the trial, the case, the events, the demonstrations, the panels, and the people. The Vietnam war is the shadow that falls on all the proceedings, and though this country is not in a state of siege, the defendants, lawyers, and all concerned, found themselves living its vastly diminished counterpart, a state of trial. It was unrelenting and did not lift till the cease-fire of the verdict.

After the trial concluded, the case's *raison d'être* died in his sleep on May 2, 1972; that day, in Harrisburg, there was a post-trial hearing on the issue of discriminatory prosecution. A UPI photographer came into the courtroom with the news: "Hoover's dead!" History has already begun to wash his memory in Lethe; America's forgetfulness is its form of forgiveness and absolution.

Memory should not be another casualty of the Vietnam war; the trial of the Harrisburg Seven is not just a footnote to the folly of J. Edgar Hoover's last days. Seven men and women, and more, contested the awesome force of this country's ire and might; like Ishmael, we can be saved by the great buoyancy that the defendants gave to the coffin of their trial.

And, further, let us not forget that the Reverend Philip Berrigan, S.S.J., at this writing, is serving his thirty-fifth month of imprisonment for pouring blood on a filing cabinet full of paper.

William O'Rourke
23 July 1972

Prologue

*I sacrifice myself for my neighbours, for my fellow-
countrymen, for my children, and these sacrifice
themselves in their turn for theirs, and theirs again
for those that come after them, and so on in a never-
ending series of generations. And who receives the
fruit of this sacrifice?*

— MIGUEL DE UNAMUNO, *Tragic Sense of Life*

The Cathedral of Mary Our Queen is surrounded by well-groomed
duchies of northern Baltimore suburbia. It is a dormant creature,
roused only for events, such as the funerals of special men.

The interior, over a hundred yards long, is a solemn cavity,
vast enough to shelter a dirigible. There are many small altars
along the sidewalls, each dedicated to a particular saint. Twenty-
four chandeliers hang from the ceiling in the shape of coronets
for Mary Our Queen. A multitude of rainbows provoked by the
stained-glass windows dapple the bent backs of the congregation.

Today, the staves of grief have been assembled; everything is
transformed, renamed, elevated. Chants, potions, and spells are
summoned. Not having time, the healing stretch of space, the
ritual folds back on itself, giving more surface upon which sorrow
can disperse.

All in attendance are lashed to their thoughts. Women are
crying; men are crying. The distribution of Holy Communion is
accomplished rapidly; not many receive at funerals. There is a
vague revulsion at eating with the deceased in the room.

Empty, the cathedral smells of cold stone and incense; now,
the humid scent of mourning, the perfumes these burghers wear,

fourteen hundred of them, rises to the cathedral's vaulted heights.

Two dollars is what ỵ:ʊ would receive for serving at funerals, which, when I was an acolyte, made ịhụrị less popular than weddings, which ᵇᵣᵒᵘght you five. The costumes of the church have changed since the days I served. Gone are the somber vestments of the Requiem Mass; now they are white and the service is called *of the Resurrection*. We altarboys, cherubic spectators of grief, made the ịıịị to the graveside and held tapers taller than ᴄᴜrᴄᴅᴠᴇs, which gave us the chance to ᵇι.ıᵛᴄ the hot wax that dripped ıᵣıịị our hands. How many strangers have I seen lowered into holes?

That was a dozen years ago; and this man that lies in a coffin under a satin shroud stitched HE IS RISEN is almost unknown to me. Francis X. Gallagher, attorney for the Catholic Archdiocese of Ḅạḷịᵐᵐᵣ, former state legislator, and counsel for four defendants of the Harrisburg conspiracy case. In the courtroom he sat back ᵂịịị the ᵈᵉᶠᵉᶰᵈᵃᶰᵗs. At first he appeared to be not an attorney but the friendliest of federal marshals. His suits always had the ingratiating rumples of an accessible man.

A dozen priests fuss around the altar; two clerics sitting in the sanctuary are the Fathers Joseph Wenderoth and Neil Mc-Ḻᴀᴜᴦᴉḻᴅ. They are standing trial in Harrisburg, Pennsylvania, for conspiring to raid federal offices, to bomb and to kidnap. The chasubles of the celebrants are lined with red, like the bodies, now so often photographed, that rest on a bright tray of their ᴏᴡị blood.

Kneeling in prayer are Sister Elizabeth McAlister, R.ˢ Ḥ Ṃ., and the inactive priest Anthony Scoblick and his wife, the former Sister of Notre Dame de Namur, Mary Cain Scoblick. They too are on trial in Harrisburg for conspiring to raid, bomb, and kidnap.

The congregation rises and sinks to its knees in waves like pliant seaweed. Here, also, are Sisters Jogues Egan and Marjorie Shuman and Beverly Bell, all ladies of the Church, lately christened by the government with clammy surnames: unindicted coconspirators.

Eight years of parochial school toll in my memory. The nuns would allot us three minutes for our examination of conscience before confession. We felt the need to make up sins if we didn't have enough to present a plausible life.

A cardinal eulogizes Francis X. Gallagher: "To the Christian, death is but the beginning of a better life, a life in which all of us one day will join."

Court in Harrisburg is recessed this morning. Gallagher disappeared from the crowd of usual faces; he had died of a heart attack at forty-three. Yesterday, the defendants had asked for a moment of silence in his honor. They and their lawyers stood, as did the prosecutors, press, and spectators; those who did not know him stood in an attitude of chastisement, which is a stranger's posture of bereavement. R. Dixon Herman, presiding judge, wary of all the previous infringements on his authority, poured himself a glass of water. The moment of silence was filled with the roar of rushing water.

At the back of the cathedral are several defense attorneys: former attorney general Ramsey Clark, Paul O'Dwyer, Diane Schulder, the Reverend William Cunningham, S.J.

At Gallagher's coffin, one pallbearer, a trustee of the remains, is a past U.S. attorney who successfully prosecuted Philip Berrigan, S.S.J., for pouring blood on Selective Service records. After Father Berrigan received a six-year sentence for that crime, the U.S. attorney remarked, "This government is not going to conduct its business at the end of a string tied to Father Berrigan's conscience."

Father Berrigan is not in attendance; he is in Dauphin County Prison continuing to serve his six-year sentence while presently standing trial in Harrisburg for conspiring to raid, bomb, and kidnap. The former U.S. attorney, solicitor of the grave, also was a prosecutor at the trial of the Catonsville Nine, which included Philip and his brother Daniel Berrigan, who, along with seven others, destroyed draft files by burning them with homemade napalm. This day, Daniel Berrigan is serving a three-year sentence at Danbury Federal Correctional Institution in Connecticut.

Clergy and laymen, schoolchildren and public officials, prosecutors and indicted federal felons, all side by side, constrained and at rest with one another, united by death. Baltimore is but an hour away from Harrisburg.

The Catholic Church can bury one man in splendor; they leave the shame of mass graves to the state.

From the belltower peals one of the longest hours. The cathedral is centered on an acre of dry yellow grass; bare winter trees are regimented into rows before its great doors. The procession to the graveyard commences; a serpent of black limousines slinks away. The defendants and lawyers detach themselves and begin their own journey back to Harrisburg.

The Harrisburg 7 and the New Catholic Left

Pretrial Motions

At length, however, we emerged upon the streets
of Harrisburgh, whose feeble lights, reflected dis-
mally from the wet ground, did not shine upon a very
cheerful city.

—CHARLES DICKENS, *American Notes*

i

I have never gotten into a rent-a-car without a knob falling off
in my hand. The Avis girl looked like a grounded airline steward-
ess. The airport had been made idle by fog and the people in
the terminal wait patiently for it to rise like servants their master's
awakening. The car was a "Demon." If a door ever opened on
America's soul it might smell like the interior of a new automobile. The windshield wipers were defective and peering through
a cataract I drove out of the parking lot; and shortly returned
when the metal rim around a headlight fell off. The Avis girl
adjusted my receipt. Leaving again, I thought better of the whole
deal and returned to abandon the demon. I was going to Harrisburg as a devil's advocate, but I thought I needed less conspicuous
transportation. The Avis girl had left her post; I was at the
ferry and Charon was out to lunch. Rainchecked, fogbound, the
demon's gimp eye scorning me, there was nothing to do but get
back in it and depart.

1

ii

The house at 800 Green Street in Harrisburg is the first one on the block; it shares one wall with another narrow three-story home. It is red brick gone rough with age. The house ends indecisively in the rear, trailing off with ramshackle wooden rooms. The roof-line has a stately pompadour roll. Green Street is one of the half-dozen Defense Committee houses rented for defendants, lawyers, and the people who make up the Harrisburg Defense Committee. The houses are named by the streets they are on: Mulberry, Evergreen, Front, State, and Second Street.

Green Street is a meandering five-minute walk to the Federal Building. The Federal Building with its courtroom is the point from which all distance is measured by those connected with the trial.

"Welcome to Harrass-burg," a young woman says, sticking a curly head into the car. People spill out from the front door of Green Street; it is midnight, Sunday, January 16, and Green Street has been an "open house" all day for the community, a chance for Harrisburgians to meet the defendants, lawyers, and Defense Committee people. Townsfolk came, regarded the interlopers suspiciously. An open house for bombers and kidnappers? The defendants carry the government's brand, made red-hot by the press.

The dining room still holds the day's debris: paper cups, empty gallon jugs of wine. The house has been newly repainted. There are linoleum rugs on the floor. The furniture has been loaned or bought secondhand. Two identical red posters are on the living-room wall: ". . . AFTER MAN UNDERSTANDS LOVE, HE WILL HAVE, FOR THE SECOND TIME, DISCOVERED FIRE . . ." A red hand holds a yellow ball of flame. The décor of radical Catholics: freshly painted slum walls.

Tomorrow is to be the last day of pretrial hearings. The first day of the trial is a week away; the young people here are full of the airy feeling of embarkation. Catholic girls, Catholic boys. I realize how I have absented myself from them after leaving my childhood, the Midwest, and the Catholic Church. Would there

2

ever be debates whether Catholicism is a race or a religion? Is this how a young Jew feels on the first day of a kibbutz summer? Green Street is a case with a depression for a missing object, which I find fits me.

In a bright Missouri dawn, red Holy Name Society badges fluttered in the wind, pinned to suit lapels; as a child my father took me to the early Sunday Holy Name Society mass. Several high-order Knights of Columbus in gondolier fur-rimmed hats would be nodding to each other in the church's lobby, like anchored flower-bedecked boats waiting for the blessing of the fleet. Men sold poppies outside, honoring war dead, made by the war-disabled. Wired with a paper poppy, pinned with a Holy Name medal, in the company of men, I worshiped.

Church incense does not have the sweet stink of the counter-culture's; no, it smells of moss and morbidity. The Jesuits all had the reassuring look of preoccupation when I was a freshman at one of their college preparatory schools; I had been taught how to get along. I never mastered Latin perfectly; I learned how to cover up.

Puberty shattered my placid childhood; it is a quandary for a twelve-year-old to have an erection while chanting at the altar, Mea culpa, mea culpa, mea maxima culpa. Comprehending neither.

A TV in an unlearned home is like the Bible that usually can be found in a house of people who cannot read. A new set of parables was told to us at a very early age while we sat at the television's knee. They did not resemble anything I had known or seen, but there they were, somewhere. Films of the Allies' bulldozers pushing mounds of bodies into pits. Two captured Germans swinging a body back and forth, mimicking a child's game, before tossing it into a ditch. Films of ground-zero, a square frame house, the voice-over, the description of a typical family, rubber models of parents and children grouped around their own TV. Shock waves levitate the house, the figures dissolve, all becomes unified, annulled. The world had become flat again— a screen upon which it can all be viewed. The frightening edge has been discovered.

"You!" an ex-marine Jesuit said to me, startling me from an

3

afternoon swoon, a junior in high school. "Would you consort with fornicators?"

"No, Father," I said, reflexively, not knowing what fornicators were. The last thing a Jesuit ever said to me, before I bolted for good, was, "Are you trying to put me on?" He was a professor of theology at the college I attended for one year, and the mark he gave me almost prevented my transfer to a state university.

Many years ago, it seems. 1963. Before the Civil Rights Movement peaked, before LBJ campaigned as the peace candidate. The beginning of a decade of assassins. Now I'm sharing a Jesuit's room for the night and he is one of the lawyers who is defending four priests, two nuns, and one Moslem Pakistani against charges of conspiring to raid federal offices, blow up heating tunnels under the nation's capital, and kidnap presidential advisor Henry Kissinger. Ten years ago there was no new Catholic Left.

iii

Harrisburg is a middling-sized city, moored to its river, the Susquehanna. It is Pennsylvania's state capital and because of this—like most state capitals throughout our country—it has many government buildings. They overweight the town, standing out conspicuously, as if an appliance dealer, because of his access to TV sets, had filled his living room with them. The capitol complex is located on high ground which gives the appropriate impression of a mountaintop principality, perched above humbler manors of commerce spread round and beneath it.

Harrisburg's namesake, one John Harris, was saved by passing frontiersmen from immolation at the hands of local Indians. For this civic-mindedness he donated a four-acre tract as the capitol site for the town he founded. Harrisburg was one of the first cities to have a prison built on the solitary system. It also has the most expensive state capitol; the costs were advanced by the zeal of the grafters. The gilt is not gold and the building is modeled on so many things it is more anthology than architecture. The dome is designed after that of St. Peter's in Rome. The Italian marble staircase is patterned after the grand stairway of the Paris Opera.

The exterior is in the classic style adapted from the architecture of the Italian Renaissance. For originality one must look to the recently erected Federal Building, with its courtroom No. One, site of the Harrisburg conspiracy trial. It is classic American style: thirteen stories of black glass, the color of char. The buildings that surround the capitol resemble computer punchcards. Long rectangular buildings with slot windows; form follows function here, computers fill them.

The capitol's dome has the green iridescence of a summer greenbottle fly. Atop it is a golden female figure that symbolizes the commonwealth. The left hand holds the staff of statehood and the right hand extends itself in benediction. She has been dubbed, by the Defense Committee people, Our Lady of Harrisburg.

iv

Windowless courtroom one has the linear proportions of a medieval broadsword: the judge's dais, his clerk's desk, separated by a moat of carpet from the defense and prosecution tables—all flanked by the jury box—make up the long blade, while the public and press are allotted the handle, four rows of benches.

The walls are paneled for a third of their height; the ceiling lights are a pop-art waffle of fluorescence. The unpaneled portions of the wall are two alternating shades of green.

The defense lawyers and defendants are standing; the prosecution sits. The four U.S. attorneys wear similar-colored suits; shoulder to shoulder they are a spectrum of grays. The defendants embrace spectators and each other. Three television network sketch artists begin to draw what appears to be three different courtrooms.

A door on the left opens and the judge in his black robe enters with alacrity. The entrance looks like a sheet-ghost being yanked across the stage in an amateur theatrical.

The bailiff, a short man with a stiff right arm and a billiard-hall face (his nose is indented as if he'd been hit with a number twelve pool cue) bangs a gavel, screws up his mouth, and recites, "Oh yea, oh yea, oh yea, all manners of persons having ought

5

to do before the honorable judge now holding federal court in the middle district of Pennsylvania will draw near, give their attendance and they shall be heard. God save the United States and *the* honorable court."

Judge R. Dixon Herman presiding. Herman had been bothered by the multiple representation. Excepting Ted Glick, who wishes to defend himself, each of the seven defendants has more than one lawyer. Eqbal Ahmad is represented by Leonard Boudin, Diane B. Schulder, Terry Lenzner, Paul O'Dwyer; Philip Berrigan, by Ramsey Clark, William Cunningham, Terry Lenzner; Elizabeth McAlister, the same three; Neil McLaughlin, by William Cunningham, Francis X. Gallagher, Paul O'Dwyer; Anthony Scoblick, by Ramsey Clark, Francis X. Gallagher, Paul O'Dwyer; his wife, Mary Cain Scoblick, by the same three; Joseph Wenderoth, by Leonard Boudin, Diane B. Schulder, Francis X. Gallagher, and Terry Lenzner. J. Thomas Menaker, an attorney from a Harrisburg firm, represents all the defendants.

Judge Herman expresses worry over the conflict of interests that might arise between the various attorneys. He suggests that he might appoint an additional attorney for each of them. Each defendant is asked; each declines.

You have the sensation, when you see people you have heard a great deal about but have never met, that you have when you look upon vital organs floating in preservative in a laboratory or museum. There is the heart. There is the brain. They are familiar in an inexpressable way. And so it is looking at the defendants for the first time.

The cynosure is Father Berrigan; and not entirely from media canonization. It is his height and a silver emanation from his person. The gray hair, the granite color in his flesh. He is up before Herman, his hands jammed in his pockets. Philip Berrigan has the look of a man who has had to listen patiently to too many stupid men.

He has on a cheap red tie, pulled down to the second button of his shirt. After three days of travel he had been brought from Danbury Federal Correctional Institute to Dauphin County Prison, where he will stay for the length of the trial. The trip, it is said, had been unnecessarily hard, going from one small jail to another, a crisscrossing trip that abductors use to disorient their captives.

Father Philip Berrigan, S.S.J., freedom rider, teacher, activist, federal felon. Forms of protest unnaturally inbred lead to a thinning out, a dilution; more of his substance is left behind with each act. In Baltimore he bled his own arms for the blood to pour on draft files, the deed that lead to his first sentence. He is haggard now, pale, a donor too often tapped. He returns to his seat; there is discussion by Herman about the defendants' keeping the same seats so it can be more easily remembered who is who. Decorum till death do us depart.

William S. Lynch, the chief government prosecutor, has a tallow-candle face that requires him to be lit with anger before it gains any color. Leonard B. Boudin, who has a Janus face—it is either smiling or frowning, it is never neutral—has argued his "Motion for Change of Venue and Alternatively for Severance of Counts." It had been discovered by Boudin's associate, Diane B. Schulder, that the statute set forth under Count II of the indictment requires that the defendant be tried in the district in which the matter (here, a "threatening" letter) was mailed. Boudin contends that the government knows whence Elizabeth McAlister's letter had been sent (from New York City). He reads from the statute, "[the defendant] upon motion duly made, shall be entitled as of right to be tried in the district in which the matter mailed or otherwise transmitted was first set in motion"—not, he stresses, *even* from where it was mailed, but from where it was set in motion. He recites cases and presses his argument. Herman turns his attention to the prosecution and says, "Well, Mr. Lynch?"

Lynch rises, face flushing, a vacuum tube filling with vapor, and complains of the defense's eleventh-hour "flurry of motions," and mocks Boudin's recitation of cases by saying, "And Your Honor, it is *just* a recitation." He argues that to sever the count would be a "waste of money," and that this motion is just another of the defense's obstructionist and delaying tactics. He resumes his seat and the color fades from his face.

Menaker, the local defense attorney, rises to complain that the prosecution is adding witnesses to the list they turned over and that should not be allowed. Lynch partially rises and turns to his left and right as if to find something and then sits and says, "Your Honor, we have one more possible witness, but we don't know who it is."

When court is reconvened in the afternoon, Ted Glick is severed from the trial; he is sent into deep space until this trial's outcome is known.

"Why have I been severed?" he asks Herman in a low voice, deflected off the floor.

"You're severed; I've ruled; you'll have the written opinion later."

Glick has the look of a tryout player who has not survived the last cut; he knows why and he doesn't like it. Glick had wanted to defend himself, be a David confronting the Goliath of the state. The other defendants are saddled with attorneys; Glick was the unbroken defendant. Herman is afraid he can be spooked, cause a scene; severed, he is no problem. The Harrisburg Eight is now the Harrisburg Seven. The Goliath of the state is not to be confronted by any scrub David.

When court adjourns for the day, Philip Berrigan is taken away by the marshals, unable to talk to spectators or press. The other defendants, out on bail, return to the lives they have started in Harrisburg. Berrigan, like a precious gem, is locked away at night after being on display during the day.

V

Mary Cain Scoblick, a former nun, has sat on pews as often as she has in chairs and now she is sitting on a pew again at eight in the evening at Bethel AME (African-Methodist-Episcopal) Church ready to participate, along with Fania Davis Jordan, Angela Davis's sister, in tonight's program.

The Bethel AME is located at Sixth and Herr Streets, on the edge of a neighborhood of low, abutted housing, most of which is abandoned and marked with tin real-estate For Sale signs. So labeled, they stand like trees marked for cutting. Across the way from the church are high-rise buildings: offices and a development called the *Towne House* apartments. Harrisburg's urban renewal projects have left the city with a divided, though wall-less, aspect.

The church is the kind that can easily be turned into an off-Broadway theater. A rise of pews surrounds a platform on three sides. The fourth wall is a backdrop of dull gold organ pipes. In front of it are two rows of straight-backed chairs, the outline of a jury box. Mary Cain Scoblick cannot escape running a symbolic gauntlet. Augurs of the defendants' fate are everywhere. There are two red velvet chairs on the platform, by a lectern with an old mortar-shell radio microphone. A small altar with a silver cross and in front of it, a large opened Bible, its pages fall equally to both sides like the wings of a gliding heron. Two cone vases are filled with plastic ferns. Gold candlesticks left unlit. The church is paneled in dour cherrywood and it serves for somber reflection.

By the front door a table is filled with posters, leaflets, and buttons: FREE ANGELA.

The small audience is half white and half black, the constituencies equally divided on account of the speakers, an arranged coincidence, though it smacks of filling out a ticket. Who is to be the main contender?

The young black organizer who arranged the event through the local Angela Davis Committee announces at the lectern that Fania has not yet arrived in the building, but she will. First there is to be a film entitled "Justice?" and then Mary Cain Scoblick. The organizer wears a fringed suede vest and mercury-tinted sunglasses. It is to be Fania's evening, based, if on nothing else, on her awaited, last-minute arrival.

The film "Justice?" is shown on the wall. A living poster, hanging crookedly on the wall of Bethel AME. Scenes of barred doors slamming; men parade around a courtyard, chain-gang fashion. These are interspersed with interviews around the UCLA campus. Angela Davis's face appears. Her lawyer talks. Jonathan Jackson's mother says, to the discomfort of the white women in the audience, "I know my boy wouldn't listen to what any woman told him to do." The film recapitulates the events surrounding

9

the Angela Davis trial, yet to begin. The Marin County Courthouse shootout and escape attempt on August 7, 1970; two convicts dead, seventeen-year-old Jonathan Jackson dead, the trial
judge, a sawed-off shotgun taped around his neck, dead. A week
later a warrant is issued for Angela Davis on murder and kidnapping charges, under a California law holding that anyone who
aids or abets in a major crime is equally guilty with the direct
participants. She is accused of supplying the guns and directing
the escape attempt. For two months she eluded the FBI. The
lights come back on in the church and reveal grim, set faces.

Fania Davis Jordan comes into the church; her arrival lifts the
depression the film caused. She is very tall, wearing jeans, clogs,
braless under a blue jersey. She mounts the stage and sits down
on one of the red velvet chairs. Mary Cain Scoblick sits on the other
and on her hands.

The organizer introduces Mary Scoblick as one of the Harrisburg Eight (uninformed about today's severance of Ted Glick)
who had allegedly planned to kidnap someone, and something
about blowing up some buildings in Washington. He starts to
laugh, senses it impolite for some reason, and excuses himself.

Mary Scoblick begins to speak, slowly and nervously, pulling
at the cardigan sweater she is wearing. First, she says, she will
not speak long, she will defer to Angela Davis, who, being in
prison, and not out on bail, deserves the greater attention.

She says that she was troubled by the film, by the idea of trying
to make prisons better, more humane, instead of trying to elimi-
nate them altogether. "I don't believe in punishment," she says,
"because it doesn't work . . ."

Her speech is not prepared, nor is it extemporaneous. She seems
to recall things she has said before, ideas solidified, though not
necessarily made clear by repetition.

"I have trouble enough with the infallibility of the Roman
Catholic Church," she says, leaving open the possibility she still
accepts it, "but the infallibility of government, institutions . . ."
She lets it trail off with incredulity.

"I am also tired of those people who say we have a martyr
complex. They forget it was the Romans who created martyrs;
they had to be found, sought out. I am also tired of people who

10

say they support us, but continue to pay their taxes. We should not mince words, or worry about the technical transgressions of abominable laws. When people ask if we should do those things, I say, yes, do them."

Her voice is low, and breaks with exasperation. She is tiny and seems sapped of energy, though the words are stern and adamant.

"It is those who say they support us who have the greatest responsibility. You should let nothing get in your way, including the deaths of your loved ones; if you have this vision, nothing can take away your spirit."

What vision was she seeing? The vision of the film just shown was Jonathan Jackson dead and George Jackson dead; a shotgun taped around a judge's neck. The mortality rate of the Catholic Left is low. Does death need to be the price of legitimization? The organ pipes with their necks notched for lamentation are silent behind her.

"I feel the presence of evil in the court building; such a presence of evil. It's impolite not to tell the judge he's terrible. Riding in the elevator with the prosecutors . . ." She leaves the thought with a shudder.

The audience has begun to fill her pauses with murmurs. The whites are rapt but the blacks are impatient to hear Fania.

"Well, the movie was about the Communist party," she says, as if she is announcing a topic, though no discussion is to follow. She sums up by stopping. The applause lasts as long as it takes her to sit down on the chair, back down on her hands.

The organizer returns to introduce Fania. A graduate of Swarthmore, he says, a member of the Communist party, who has recently returned from Europe where she had an amazing reception. In Paris over sixty thousand people were on hand to meet her at the airport. Fania smiles ironically at this. The glamour of the Paris airport and sixty thousand fans does clash with the audience of sixty and the humble dais of Bethel AME.

"So, it is my pleasure," he continues, "to introduce Fania Davis Jordan, a courageous-black-woman-freedom-fighter."

The audience applauds the attractive surrogate. Though exhaustion has been claimed for her, she seems flushed. The clapping is a draft of pure oxygen to her. She would never wear a cardigan sweater.

"My sister," she says, her voice embracing the crowd with the glad tidings of reunion, "sends you her warmest revolutionary greetings."

There is a party to go to. The speeches concluded, two knots of people gather at the front of the stage. Mary and a few young women from the Harrisburg Defense Committee speak together for a minute and then leave. There will be no court till next Monday, though these pauses do not provide the defendants any rest; anxiety has turned into desire; it has been a year since the first indictment was handed down. All the days resemble waiting rooms and time has become the preoccupied stretch before an appointment that must be kept. Fania is traveling, speaking, raising money for her sister's defense. Her speech was aggressive and angry, full of scorn. Her sister had been moved from dungeon to dungeon, she had said; deprived of light and a view of outdoors, she is losing her long-distance focusing. Nixon had apologized for saying Manson was guilty, prejudging him, but he didn't apologize to Angela Davis for saying, before he signed an anticrime bill, "Let this be a warning to Angela Davis and to all other terrorists . . ." Fania had filled the space around her with a dancer's gestures. "Here's a man," she said of Nixon, "here's a man—you can disregard that . . ." The arbiter of man's virility is woman. Early in her speech she had said, "I salute Mary Scolic"; that she got the name wrong didn't seem to matter; she was honoring acts, not people.

It was hoped that the two trials would naturally link themselves. An unnatural chain-gang bondage. The government provides the unity. Angela, Fania reiterates, after lauding the escape attempt, is completely innocent of the charges brought against her, thereby having it both ways. Angela has been framed, says her sister. And the Harrisburg Eight have been framed. And the frame is the government. Fania's face could certainly launch a thousand Right Ons! Fantasy ships riding high on night seas. Mary, an astringent to Fania's warm oils, counsels action, but not excess. Don't pay war taxes. Told to this audience of poor blacks it sounded like an imperious "Let them eat cake," to *mères* marching for bread. Fania, preacherlike, left the audience roused, the frenzy the aim and result—exhaustion and excitement signal something has been accomplished. Mary's talk was unfulfilling—though that was its moral. Talk is a feast of dust.

Eqbal Ahmad, no doubt, is tired of being the piece of exotica every hostess longs for at her party. This fête does not promise to be fashionable. Fania wants to talk to Eqbal, or so the word goes, a movement summit.

We drive through Harrisburg with the exaggerated interest of occupiers. Landmarks are recognized. The map of the town begins to unfold.

Mulberry is another arc on the crumbling circumference of neighborhoods that circles the capitol complex. Row houses, some abandoned, others derelict. The Mulberry Street house, rented by the Defense Committee, is again on a corner. The first floor had been a candy store; its large window is faced with plywood. It serves as an office for the lawyers. Mulberry Street is full of "heavies," as the kids of the Defense Committee speak of them. Ramsey Clark and wife; Leonard Boudin and wife; Sisters Elizabeth McAlister and Jogues Egan; and a few young lawyers and investigators.

We park. Our driver gets out and is admitted into the house.

After Ted Glick was severed from the trial this afternoon, Eqbal had said, "I am having an identity crisis; just who am I supposed to have conspired with?" Eqbal Ahmad came to the United States in 1957 on a Fulbright Grant. He received a Ph.D. from Princeton in 1965. Judge Herman had wondered if Eqbal's degree was real, or if he understood English well enough to follow the proceedings. Herman's idea of being fair is to be outlandishly condescending. During court today, Eqbal touched all the women he talked with, delicately and abstractly as people do with children; they all responded with easy compliance. His dark black hair has streaks of pewter through it. He has the deracinated look of a British-educated Third World subject. His voice is unique—a new piece of music.

In the car waiting are three members of the Defense Commit-

13

tee. They are discussing whether Eqbal is going to be too loaded to make it to the party. They think of the defendants as a country: each one is a state within it, and each is assigned trademarks: the state bird, flower, tree. They joke about Ahmad's voice, his drinking, his tendency towards long speeches. "I have two points to talk about. P-want One. P-want Two. P-want Three . . ." It always gets a laugh among Defense Committee People. The young people of the Defense Committee, their numbers rising and falling, but hovering now, locally, around twenty, are possessive about the defendants. They are *their* defendants. They need to be tended, maintained, and often repaired. Symbol machines.

Ahmad comes out of the house not wearing a coat, even though it is cold enough to frost his breath.

"Look at him, no coat," a young man says, actually hurt, flustered that he is not taking care of himself, that he might break down and somebody in the Defense Committee will get a memo: please make Eq well. The Humpty Dumpty Committee; put the defendants back together again.

Ahmad gets in the car, clapping his shoulders.

"We were just commenting on your summer wardrobe."

"Well," Eqbal says, in *the* voice, "I've just come back from Chicago where it was ten degrees below zero; so this is like spring . . ."

He had been introduced to me earlier in the day; I, a member of the friendly press; he looks again, some decision has been made; am I to be trusted? My letters of transit have the proper seals.

It is the first question everyone has as they meet "new people." A world of informers, listening devices, spies. A diet of leaks and plants. The prime mover of this case is an informer. Such a cause, the uncaused cause, produces a medium of suspicion that affects everyone. It is a fog through which we all pass. Will it lift? Bleating horns blow. Weak yellow lights shine through the haze. Wary eyes pass and pass on.

"Do you know what they're doing in there?" Eqbal asks, gesturing back toward Mulberry Street we have left behind. "The government has given us the telephone records they secured and

14

we have to go through them; records of pay telephones, thousands and thousands of numbers, and we have to search the lists to see if any of the numbers have anything to do with us. The others are going over them meticulously; but I could not do it. I made a list of only the telephone numbers that would have anything at all to do with this case. A few dozen numbers and I have run through the lists looking for those. You would spend hours, days, going over the list completely. It is not worth it. The loss of all that time; checking numbers! Ah, what we've been reduced to. Well, hopefully, I haven't let an important number slip by. We shall find out," he said with the smile of a man who has just placed a reckless bet.

"It's terrible about the theft," he said, as if just recalling. "Why was that money left in the office?"

"It was mostly checks, Eq," someone says. The New York City office of the Defense Committee had been burglarized.

"The checks can be stopped . . ."

"Even if it was just checks, imagine having to write those people to tell them to stop payment and asking them all over again to write us another. I wouldn't want to do it . . ."

We are driving out Cameron Street, a wide commercial ditch. Neon graffiti scratched into the night sky.

"There is no time; I neglect my work; the speeches I give are all beginning to be the same. I can't sleep in airplanes; I don't know why, I'm just unable to sleep when I fly. Traveling from engagement to engagement. Boring your audience is one thing; but when you begin to bore yourself . . ."

He looks at the canted reflection of himself that rides along outside the car window.

"Our lives have been completely disrupted . . ."

The defendants are the new refugees, forced bodily from one town to another, filling the roads, airplane credit cards bundled on their heads. This prosecution has made displaced persons of them all.

"We have such limited resources; and the government's . . . ! Ramsey Clark told me, based on his experience, that this entire prosecution, investigation and all, beginning with Daniel Berrigan,

15

will cost the government around eight million dollars. All the surveillance, man-hours, technical work. Just one example. They
have over sixty photographs of Tom Davidson's farm. Tom Davidson's farm! Sixty photographs. All showing the same thing . . ."

Eqbal looks disgusted; his face soured by the scent of spoil-
age, the malignant redundancy.

"American bureaucracy. I met it for the first time when I was
in Rhodesia; I was on a project that required me to secure certain statistics. I went to the American Embassy; they sent me first
to one division and then to the next. Endless filing cabinets. Bu-
reaucrats behind the desks. They still couldn't locate what I
needed. I then went to the British Consulate, where there was
but one man behind one desk in an uncluttered office. He swung
around in his chair and by the time it took to swing back he had
the information I sought . . ."

We pulled into the Minotaur Arms Apartment Complex: four
stories high, the unconnected buildings separated by parking lots
and narrow alleys of grass. The party was in one of them; each
building was identified by number.

A door opens; introductions are made. Eqbal repeats his last
name for his host, a black connected with the Angela Davis
Committee.

"It's Eqbal *Ahmad* . . ."

"Ah," his host says, "Eqbal Muhammed, come right in . . ."

Fania is sprawled out on top of a friend who serves as a chaise
longue. Eqbal is led over to her and the entire conversation is
conducted while she is on that throne.

The room is furnished in a black caricature of white middle-
class taste. They are the same except here everything is sheathed
in clear plastic covers. Ike and Tina shake the stereo speakers.

Ahmad kneels down in front of Fania. Her head is held up by a
crooked arm, her elbow in the center of her friend's chest. Columbus before Isabella trying to book passage to the new Third
World.

"Are you Indian?" she asks Eq.

"No; Pakistani."

"Bangladesh?!" she says enthusiastically.

"No," Eqbal says, somehow failing her, "West Pakistan."

vi

Front Street is lined with the mansions of the robber barons; their magnificence hard to support they have turned into offices for lawyers, doctors, insurance and real estate companies. The servants now occupy the homes of their masters. Every river town has a "Front" street; the Susquehanna flows by and these grand homes are a reviewing stand from which the passing riches can be applauded. The Susquehanna was the principle entry way into Harrisburg in the late eighteen-hundreds. Further up the river from Harrisburg, the Confederate and Union armies fought over the bridges that spanned it.

The south end of Front Street reaches the ganglia of the interstate highway system. The north travels toward rural Pennsylvania; the opulence thins out in this direction. Some old manor homes have been demolished; gas stations have sprouted there. Fast food drive-ins, roadside taverns, all bathed in colored lights, the electric Sirens that lure the Detroit Argonauts.

Under moonlight the Susquehanna, filled with ice, moves, a conveyor belt heaped with broken glass.

vii

The Defense Committee's offices are on the third floor of the Payne-Shoemaker building on Third Street. An undistinguished building, two elevators go up its center. A miniature of the Empire State Building. The Defense Committee has volunteers and those that get paid receive housing and twenty dollars a week sustenance. Some receive fifty; a few receive more. A "defense committee" is a natural offshoot of the Catholic Resistance. It taps the auxiliary population, appeals to the bake-sale and rummage organizers, and generally puts to work the peripheral people who surround the defendants. Individuals confronting criminal charges have, at best, only their immediate families for support; but here the circle is wider. Priests have congregations, and

17

nuns have communities. Teachers have students; students have friends. Defense Committees are the bureaucracies of the Resistance. They have evolved with the forms they complement. The defendants decree the kind of defense committee they will have as the foot outlines the shoe. There is some pain in breaking them in.

Defense Committees are the sum of many parts: draft counseling offices, civil rights headquarters, graduate student seminars, underground press publications. Three things fix it in time: the faces on the posters and the electric typewriters and multi-buttoned telephones. Everything can be folded up and trucked away. Except the phones; they would leave the immutable traces, like the carbon in a skeleton's bones.

And the posters. Individual frames spliced out of the reel consciousness. The adage has become self-contained; the motto an entire tome. A poster dies like a flower: it yellows with age, or bespeaks one. They are not simply small signs, but the plaques and memorials for a disposable age that no longer sets in brass or chisels into stone. Every poster is an epitaph to something and that is why they are the size of gravestones.

Posters cover the walls. The Harrisburg Eight's own: "In giving their lives they find life, in serving others they lose the fear that cripples freedom / in reaching for the best in every person they make each of us more human / in respecting the life of every man and woman they make LIFE more precious for us all. Chavez." Their pictures are beneath. Informal mug-shots. A nun's handwriting is the graphic style; the script of Chavez's injunction; the word LIFE as large as skywriting. A statement is beneath:

> We state with clear conscience that we are neither conspirators nor bombers nor kidnappers . . .
> We believe in the holy commandment: thou shalt not kill—a commandment which our government has violated with impunity a million times . . .

A poster, not this one, was one of the government's earliest exhibits in pretrial motions. Prosecutor Lynch referred to it as an example of the wholesale propaganda engaged in by the Defense Committee.

And on another wall is *the* poster. A blowup of a color photograph of a trail leading out of Mylai 4. "And Babies?" it reads above. "And babies . . ." it reads below. A peasant of Guadalupe, some believe, had a portrait of the Madonna imprinted on his tunic; that is preserved in a gold-encrusted church, where art experts climb up and peek at it under glass. Our Lady of Guadalupe. Would God work in oils? has been their judgment. The peasant believed; his cloak opened and out spilled red roses, and on his tunic the portrait. Painted with brushes made of red roses. Oh, I can hear the nuns, telling the tale. Miracles were *proof*. And in many places this poster is venerated, as in the Defense Committee office.

It is smeared, slightly out of focus; a wash of green and red. The dirt trail narrows, lies across the poster like an arrowhead, the tip disappears at the top out of sight. There is a short fence on the right, shorter than the high grass around it, two strands of barbed wire. Is it there to impede water buffalo? The fence, near the bottom, is bent back, by the bodies that are against it. The colors of the clothes the dead are wearing are muted: purple, maroon, dark browns and greens. You notice the bare feet. They are the dangling strands you would reach for in trying to unravel balled string. Across the heel of one foot are three slashes. No warrior will give his name to the tendons that were cut. The wounds are as dark as the clothing. To the left of the center of the photograph is an example of death's singularity. A bare-legged adolescent is clutching his genitals with both small hands while his legs are bent up at the knee and spread apart in perfect symmetry, the outline of a moth's wings.

The Defense Committee runs its own security clearance. Gets background, checks references. Because of Douglas, the informer in this case, they act the betrayed maiden, who will be forever suspicious. The Return of Boyd F. Douglas, Jr., is awaited by his people no less than the Second Coming.

"They still want to save his soul," a Defense Committee member says.

There are three distinct groups to the Defense Committee: "Crossroads: the Counter-Trial," a series of panels to be held throughout the length of the trial; "The Pilgrimage Committee," which is handling the anticipated crowds and speakers that will be lured or moved to come to Harrisburg during Holy Week; and the Defense Committee proper, consisting of press and publicity.

There is grumbling about the paranoia in the security checks. "We are becoming what we are attacking," is most often the complaint. The three separate divisions of the Defense Committee are susceptible to attacks and gripes along the lines of "power trips," "ego trips," and "male trips."

Mail is being sorted out, placed in a hotel mail-hive made out of white pine. Each phone is in use; a mimeo machine is thwacking. The logo of the Defense Committee is Daniel Berrigan's manacled hands, the right lifted up, giving the V sign. The hands are disembodied; they swim before you everywhere like the colored amoebas you see after staring too long into the sun.

viii

It is not the skimpy crowd that was here for Mary Cain Scoblick and Fania, who had seemed to be huddling from the night's cold, more than anything; Bethel AME today is full of smiles; people skip up and down the aisles, darting glances to familiar faces. Reunions occur. Backslapping raises the dust on neglected friendships. Tomorrow the trial begins in earnest; the press has arrived, the harbingers of notoriety. A row of cameras has been set up in the middle of the pews; the dais is bathed in their high-intensity lights. Cameras are the new Trojan horse; they gain admittance to any armed camp. Speeches, a communal supper, then a vigil at Dauphin County Prison, where "Phil" is being held.

The black pastor of Bethel AME gives an introductory welcoming address; he characterizes these radical Catholics as Marys and Josephs trudging through Bethlehem, unable to find shelter. Bethel AME is the stable provided for them. His remarks have the rounded pronunciation of the evangelist. He finds it unusual to look upon all these white faces that he is harboring; outcasts of Harrisburg to whom he is providing succor and a hall. The dark cherrywood glistens in the lights. The gold candlesticks gleam. The red velvet glows. Hooray! is the mood; it's starting!

Sister Elizabeth McAlister is introduced; receives a standing ovation. She makes no personal remarks, but reads a prayer, an invocation, with the hesitation of a novice translator. Its vocabulary remains stuck in the mind, stones that will not pass through a screen. Beseech. Light. Strength. Confusion. Darkness. Despair. Engulf. Survive. Fulfill. Trust.

Children scamper up and down the aisles. They are a focus of attention. They locate the dream.

Howard Zinn, a professor at Boston University, fellow traveler of Daniel Berrigan to North Vietnam to gain the release of three downed American fliers. They met for the first time, on 31 January 1968, at their embarkation for Hanoi. Two animals of the same species meeting at the ramp of a special arc. It makes for friendship. Zinn is all black-and-white lines of an etching. A New England preacher; Cotton Mather with a visa stamped Hanoi, frenzied intellect, enunciated wrath. The crowd had sunk during Elizabeth's incantations; but Zinn picks them back up. He scorns the court proceedings, calls it "a little totalitarian room." He bellows at the insidious evolution of power: one political official appoints another political official, appoints another. He mocks the hysterical labels of secrecy: "The more imprints it has, the more stamps—Confidential, For Your Eyes Only, Secret, Top Secret—the more likely it is to be a lie." Zinn speaks for fifty minutes, unable to break a lecture-course rhythm.

A member of the Defense Committee Pilgrimage staff gets up and explains the aims of that project: forty-day committees, named for the forty days of Lent. Caravans coming to Harrisburg from numerous cities. All to converge here during Holy Week. Thirty thousand pilgrims marching for peace. The TV lights go off. Without their heat a chill reenters.

The communal supper begins in the basement. A speaker who arrived late, a minister from the National Council of Churches, exhorts the diners while they drink pink tomato soup out of paper cups.

Maps giving directions to Dauphin County Prison are passed out. "All those who have cars, don't leave till they are filled up."

21

The poster-and-button table is doing a brisk business; cars get their passengers. A long procession sets off bumper-to-bumper down a narrow street, then out Front Street, heading for Dauphin County Prison, tonight's Bastille.

We are lost. A woman from Connecticut and her friend who have taken us up have disregarded the map and followed a car with a peace sticker on the back window. "Was it 23 or 83 that we were supposed to have taken?"

Other cars trail into the parking lot we have stopped at to reconnoiter. They circle like Conestoga wagons putting up for the night. One driver gets out and stops a passing motorist and asks for directions to the prison. Redirected, everyone starts out again.

We arrive at the Harrisburg East Shopping Mall, a rising knoll of asphalt peaked with stores. The parking lot spread around it is bright with outdoor lighting. Everything has a blue cast. The cars are parking at its farthest edge. Across a greensward is the prison. It looks like a new public grammar school. A hurricane fence is around the back and sides, lined at the top with a small roof of barbed wire. Concentration-camp trademark, that wedge of barbed wire. Seen from Gimbels on the shopping mall, the fence is the only thing that distinguishes Dauphin as a penal colony. There are no windows at Gimbels. Shoppers prefer the blinds pulled when they buy.

The distance traveled induced a false euphoria. Stirred, everyone went into the lobby of the prison. Give us Phil. They were ejected like foreign tissue and then were told by the Defense Committee people that they should assemble for the vigil in the grass beyond the fence, where sound speakers had been set up. Candles begin to flicker in the dark.

Empty, the lobby is undistinguished. A great counter covers the length of one wall. All personnel had retreated behind a thick glass wall, through which barred doors could be seen, though there was no direct view into the prison interior. Tom Menaker, the local attorney, arrived with his wife (who is also an attorney); they are admitted. Above the counter was a large scroll upon which the warden had ordered printed:

When you enter this institution, you leave behind your race, creed, color, social and economic status, you become merely a human individual and will be treated as such. There is no place in this institution for prejudice or favoritism, each individual will be treated the same, with understanding, consideration and dignity.

Every harrowing portal requires a warning inscription.

A crowd of around three hundred have come from the church. They were gathered around a microphone like a spread-open fan. Their candles flickered, making them look like the lights of a seaport town carved into the night. The cyclone fence is starkly lit by the beams of light that came from each corner of the jail. That barbed wire fence echoed down a thousand movie frames, changed geography and country, went over from the Axis to the Allies, freed of nationality; that fence is universal, has been seen by all men.

TV crews arrive and their lights center upon the speakers and guitar players. A priest reads from the Acts of the Apostles: "The kings of the earth stood up, and the rulers were gathered together against the Lord, and against his Christ. And now Lord, behold their threatenings; and grant unto thy servants, that with all boldness they may speak thy word."

Tom Menaker came out from the jail with a message from Father Berrigan. "I'm playing Boyd Douglas," he says to a friend, referring to the smuggling of letters out of the prison, seven counts of the ten-count indictment. Menaker reads:

"Peace and love from Dauphin County Prison; and gratitude to you for coming.

"I hope you're dealing with your lockup as well as I'm dealing with mine. I'm not trying to be flippant!"

Berrigan had correctly anticipated the chuckling of the crowd.

"I am trying to say that any American not in serious resistance against this government is in lockup. And in lockstep."

The crowd compresses and expands; reacting together, the respiration of remonstrance.

"I hope also that you're not worrying about us seven or about

23

Ted Glick. We're o.k., getting it together, and we'll get it more together as the courtroom débâcle develops."

Getting it together. The philosophy of the streets. Things are apart, fragmented, separated, shattered. Pick up the pieces. Get it together.

"After all, we have one another, our lives in resistance, the best of lawyers, you and thousands like you. That's more than enough going for us.

"Instead of overconcern for us, how about using the trial as an occasion for giving rebirth to the movement? How about giving movement to something that never really moved, or at least in a sustained way? How about saying this time that our lives are truth and peace—both of which mean resistance. How about beginning January twenty-fourth, building a force of community and continuity capable of holding accountable even one of Richard Nixon's uh! cough! versatility? We're liable to have him another four years, you know."

A farewell address to his troops?

"Wherever one can share one's life, in jail or out, wherever people are, there is ignorance to be fought, fear to be dispelled, culture shock to be eased. Let's reteach the ABC's to our sisters and brothers—the ABC's of compassion and resistance, of risk and expense, of courage in the face of the warmakers! Let's remember our Indochinese brothers and sisters—living and dead."

Who can remember what one has never known?

"Let's make our rhetoric very good and very real, but let's back up rhetoric with our lives. Let's conspire with truth and justice to withstand the real conspirators!

"Let's build a real movement by building real people. Let's give one another hope and love, that's all people need, hope and love. Let's push back the darkness! That's what they said about Christ, you know, he pushed back the darkness—once and for all!

"Peace and love to you."

Menaker puts away the speech, (glad to have only read it).

The crowd is burdened.

"That should've been written on stone tablets . . ."

"Philip Berrigan in jail is like Christ walking on the water;

24

you're tempted to join him, but you end up just getting wet . . ."

The crowd begins to break apart like a pill disintegrating in water. Some young people go up to the cyclone fence and hang on to it, arms outstretched. Two small girls wander up to it, with flowers in their hands, and the TV crew follows them up. The tots realize they are being filmed and begin to preen, pull petals from their flowers.

People head back towards their cars in the Harrisburg East Shopping Mall lot. Their expressions are preoccupied, perplexed. The candles go out, one by one.

"Is it breaking up already?"

"It's a vigilette."

Jury Selection

*Americans, while occasionally willing to be serfs,
have always been obstinate about being peasantry.*
—F. SCOTT FITZGERALD, *The Great Gatsby*

i

"You're number thirteen," I am told, coming up to the short
queue. It is six thirty in the morning and a cobalt blue band rings
the horizon.

"Someone has been here since four."

"Get his name; it should be recorded for posterity."

"You're number fourteen," the St. Louis *Post-Dispatch,* the
number-giver, tells another. "Two more to go; then that's it. The
press section of the courtroom can hold only forty-two people."
Those who were not given permanent seats were left to line up
to get in on a first-come-first-served basis, for the remaining sixteen unassigned seats. Hence, this dawn shape-up of the Fourth
Estate.

"When they open the doors to give us our passes, let's all keep
our places; if we can't maintain order and a gentlemanly spirit,
who can?"

Last Monday, the press section was sparsely filled; it was only
necessary to wait for court to open. Sketch artists, TV cameramen,
commentators, passed the time waiting in the Federal Building

lunchroom. It looked like the commissary of a film studio. Passes act on the guards like laminated electric messages. Flash one, the elevator starts up. Without it nothing works.

"Ten till seven," a crier sang out, reading the clock face on a building across the street.

"We *can't* do this each morning; they *couldn't* make us do that."

Media derelicts waiting in the information soup line. Print addicts hustling their daily fix.

"That's it," the *Post-Dispatch* says as fifteen and sixteen file on.

Sixteen, the New York. *Daily News,* says, "Tell me I'm too late so I can go back to bed."

The sky brightens. Early morning passers-by stare at the tail of people hanging out from the Federal Building's front door.

Lights come on inside the foyer of the building. Uniformed guards swim up out of the inner darkness like tropical fish peering out of the glass of an aquarium.

"Aren't you going to let us in?"

They shake their heads somnambulantly.

The door cracks open and the end of a long stepladder appears. Two guards carry it like a battering ram. Another follows with a wedge of flag. They lean the ten-foot ladder against an aluminum flagpole anchored to a marble ledge. One guard holds the ladder steady. The other struggles on his perch to fasten the flag, while it covers most of the ladder like a dustcloth.

The original location of the tie-off cleat has been moved upwards. Two bolts that once held it where a standing man could reach it were still there, but it had been raised, so that a ladder is required. The flag jerks up the pole. Two reporters simultaneously begin to hum "America the Beautiful."

The hoisting completed, the ladder is removed. The cleat had been raised out of fear that demonstrators would be able to reach it and molest the flag.

The reporters file in, receive a daily pass, and then disperse as quickly as birds when the crumbs are gone.

Two spectators have arrived and begin their own wait till court opens at nine thirty.

27

ii

From the floor referred to as the "Penthouse," atop the building at 100 Pine Street that houses the law firm of McNees, Wallace & Nurick, of which J. Thomas Menaker is a partner and out of which the defense lawyers conduct their legal business, all of Harrisburg is visible. At seven thirty in the morning, traffic is an unbroken chain coming across the river on the Taylor bridge. There is a cleft in the mountains that encircle Harrisburg through which the ice-filled Susquehanna flows. Mist is parted by a comb of trees that ridge the hills. Church spires and cupolas are green with the patina of public places. The secular rooftops are low; they and the buildings that support them are Mediterranean colors, pinks, yellows, olives, made luminous by the low winter sun.

The room has small tables and two women who will prepare you breakfast. Ramsey Clark and Leonard Boudin are sitting here. They are talking about judges. Clark uses adjectives of approbation like a diamond cutter announcing the number of carats a gem has. He can make a word like *distinguished* seem to be an exact quality. The words are generalities but his application of them is not.

Both of them are, in a phrase Boudin himself is fond of, *men of the world*. Officers, who after commanding opposing armies that have since dispersed, who can meet with the ease of having shared the same rank. When Clark was attorney general he approved the prosecution of Dr. Benjamin Spock and four others for "conspiring to counsel, aid and abet diverse Selective Service registrants to . . . neglect, fail, refuse and evade service in the Armed Forces of the United States . . ." Their conviction was reversed; Boudin, who was Spock's lawyer and won the appeal, was sure it would be; what he was not sure of was on which grounds it would be reversed, since he provided so many. Clark had allowed the first of the government's conspiracy trials of anti-war defendants, and by chance or purpose he is a member of the defense team for what might be the last.

28

Lawyers diagnose a case like physicians: the indictment is the disease; the cure requires various remedies. The serum is some part judge, some part jury, some part press, and perhaps the ear and tail of the prosecution. Reputation that the defense lawyers might have is an anodyne; here, some balance of power has been achieved. Ramsey Clark carries with him the shadow of the government. This is a trial built on informers. The government has theirs: Boyd F. Douglas, Jr. The defense has theirs: Ramsey Clark. A spy has been in both houses. Clark can clean the government's face as he smears it.

They both return to the offices on the floor below, leaving behind the view. Become a lawyer and you will have all that you can see before you. The dominance of height; the possessiveness of sight. As far as the eye can see. Heights inspire temptations. Lordly. Pinnacles. Peaks. I have seen from the mountaintop. Dead black Moses, never to enter the promised land. The courtroom has no windows, no view; it is blind, like Justice.

iii

At the YWCA at Walnut and Fourth Streets every room resembles a parlor. Upright pianos are more common than ashtrays. The blinds remain drawn; the light that is admitted is yellow as old silk. The stairway is sealed off beyond the third floor by glass. A sign on the gym door reads: NO SPECTATORS DURING BALLET CLASS.

The women who stay here are diffident in the wake of the invaders. The Defense Committee has gotten the second-floor auditorium to use for press conferences.

Press packets are on each folding chair like party favors. On stage are defendant Sister Elizabeth McAlister, Tony Russo, Professor Richard Falk, Michael Ferber, Professor Howard Zinn, and defendant Father Joseph Wenderoth.

A forty-one-year-old Puerto Rican, under indictment in New York City, reads a statement of solidarity signed by those on the stage who are not defendants. He wears a pleated white shirt, black pants and jacket, and a black bowtie. The allegations against him resulted in a bail first set at $150,000. The New York district attorney, John Fine, charged that he was responsible for the attempted bombing of thirty-five public buildings, including the New York Public Library.

He reads the statement, thick rhetoric thickening still with his accent. On stage in his black-and-white outfit, surrounded by priests and nuns, he looks like God's busboy.

He finishes with the prepared statement and breaks into an emotional discussion of his own case. The press secretary (defense committees, like presidents, have press secretaries) comes up behind him and extends his arm around him like a vaudeville hook and extracts him from the podium. He is replaced by Tony Russo, indicted in California for allegedly defrauding the United States.

"I see two things happening today," Russo says. "At home the U.S. Government starts the trial against the Harrisburg Eight and abroad we are starting new forms of exported violence, the electronic battlefield . . ."

Each time I hear *electronic battlefield* I think television is being referred to; but it is the computerized air strikes, the heat-detecting sensors dropped into the jungles.

"They're bringing home all the boys that pull the trigger; he wants to end the war in your perception. We're closer to nineteen-eighty-four than twelve years."

Russo has been baptized in the green river of a Xerox copier. Alleluia. He and Daniel Ellsberg struck down on the road to Santa Monica on the way to the RAND Corporation. Saul lost his sight; Daniel Ellsberg worried about going blind from the light of the Xerox machine while he copied the RAND study that came to be known as the Pentagon Papers.

Russo has both hands tight on the lecturn, leaning forward as if he is just about to begin a gymnast display. His hair is tied into a ponytail, the scoff-lock of the exestablishment bullfighter. He finishes, saying, "After you've come to Harrisburg, come to Los Angeles. This is going to be a big year for political trials."

The press secretary asks if there are any questions. There are none.

From the back of the room, a handful of Vietnam Veterans Against the War, in mufti, beards, and long hair that gives them the wild look of deserters, though they are that only in spirit not body, come forward bearing a coffin, a homemade box looking like a prop from a high-school production of *Our Town.*

It is placed in front of the people on the stage, its lid braced open like a grand piano's. A number of people file by the coffin and drop things into it. A statement is read:

> We take this act of depositing draft files as local residents showing our solidarity with the Eight Harrisburg defendants. Our action demonstrates the effect of the Harrisburg trial is to enlarge the community of resistance rather than to diminish it . . .

The press secretary, acting as narrator, announces they are putting in the coffin "various instruments of war made of paper."

The coffin is a donation plate. The people are making an offering. *Paying their dues.*

Newsmen down front stir for the first time this morning.

"What are they putting in there?"

"Are they draft cards?"

"They *look* like draft files. Are they stolen?"

"Is this illegal?"

There is a commotion. Those who cannot look in the coffin ask questions. Howard Zinn is asked, "What about the explosives? If there's proof they got explosives would you support them as you do now?"

"I don't expect my support of the defendants to waver. If the very worst of the government's charges were true, they would still stand as the abolitionists did, as the Underground Railroad did, as John Brown did. While we're sitting here, tons and tons and thousands of tons of explosives are being dropped on the people of Southeast Asia."

A crowd of reporters circle the coffin like apple-dunkers around a barrel. One comes up with a question: "How were these acquired?"

The press secretary answers, a glint in his eye, "There are other agencies to ask those kinds of questions."

One reporter queries another, holding an armful of draft files: "Is it legal to steal stolen draft files?"

A procession is arranged. The VVAW shoulder the coffin and

march out of the YWCA. Everyone leaves to follow them to the federal building two blocks away. A circuitous route is picked to show the morning crowds going to work that the trial of the Harrisburg Seven has begun.

In front of the coffin a Revolutionary War flag is carried, the coiled snake and the inscription: DON'T TREAD ON ME. These are followed by about thirty supporters and thirty members of the press. The ratio of press to supporters is considered as important in educating the public as the ratio of teacher to students is in the classroom.

The citizens of Harrisburg do not gawk. They have been warned. Not by leaflets dropped on the village advising them to evacuate, but by their daily press. Rumors have been at large for some time; the citizenry are galvanized, prepared to be struck. Any shock on their faces is from realizing the blow is so soft.

At the corner of Walnut and Third I see the first Harrisburg policeman visible at any event thus far; he has been directing traffic at the busy corner and he now stops it and waves for the tiny parade to cross.

iv

"You'll have to work it out among yourselves."

The man from GSA (Government Services Administration) stands with a list in his hand, high up, as if it were about to be identified.

"We've had numerous complaints," he says and that is greeted with affirmative mutters, "about having to line up to get daily passes. So we've arranged a pool system for the unassigned seats. We've put people together on the basis of similarities. This can be altered slightly. But we will give you the pool passes, to a chosen representative from each pool, and you can work it out among yourselves who gets in and when."

The group begins to form its pools.

"Who's here from the Philadelphia *Daily News*?"

"Christian Science Monitor?"

A chain of press-islands appears; each elects its chief.

"It will be impossible to let you up this morning; the court-room is full of prospective jurors; we've allowed three reporters up, UPI, AP, and the local *Patriot-News*. They will act as a pool for all of you, and report back down at each recess. Any questions?"

He is surrounded as if for a ritual killing.

GSA is to act the liaison between press and the federal mar-shals, who have jurisdiction over the courtroom. Two men have been sent down from Washington, and they appear very much like continental tour guides. They are not homegrown Harrisburgites, but slick government men, with Georgetown polish. The younger and friendlier of the two wears black patent leather shoes and counterculture jewelry: a large burnt-metal belt-buckle, small remnant of someone's scorched-earth policy. They are public relations men, trained to deal with the press, and in our informer society, they are suited for the job, blending in as they do with the mixed styles of the press corps. The passes are no longer called press, but MEDIA. The institutions are the first to adapt: media. Talk their language.

Three rooms on the third floor of the federal building have been outfitted for the press; in the largest, the walls are lined with tables; little pup-tent name cards have been printed up, to sit in front of each chair. Telephones have been arranged for; it has been advised that small cylindrical locks be bought for them to prevent unauthorized calls. No honor among thieves. Soon they do sprout protective warts.

The GSA men are imported crisis-managers, press level. They sympathize. Privately they say that the man they have come to supersede has, as one of them puts it, a size eighteen neck but wears a size three hat. The GSA men are here just till things get moving, then they turn it over to the locals. They are architects, not laborers.

Court is in session, but the press is not let up save for the three pool members, and they are as impatient as musicians left without their instruments. Variations of pacing the room are plotted. A petition circulates, requesting that a sound system and closed-circuit television be installed into an overflow newsroom. The pool system has gone down easily; no one wants to stand in line at six thirty in the morning. The implications of being shut out of the courtroom harden in some of their minds. The GSA men commiserate, forecast but a short ban. A document is brought into the press room and pinned on the bulletin board.

> Until the jury in the above-captioned case is selected and sworn, it is requested, and strongly urged, that no representative of the news media report or publish in any manner the names of any of the prospective jurors or the questions asked by the court nor the answers given by any prospective juror on the voir dire examination held for the purpose of selecting a fair and impartial jury to try the issues involved in this matter. (Signed) R. Dixon Herman, United States District Judge, Middle District of Pennsylvania

"Is he kidding?"

" 'Requested and strongly urged'—that's not a court order."

"Even if it was, who cares about their names; but not to reveal the questions!"

"Are you going to abide by that?"

"Not me."

"Nor I."

"We might not ever find out what the questions are."

The agitated talk and wanderings increase till the door opens and the three pool men come in, quickly, as if out of a storm.

They take a place in a corner and the rest of the press spreads out before them; there are about sixty people in the room. Notebooks spring open like trap doors.

The man from the local paper begins:

"The judge entered at eleven sixteen A.M.; there were one hundred forty-four prospective jurors present at the roll call; there is a preponderance of substantial-looking middle-aged people. There are eight blacks, eight people in their early twenties, and roughly eighteen in their early thirties. The judge welcomed them, told them it was a privilege and a duty to serve on juries, described the jury system to them, said that Japan was considering adopting it . . ."

Each took their turn. The recitations and questions left off. The newsmen began looking back over the notes they had just taken. The three pool men look at each other like a comedy team that has just lost its audience.

"Shall we tell them?" one said to the others, a nervous laugh nudged out his words. "Well, I'm not," the local man said, turning away, flipping closed his long narrow notebook.

"Not tell us *what*?" the Los Angeles *Times* said, grabbing onto the coattails of the exchange just before it got away.

"Yes, what is this, tell us," the Chicago *Daily News* said. It was now a looseball spotted by everyone; the pile-on began.

"What are you holding back?"

"Tell us everything."

The three conferred, shrugging their shoulders, mumbling.

"Well, it was really nothing," one of them said.

"Let us decide what it was . . ."

"We want to know what went on there . . ."

"This was before court even began, so technically . . ."

"Bullshit; you wouldn't have been up there at all without us being down here. Give."

"Well, it was like this," AP said. "Eqbal was talking to us and said, 'Would you like to meet Philip Berrigan?' and he took us up to the rail. The marshals didn't appear to pay any attention; and," he said, pausing, "we had a discussion; then the marshals saw us and said they didn't want it published, since we're not allowed to talk with him, he being in federal custody . . ."

The local man said, "So we agreed; said we wouldn't publish it; so for me it's a closed case."

UPI, the other pool man, nodded his head.

AP said, "I didn't say anything; I didn't affirm or deny; I'll let my office take care of it . . ."

"Well, we did agree," the *Patriot-News* said.

UPI nodded again; AP smiled broadly.

"What did Berrigan say?"

"Oh, nothing, really," the AP man said, "Just the same old stuff . . ."

Typewriters began to clatter; their hammering cracked the group apart. The local man and UPI went to their desks. The voices diminished as the sounds of the machines increased.

"Don't you find them charming; they're being so sweet," F. said, referring to the GSA men. "They've never been this cooperative before."

"I think they're treating us like doctors and nurses treat the relatives of a patient who has a terminal illness."

"My, you think it's that bad?"

"They just want it cooled; they expect it to die as long as there's no provocative transfusions. The local police have word from Washington not to do anything without it being cleared there first. Their profile is so low that it wouldn't even show up on a coin . . ."

"Well, the press is certainly different. It used to be so terribly *polarized*," F. said, tasting her words, "when these Catholic trials began; it would really show up; those who had any sympathies at all with the defendants would be ostrazied; it was bad at Catonsville, but worse at the trial of the Milwaukee Fourteen. You would have thought we had the clap . . . or something. But here; well, it appears to be a friendly bunch. Now; I'm going to be here only on Tuesdays, so if I could be assured the pass . . ."

"That's funny," a woman from a Baltimore paper said, "I just called my office with my story and they said, don't bother; we topped it with the AP wire, that carried Father Berrigan's confession . . ."

"What!"

The rumor fuse burned instantaneously; the AP man was sought out; the explosion went off there.

"You filed a story on what Berrigan said?!"

"I didn't say I wouldn't; I said I would let my office decide . . ."

"You'd better come across right now—with everything Berrigan said."

"Don't you realize what you've done?!"

"It's like a hockey game," F. said, standing back of the circle of reporters that surrounded the AP man. "It's like the Boston Bruins. What do you call it, when they surround the puck?"

"A face-off."

"Yes, that's what it is; just like the Boston Bruins."

The AP man began to read from his notes.

"This was just a short conversation; I asked Berrigan if there was any substance to the charges and how the case looked so far. He said, 'It looks good. It's,' he said, meaning the indictment, 'a catchall, highly fabricated. Everything we've done we've acknowledged publicly. There was a discussion similar to discussions by millions of people who have had these kinds of ideas at one time or another. It doesn't mean they would act or really want to act. Part of a discussion . . .' "

"Slower!"

" 'Part of a discussion, if it is to be real, is to investigate the feasibility of it. There was no planning'—it's not really an exact quote here—he said they were trying to find out what they did in Quebec, about political kidnappings . . ."

"The FLQ . . ."

". . . and Uruguay."

"The Tupamaros."

"Thinking about the feasibility of it. And then he said, and this is more or less straight, 'I've been in federal buildings all over the East Coast . . .' "

"He said *that?*"

"Overt act number four."

"Shut up. Go on."

" 'If you are a peace-movement person you are trying to find out what is going on, to see if you can do what others are doing and whether you should do what they do.' End of quote. That was about all of that. Then I asked about this trial and he said, 'It's not a priority of ours to win an acquittal, but to conduct a political trial and get the issues before the American people.' "

"Yeah, just the usual stuff . . ."

"Then the marshal came up and separated us; asked for our notes and made us promise not to publish what he said . . ."

"You should have told us . . ."

"Court hadn't begun, so technically," he began again, "I wasn't responsible . . ."

"Bullshit . . ."

"Man, I don't want you in my pool; you're not going back up there for any of us . . ."

Affirmative shouts seconded this.

Three others were selected as replacements. The AP man could not stop smiling. A Cheshire grin possessed his face. The reporters drew back and left him an iron stake, rung by a horseshoe of isolation.

Discussion groups formed.

"How do you think Berrigan could say all that in a two-minute conversation. Just launch right into the heart of the matter?"

"He hasn't been allowed to talk to the press all this time; just pressure, building up. The need to explain. All that being dammed up for a year. Thinking about something so much that you blurt out the answer before the question."

"A pool system is in effect and in two hours the greatest fault of the system appears . . ."

Reporters are angry—at AP and at themselves for not pressing harder when it was first mentioned. The press room is a blinking light of alternating tension and torpor.

They return to their typewriters the way any worker goes back to his machine.

"We should send a pool man down to a bar . . ."

"If you send AP the only thing he'd bring back would be the hangover."

"The word from GSA is that that story going out has jeopardized the entire coverage of this trial. They are mad and upset . . ."

"Gentlemen," the New York *Times* says, "here is the AP dispatch that went over the wire; you might be interested in seeing the last line."

He hands it to the New York *Daily News,* who reads, " 'I've been in federal buildings all over the East Coast, checking them out.' Checking them out! He didn't tell us that."

"I think," the New York *Times* said after a federal marshal had come and gone, "that we should give a vote of thanks to the man from AP; he's the only one who got a public official to talk to us today."

A posse of press begins to approach the man from AP. A journalist looks up from reading a copy of *Comedy of Errors,* which serves as a subtitle for the silent scene that is creeping up on AP. In appropriate melodrama style, the *dei ex machina* appear. The door opens and the three afternoon pool people come in, breathless with their report.

The vendetta is put aside; the reporters turn towards their peers.

At court's adjournment for the day, four of the defendants came down to the third floor for a press conference. In the room reserved for this, cameras remain set up. A table is there, fixed with bouquets of microphones. The conference is to be held to protest the judge's intention to sequester the jury. The defendants did not know that the stories sent out today had little to do with the entire day's proceedings, but were pounded out of the two-minute conversation with Philip Berrigan. They were not concerned by it, because they did not yet know it. Eqbal Ahmad, who had introduced Berrigan to the three members of the pool, thought it had gone no further than an exchange of pleasantries. Sequestration was on their minds and the effects it would have on the jury. Eqbal was their spokesman, and in his elegant voice which seems to choose the words for his sentences the way flowers are arranged in a vase, spoke: "First, we want to express our disappointment that you were not with us in the courtroom today . . ."

The press corps smiled collectively, ruefully.

But Eqbal, knowing nothing of what had happened, looked towards the man from AP with a smile that seemed more blissful because of his ignorance and said, "but I am sure you have most of this information, information your colleagues of the pool have already given you . . ." Eqbal's smile turned towards the man from AP as did all the other heads in the room, but not with the same expression of fellowship.

"The pool," G. says quietly, "has turned into a well."

V

There has been singing on the steps of the federal building all day. Music is no longer the food of love, but the balm of catastrophe. How many ships have gone down to the sounds of singing? Singing is the reasoning of lost minds; the daughter of Polonius warbles

39

wandering to her riverbank. Song is the word honored. This trial begins with song in the streets; a bit more than two years ago the Chicago Eight conspiracy trial began in Chicago and was baptized with the organized riot known as "trashing," by the Weathermen and their "Days of Rage."

"While Peter was singing this afternoon two men kept saying, 'Isn't he the one who was jailed on a morals charge?' 'Yeah, some minor, some fourteen-year-old.' It didn't matter to them that she was a groupie; just that he'd been arrested."

Peter Yarrow, of Peter, Paul, and Mary, the folk-song trinity that tutored an entire generation of college students. Who made the lyrics of Bob Dylan come out from behind his abrasive voice when they recorded his "Blowin' in the Wind." The answer my friend. Success, like the duration of the first airplane flights, was measured by the time your tune could remain on the airwaves. Tape was introduced; seamless continuity cried out for; the ear could not stand cessation. Peter, Paul, and Mary, two men and a woman, which would now only bespeak some sexual triangle, but then, they were clean, witty models for hosts of middle-class whites. The sound they made was so *pleasant*. The postwar college generation was watered with their clear flowing voices.

They broke up; every music group that rises must sooner or later break up. The dénouement was Yarrow's conviction in Washington, D.C., in the fall of 1970 on a morals charge. Paul O'Dwyer was his lawyer. One magnet that attracted Yarrow to Harrisburg. The judge at his trial expressed his shock at the low point this country's morals had reached. Yarrow had a psychiatrist plead for him. The Folk-music Scottsboro case; how could a groupie be molested? Her sister was a witness. A sorry incident. Yarrow was cast as the Magdalene of the Movement. Here in Harrisburg washing feet at Augsburg Lutheran Church at Fifth and Minnich. Do people expect to take away a glow coming from hereafter basking under the saintly sunlamp? Tony Russo's presence was assisted by about four hundred dollars. Travel expenses. Lecture fees. Will Harrisburg be the American Lourdes for the next three months? Will a wall of abandoned crutches be left behind?

Yarrow is singing; the audience claps, rises from their seats and begins to dance. They link hands and form a moving circle.

Yarrow is signaled. He has a flight to catch. He has just found out his wife is pregnant and he wants to be with her. We drive to Harrisburg's international airport. When it was an air force base, the Berlin blockade airlift originated there. Blockades. Airlifts. The Cold War is dated from the start of the Berlin blockade.

We speed through the night, watching out for police. Running down corridors to catch the plane. Just in time. Allegheny Airlines. Off to a pregnant wife. Absolved. The wall is being built.

Tony Russo had not yet finished talking when we returned. "I've seen it man; I know what I'm talking about."

Russo had worked for the RAND Corporation; had gone to Vietnam to conduct various studies. Had allegedly assisted Daniel Ellsberg in copying the RAND study ordered by Robert Mc-Namara. TOP SECRET. Published in a continuing series by the New York *Times*. There are other studies, he says. Strange aquatic creatures from the lowest depths of the think tanks. The monsters are there, he implies. They glow with their phosphorescent secrets; intelligence now means facts.

Russo has grafted a hip argot onto his speech, though it sounds as unnatural as a foreign language learned by only memorizing its idioms.

"Dig it. The electronic battlefield; the pigs have sensors, they can smell us. We all have a little pig in us, like we all have a little angel in us. Dig it. This will be a console war. Dig it." Russo is a social scientist. Dig it. "Dig it," is digit. All is number.

I'm dropped off at the hotel where I've gotten a room for a week. A rule has come down: no press are to live in Defense Committee houses. Russo's "partner" is talking about Tony. The experiences he had in Vietnam which changed him.

"He just got to the point when he couldn't stand to see another Vietcong suspect being brought into the interrogation room. Dragged in, kicked in, tortured. He couldn't stand to hear them asked the questions. That had the biggest effect on him."

"Good night. Good night."

Crossing State Street, my head swims with interrogations—

Russo's distress. You see, we're doing this *study*. The RAND Corporation; we're going to think about this for a while. Peter Yarrow's voice trails overhead like a kite tail.

Russo's sensors smell my steps into the Hotel Packer House's so-called lounge. The AP man's Cheshire grin appears above a limb of a blasted tree. The hotel would pass for mortuary fallen on hard times. It had a restaurant, which has been shut down. A bar has been built into what was once the dining room of a good-sized house. It fits as well as would a pickup truck.

There are four other patrons besides myself. An elderly black woman is buying a six-pack to take out. A white woman, middle-aged and afflicted with a nonstop palsy; a man with one arm; and a salesman who stands up at the elbow of the U-shaped bar, talking to all and sundry, taking stories of his life from out of a sample case of failure. A color TV set shows a movie. White mountains, ski slopes, blue-eyed people sleek with adventure. The patrons are regulars who pass their nights here. The black woman chats with the woman who vibrates with her affliction. The tip of her cigarette waves frantically like a warning torch. Hungry, I order a sandwich that comes wrapped in cellophane, then it's stuck in an orgone box for three minutes from which it emerges thawed. Should the RAND Corporation interrogate these folks? The stump of the one-armed man looks like the bottom of an apple. Harrisburg's infrastructure. They all discuss a mutual friend who they fear is shooting heroin. One of the TV movie's skiers leaps into the air, bent over the two slats, forming the Greek letter lambda, the mathematical sign for longitude, flying over a landscape perfectly white. All the eyes in the bar look towards his flight.

vi

As I walk to court in the morning, it becomes obvious that a notorious trial to a town like Harrisburg is as much of a mixed blessing as a national political convention is to large cities like Chicago or Miami Beach. The merchants have accepted this trial as an unexpected tourist season. Motel business was down; it is now up. Department store windows all sport sales, and though they are not advertised as "Harrisburg Seven Sale Days," that impression is hard to avoid.

The press, still confined to their press room, hear another pool report.

"Herman then introduced the defendants, asking if any of the prospective jurors were related to any one of them. Each one separately beginning with Ahmad. 'Are any of you related to Eqbal Ahmad'—figure the odds on that—'are any of you friends of his' . . . etc. When he got to Tony Scoblick, he added 'Mr. Scoblick was a priest, he left the order,' and asked if his not being a priest any more would prejudice any of them against him. Scoblick then said, 'Your Honor, you're always a priest.' And Herman shot back, 'All right, you're a priest.' "

"Does that make the judge a bishop?" ABC wondered.

"Then when Herman got to Mary Scoblick, he said the same things about her leaving the order and then he added, 'Or are you still a nun?' He then introduced the lawyers, asking if any of them knew them, were related, ever had any business with their firms. None of them have served in Vietnam. Quite a few of the men have been in the air force in the past. One had a nephew wounded in Vietnam; another a son-in-law killed. One man taught pilots how to fly . . ."

"That's a good thing to teach them . . ."

"A few have friends in law enforcement and the FBI. There are three black women in the array; one is quite old and tottering, and another is middle-aged, and," he said, looking at a list of the juror's addresses, "lives in a federally funded low-income housing project; and the other is young, no more than twenty-two or so, she lives in Harrisburg . . ."

"Give us a rundown on the whites!"

General laughter overtakes the press corps.

vii

If the jury was an animal on the endangered species list, it would have been extinct long ago. Here they are: the array. People plucked from their homes and jobs. They fill the back of the courtroom, transform it to the sidewalk in front of a church, wearing, as they are, their Sunday best. They are as nervous as any group of auditioners, waiting for their turn, the chance to be excused for hardship or on the grounds of preformed opinion. They are citizens, and receiving a summons, they appear. Judge Herman repeats to them the privilege of serving on a jury. It is a pep talk, to calm them, allay their fears.

The clerk of court spins the jury wheel, which is in the same wood and style as the rest of the furniture of the courtroom. Lotteries. The new draft lottery. A random selection; take it out of the hands of men and put it back into the gods of fate. A bingo-parlor Olympus. The clerk calls out a name. Part of the crowd becomes soft, begins to sink, a hole forms, someone steps out and walks up and sits in the jury box. They are to select a qualified panel of forty-six.

The press has rushed to their seats. The prospective jurors regarded the press; the press regarded the prospective jurors. The stares decreased. Herman, at that time, was still excusing people for hardship. Asked if any had a hardship, they would raise their hands slowly, cautious periscopes breaking water.

Each explains their troubles in less than a sentence:

". . . chronic bronchitis . . ."

". . . controlled diabetes . . ."

". . . an eighty-nine-year-old dependent father . . ."

Herman, the arbiter, a Solomon who sees a hundred disputed maternities a day.

A man with black hair cut straight across his neck, what barbers call the hatchet cut, says he should be excused because his fifteen-year-old daughter would be scared at night if he were not at home. Herman inquired why. The man mumbled. Herman said, "What?" turning his ear toward him. "She was raped when she was thirteen and she would be scared if I wasn't home."

When a hardship story was told the other prospective jurors would look at the teller, their eyes scales that would be weighing their own complaints against his or hers. The courtroom had become a tent healing service; each sinner confessing dislocated discs, errant kidneys, moronic offspring who could not be left unattended. Each rose up, their new clothes unwrinkled, and re-

44

cited a dole of misery. There will never be a bread line for woe; ask anyone and you'll never hunger for it.

This is not a prospective jury made up of "key men," as was the Spock trial held in Boston. These names have come from the list of registered voters; the statutory exemptions have removed professionals: lawyers, doctors, teachers. The net catches the middle swath: widows, retired men and women, the periodically unemployed, government civil-service employees who can be excused from work without fear of losing their jobs.

Harrisburg has been surveyed; studies have been done of the sociological breakdown of the population. The defense lawyers looked at the results of these investigations. A portion of a memo to defense lawyers shows their concern:

> . . . on statistical grounds alone it's imperative that we fight to see as many jurors as possible. Thus if Lynch is going to reject young people, the more frames [blocks of people randomly chosen from a population] of people we go through the more likely we are to land a young person on the jury. It is also to our advantage in other ways to extend the jury selection process. The more people we see the better feel we will get for how our estimates fit the actual individuals coming through the array. A frame of 100 people: 57 will be male; 43 will be female; 8 will be under 30, 14 will be 30–39, 23 will be 40–49, 26 will be 50–59, 21 will be 60–69, 7 will be 70 and over. 33 will have less than a high school education, 46 will be high school graduates, 21 will have some college or more.

That is predictable, and lo! it is true. The defense wants to see as many people as possible. The prosecution believes in the fears of the defense; that Harrisburg will produce a jury only of bigots, hangmen, hawks, and conservative law-and-order proponents. They do not care how many people are seen. The defense's well-announced fears have become a shield; the prosecution trusts too much in this homegrown weapon; they do not consider chance-

statisticians' figuring for them, no wild-eyed population mathematicians predicting a throwback or two with every hundred people seen. The defense has twenty-eight peremptory challenges; four for each defendant. The prosecution has six. There must be forty-six eligible jurors empaneled before the peremptories are used. The more people they go through, the more young people they will have on the jury. What the young people will quench is less specific, but that is their thirst.

The winnowing continues. Prejudice is the prospective juror's loophole. If a man does not want to serve on the jury all he need say is that he has formed an opinion as to the guilt or innocence of the defendants. Herman asks if any have formed an opinion. Hands squirm up. "I have an opinion, Your Honor." Most answers follow the model of the first.

"All right, you're excused." Faces relax into smiles. Which, if any, are lying? In so many forms, conscience is pried open, exposed in the courtroom.

The numbers are depleted. Herman announces the likelihood of sequestration. It is one of the many powers that a federal judge can use capriciously. Since sequestration of juries is uncommon, and the number of people it happens to, minute, it is treated like the tiny percentage of bad reactions to a drug universally used: it is ignored.

Herman asks, "How much severe inconvenience in your lives will sequestration cause?"

Paul O'Dwyer rises and says, "All the defendants oppose sequestration of the jury." S. John Cottone, the U.S. attorney from Scranton, gets up to object to O'Dwyer's statement. Cottone is the government attorney who handles procedural matters.

Herman again asks, "Will it cause any of you extreme hardship?" Another abject litany begins.

The prospective jurors are then begun to be lured into a vaguely Mephisthophelean pact in order to accept sequestration. Herman hints at the luxuriousness of the accommodations, the weekend trips that will be arranged, the fine foods and restaurants that will be visited. Some prospective jurors begin to settle into their seats, root down, wanting to get on for just that reason.

Sequestration for them could be the cruise they've never been able to take.

The rationale for sequestration has come full circle. In the language of the Constitution, a jury was made up of "neighbors," who would have a great deal of familiarity with everyone. Out of the courtroom you would run into his family, friends, even the accused. When sequestration began in English Common Law, trials took but one day and the jury was confined behind a rail and were, in evident coercion to hasten a verdict, deprived of "food, drink, fire or light, except by the explicit license of the court." If they did not reach a verdict before court resumed they toured the circuit with the judge, trundling from shire to shire in a cart. This was seen eventually as a defect of the system and it went out and "separated" juries that could return to home and business came into American federal practice. But it is just the fear of news saturation, the establishment of the media neighborhood, which is Judge Herman's justification for his sequestering of the jury. Feudal days have returned and the jurors need to be denied "fire and light" (radio and television: they will be forbidden to see *Mod Squad, The FBI,* etc.). The degrading cart is adequately replaced by their confined and observed status. Not to let them go to and fro in their community is to deny the health and goodness of the community in which they live. The court is showing the cynicism that has been thus far reserved for the defense. Herman has let out that he is afraid that members of the jury will be bothered by the supporters of the defendants; but more than that he is following, in calling for sequestration, a simple reflex: an important case rates a sequestered jury, just as a costume epic requires a lavish budget.

Herman is becoming miserly with his abstentions. He refuses to excuse most of those who ask for it on account of his proposed sequestration order.

Those who are turned back, turn in shame, left with having to dig deeper to find a hardship presentable to the judge. A few elaborate more fully, buying their freedom with humiliation. The judge arbitrates not only the law, but lesser and greater things. The eyes of those still retained grow dull and worried. The only thing that will free them begins to flicker: opinion. It forms,

47

ignited by the sense of entrapment, fanned by exasperation, fed by the hardships they already have taken out and broken in front of the judge.

A few announce their new frame of mind. The judge scowls at them. They say that their prejudice is irrevocable. He releases them, forced by his own dicta. Everyone learns. Those who still remain change; in the courtroom they are exposed directly and personally to unredressable power.

A political trial heard by a sequestered jury is not entirely disadvantaged. The jury has made all the acquiescences, genuflexions, and adjustments to the same system of repressions and favors, of demands and rewards, to which these seven defendants stand opposed. The jury will agree to give up certain liberties; they are enlisting to live on a government compound (though of a Holiday Inn type) and are consenting to have their entertainments and other aspects of life—including "conjugal rights," as they are called in prisons—selected and censored by what is—though one diminutive and polite—a totalitarian state. They are being inoculated; given a taste of it, seeing for themselves; it is possible that first-hand knowledge will acquaint them with something heretofore unknown. They will become veterans; and veterans these days sour.

Eqbal, at yesterday's press conference, outlined the defense's objections to sequestration. They were, in Ahmad's alphabetical form: a) Sequestration was a deviation from the norm (as you take notes you realize that his students must find Ahmad's classes easy to follow); b) sequestration is reserved for capital cases, or when lives are in danger, or for particularly heinous crimes, and this would cause the jury to exaggerate the charges against them; c) jurors blame the defendants for the difficulties of sequestration; d) the defense would be presenting its case after the prosecution and by that time the jury would be quite weary; and e) sequestered juries usually bring in guilty verdicts.

Sister Elizabeth McAlister said she was deeply concerned about the deprivations that the jurors would have to suffer.

In the trials of the Catholic Left and the Resistance the juries have in the main appeared prepackaged. In the Boston Five (Spock) trial, the first noted "conspiracy" trial, the jury was

48

empaneled almost overnight. At Catonsville, Maryland, at the trial of the Nine (Philip and Daniel Berrigan, David Darst, John Hogan, Thomas Lewis, Marjorie Bradford Melville, Thomas Melville, George Mische, and Mary Moylan, who napalmed draft records), their attorney William Kunstler said, when it came to the jury selection, "Just take the first twelve." It was cavalier; they intended to conduct a political defense and made the assumption that any jury they got would be as good or bad as any other. Here, the case was different: The Harrisburg Seven were pleading *not guilty,* and this was not just a *pro forma* plea. This case was not an action they initiated; they were not acting out of their own free will. This was something else. The Resistance and the Catholic New Left are termed by the authorities,—as are draft resisters— "criminals by choice." That preserves their sense of decency, their sanity, their will; the exericse of choice, the chief tenet of free men. It gives them a sense of control. They are governing their own lives. Harrisburg cannot be compared to Catonsville, just as it cannot be correctly compared to the Boston Five. The Catholic Left isn't the only one trafficking in symbols.

Church and State are the practitioners of myth and ikon. The activists of the Catholic New Left carry out their symbolic acts of resistance; the government, the dark half of that dualism, responds with its own: the Boston Five, the Spock trial, was a symbolic prosecution, aimed at undermining academic support of draft resisters. It was to warn upper-middle-class professors and professionals that they will be known by the company they keep. Ramsey Clark, who authorized that prosecution, has said, "The system must have integrity. . . . It never seemed wrong to me that Thoreau and Gandhi were prosecuted or that they went to jail. That was their point. They so disagreed with their government that they would sacrifice freedom itself to show their concern."

The Chicago Seven trial, another manufactured indictment, like the Boston Five, was conjured up with the skill of a casting director picking a play of types. To discredit demonstrations, to equate any gathering as single manifestations of manipulation. And Harrisburg? Who is better at rattling their symbols?

The three major conspiracy trials of the last five years have not been mounted to prosecute crimes or individuals. The stakes

49

and scales are larger. This triptych of trials has been a clash of armies. Boston was the academic intellectuals and their adherents and followers; Chicago, the unkempt and unruly masses, the youth mob, the powerless hordes; and Harrisburg, the Spirit, the Word, the fanatic Church, those who attack the Pharisees. The trials are visions the ruling élite has in its darkest hours: professors urging armies to mutiny; youths organizing other youths into armies of destruction, to vandalize the world; priests and nuns summoning their congregations to revenge wrongs, banish rulers, destroy false gods. Each of the trials has outlined a sector, isolated an allegorical circle.

"A court stenographer is a contract job," I am being told, "and they earn about twenty thousand a year; they have to be able to do at least two hundred words a minute." Fast hands; the same salary as a professional shortstop. "Herman makes wine in his basement; he has a permit from the Treasury Department for that, strictly legit. He flies small planes, has a pilot's license"— and in his chambers, a photograph of a jet dropping napalm— "and when he was a juvenile court judge he and two others gave some black kids the death penalty. The Pitts case. His brother-in-law opened an ACLU chapter up in Tunkhannock . . ."

Judge Herman is an American bestiary: he is a Moose, a Lion, a Mason, an aviator, a hunter, a fisherman, a Legionnaire, a veteran. Sixty years old. When he takes off his black plastic-rimmed eyeglasses his face disappears.

During a recess prosecutor Lynch is shown a New York *Times* editorial headlined: WASTE IN HARRISBURG. He shrugs and returns it.

"Didn't you go to the Clergy and Laymen Concerned breakfast this morning? Fifty priests were there," G. says, "The sound of breaking bread could be heard for miles."

All but 62 of the initial 175 have been eliminated. These are to be brought in one at a time and questioned individually. Will it be a citizens' tribunal on the war?

The first, a woman, is asked by Herman: "What newspapers, magazines, do you read or receive?"

50

We, her husband and herself—instead of the royal we, it is the married we—we get the local paper. But she only reads the food ads. Television news? "I don't like to listen . . . because it only confuses me." She holds her hands up in front of her face. She wears white gloves. Covering her mouth, they become an Eastern woman's veil. White gloves; a disinclination to pry. Could she be impartial? "I've been asking God's help for that . . ." When she received her jury notice a neighbor said to her, "Oh, it must be the trial about those priests and nuns," but when the neighbor inquired further of her, she couldn't answer because, "I didn't want her to know I was so stupid, not knowing anything about it."

Prosecutor Lynch asks about her husband's job and service record. "Are you able and willing to put aside your views on the war, whatever they are, put them out of your mind and decide this case before you on the basis of the evidence presented and the law as given to you by the court?" She certainly hopes so.

The defense begins. Ramsey Clark asks about her children, gets their ages, finds out she is active in the PTA, is a school aide. "Do you know what defense contracts Borg-Warner may have with the government?" Clark asks, after discovering the firm her husband works for. She doesn't know, but Clark gives the impression that *he* knows. Asked about her feelings about the Vietnam war, she says, "I never really gave it too much thought."

Menaker, the local attorney for the defense, asks her about her schooling. He is native to the area, acquainted with the high schools, the meaning hidden by addresses, regionalisms, locales. He asks when she was married. The woman blushes, looks away, hides behind her white gloves, remembers. "Nineteen fifty-five," she says. Everyone smiles.

She is accepted on the panel of forty-six. It took about eight minutes. Another woman takes the stand. The procedure repeats. "I really don't know anything." She works for the Lebanon Packaging Company. On a label machine. Her husband manages a Bargain Town store in Lebanon. Her son-in-law was aboard the U.S.S. *Enterprise* when they had ". . . those explosions, you know." The aircraft carrier, off the coast of Vietnam. Rockets accidentally shot from under the wing of one Phantom jet into another. "If that's what happens to the people we shoot those things at I don't want anything to do with it," a distressed sailor said, after handling the burnt bodies. Asked about the war: "Everyone wants it over."

She is put on the panel of forty-six. She took twelve minutes. A man is questioned. They have talked about the case at work. "I'm a Catholic," he says. Lynch asks, "Could you put aside your religious feelings?" "They might sway me a little, but I don't believe so." When asked about the war: "I'm progovernment." Lynch says, "You understand the war is not on trial in this case; there are certain criminal charges . . ."

"Gentlemen," Herman says to the lawyers, though the defense has a woman lawyer at their table, "do you want to come up here?" There is a huddle at the bench. When it is over, Herman says, "We're going to excuse you from further attendance at this trial."

He took fifteen minutes. The graph is going up; it will never appreciably decline or dip.

Jury selection turns into a procession of the mothers and fathers of the cannon fodder of this and past wars. You have to leave America to see its military might; it is hidden here in the states; one must journey to the ports of Hong Kong, Sydney, Australia, the Mediterranean. Here, though, it is translated into family trees supplied by military service. The father's service in World War II, his older brothers before him, sons and nephews in Korea, sons-in-law and grandsons in Vietnam.

The panel would give an adman nightmares. It is a demographic ground-zero. No one reads any magazines; they skim the headlines of the local newspaper, and what they hear and see on radio and TV leaves their minds as quickly as the spirit departs from the dead.

At first they are questioned gingerly; the defense soon realizes, much to its surprise, that they are to be given more leeway than they assumed. The questions become sharper. Leonard Boudin is the last to question and if they decide that a prospective juror can be removed for cause, it is Boudin's task to do it. They are archaeologists who have discovered the remains of a lost American tribe.

Lynch doesn't fail to ask any of them that even if they think the conspiracy statute a "bad law," will they nonetheless still obey the instructions of the court in how to apply that law. The judge at times reiterates that they are not charged on the first count with substantive crimes, but with conspiring to commit illegal actions. The conspiracy charge they are left with is as faint from the deeds it implies as a Xerox of a Xerox of a Xerox.

"From the papers you've read, the TV you've seen, from what you talk about with friends, what do you know about this case?" Herman asks each one. It's something to do with priests and nuns kidnapping Kissinger and blowing up tunnels. If they have any impression, that is it.

They do not know that on 27 November 1970 in testimony before a Senate appropriations subcommittee, FBI Director J. Edgar Hoover announced "an incipient plot on the part of an anarchist group . . . the so-called 'East Coast Conspiracy to Save Lives' . . . a militant group, self-described as being composed of Catholic priests and nuns, teachers, students and former students . . . [whose] principal leaders . . . are Philip and Daniel Berrigan. . . . This group plans to blow up underground electrical conduits and steam pipes serving the Washington, D.C., area in order to disrupt federal government operations. The plotters are also concocting a scheme to kidnap a highly placed government official. The name of a White House staff member has been mentioned as a possible victim. If successful, the plotters would demand an end to United States bombing operations in Southeast Asia and the release of all political prisoners as ransom. Intensive investigation is being conducted concerning this matter."

J. Edgar Hoover gave that statement during his forty-ninth year as chief law enforcement official in this country. Practically fifty years, in a country that, dated from its Constitution, is not yet two hundred years old. One man a power for a fourth of its existence. Who has ruled longer? Where? What Caesar? How young this country is, if one man can remain in power for 25 percent of its history.

The prospective jurors treat most of the questions as a test; they recall the quiz shows of the fifties; they respond as if being asked current-events questions in a long-gone civics class.

Most belong to churches, erratically named: Messiah United Methodist, Camp Hill Presbyterian, Dover Assembly, Huntsdale Church of the Brethren, Evangelical Congregation.

A law of jury selection becomes apparent: the most memorable are scratched, the least memorable are kept.

Herman had told the lawyers that anyone who has read a national newsmagazine article that included excerpts from the letters, will be automatically excused. Herman is Rousseauesque in his search for a jury; he is looking for twelve *tabularasa*. No one admits to having read the article, or to remembering it, if they have.

They toil; they send their sons to the army; their daughters marry as soon as possible; grandchildren give them some pleasure. They stay close to their land; they are not nomadic, in fact look upon wandering as fit only for tramps; they are steady. It is a compliment often paid. He's steady. Can be trusted. Level-headed. Will show up. Stick-to-it-iveness. They long for equilibrium. Are made uneasy by change. They fear it like natives an erupting volcano; their gods are stolid, fixed, at rest. The middle district of Pennsylvania. When asked how long they have lived in their county, the answer most often given is, "All my life."

And if they have departed, it is under the spell of the armed forces. They have been taken off to distant lands, but they find their way back. They look upon those separated periods like men who claim to have been taken up by extraterrestial beings, shown unaccountable wonders, and let back down in the same fields behind their houses, whence they left.

The statutory exemptions from jury duty help produce this homogeneous array. It appears to be the cross-section of a radish. They have all the disadvantages of inbreeding. As Judge Herman has told them, their names are drawn only from "the good citizens of your district."

A man asks to be excused for hardship; he was newly made a widower and had been under great strain. "We went to sleep at one o'clock and I awoke at three A.M. and found her dead. It was like a dream. It's made my boy very upset; he was close to his mother . . ."

He talked volubly, in a torrent, as if in this court was the first time he had talked about his wife's death. He was ashen, his gaze trapped by some sight not found here. But so many had been questioned, that a dying man could have been brought in, propped up, and Herman would begin, "What newspapers do you read?" It was a formula that produced each time the exact same substance. "When you go to bed at one o'clock in the morning and at three o'clock she's dead it's a terrible shock. I'm just a little mixed up." The voir dire had undone so many, that neither the prosecution nor the defense was inclined to let him go; neither was Herman. Asked if he had any predisposition or prejudice that might affect his fair and impartial judgment, he replied: "Well, the three greatest men in government that I've admired have been Adlai Stevenson, Bobby Kennedy, and Ramsey Clark . . ."

The hush was broken by scattered applause from the spectators, stones against a windowpane. All the lawyers went up to the bench for a sidebar conference, except Clark, who remained alone at the table. The prospective juror smiles sheepishly at him.

He could not be excused for that and was placed on the panel of forty-six. He walked from the courtroom, his face pale as the sheets that wrapped him and his wife at three in the morning.

"There's Mr. Cottone," Sister Jogues Egan said, as the government prosecutor, the U.S. attorney from Scranton, walked by us, standing in the hall, waiting for a recess to conclude. "He's a nice man, even if he did send me to jail." Sister Jogues Egan is Sister Elizabeth McAlister's duenna. When McAlister was a student at Marymount College Jogues Egan was dean of students; when McAlister entered the Religious of the Sacred Heart of Mary, Jogues had become its provincial. Jogues is in her fifties. She is tall, as is Elizabeth, and has the silver hair of a well-kept matron. Her light blue eyes are thin sheets of ice. She can be quite warm, yet let a cloud pass and you will find yourself standing in her dank shadow; it is the disciplinarian in her. How many young Marymount girls have stood before her, imagining that white hair to be arctic vapor while they undergo her chastisements? It would drive some of them to excess just to warm up again. It gives her a tough mettle. She was jailed for contempt for refusing to testify at the grand jury in Harrisburg; the Third

Circuit Court of Appeals voided her citation for contempt and "In the matter of Jogues Egan" awaits the outcome of a wire-tapping case before the Supreme Court. She had asked whether the questions asked her before the Grand Jury resulted from illegal electronic surveillance directed at her. Cottone smiles a great deal; but he can smile and smile and still be a villain.

The bailiff has been lured up to the press section; it took a while. Like a wary bird he remained perched by the bench, but beckoned by the suet of publicity he came down, gave the press the correct spelling of his name. "Accent *grave,*" he said, in innocent mimicry of W. C. Fields in *The Bank Dick*. He wears a tie clasp shaped like a ponderous key, given him for years of service at the Eastern State Penitentiary. Asked to repeat his "Oh, yea" speech, he begins, then stops midway, forgetting—he wanders around the courtroom, looking up in the air, till he remembers and returns to finish. "Do you know why I say *the* honorable court? Instead of *this* honorable court?" he says in his gravel voice. "Because if I said *this* honorable court, it would sound like *dis*honorable court." He starts to laugh, and going away, says, "I have to go get my vodka before I open court."

A young girl takes the stand, looking like a squashed Kewpie doll. Herman asks, "Are you a single girl?" more out of surprise at the exception. He wants it confirmed, not seeking information. She works for the state, the "commonwealth," as they call it here, and has read something about the "plot." She has an uncle who is a part-time policeman; her father was in the service during World War II, but didn't go overseas, to Germany, till after the war; he belongs to the VFW and the American Legion. She lives at home. There are two ways to get a commonwealth job, she says, that's civil service and patronage jobs. "When I graduated from high school, I applied through the Republican party for a job." She spent nine years at Lebanon Catholic grammar school. "Was there any experience you had there with the nuns which might influence you in any way?" Paul O'Dwyer asks. "No," she replies. The good sisters did not influence her enough to keep her from chewing gum in public. Boudin gets up, not too pleased with her crabbed appearance, tightly cinched with corsetry to give shape to her squat figure. A starched pink blouse; pink is a bad color for jurors. Boudin inquires of her, in a fey Oscar Wilde manner, if she is active in GOP affairs.

"At the time," she replies, meaning at the time she applied for the job, "it was a Republican administration. Then the Democrats came in. So if you want to keep your job, you must change your politics."

It is the first time an uncontested truth has been spoken by a prospective juror. Herman stares blankly ahead as if he'd just heard his name called out by a stranger.

Boudin moves on, and asks if she knows anything about Henry Kissinger. She replies in the negative.

"You did know he went to China recently?"

"No."

"Well, I know; take my word for it."

She is asked about her feelings concerning Vietnam.

"I would like to see the war over, but I feel that we need the men over there so the war can be over as soon as possible."

Boudin is inclined to get her off for cause; but her opinions are so malleable, so without shape, that it is impossible to keep any of them braced up long enough to show them to be unacceptable. She realizes Boudin is being caustic with her; she smells a trap, becomes immobile, will not respond at length to anything he asks.

After much prodding, about how much faith she has in the government and in the president and the extent of his authority in all matters, she says tartly, "He is the president of the United States and commander in chief and it's his responsibility to decide if men are needed in Vietnam."

"Not at all *our* responsibility?"

Herman bristles at the slow pace of the questioning. He tells Boudin that he's covered everything that could be covered; she is put on the panel of forty-six. Boudin turns about to the spectators and press with the expression of a man staring at the departing train he has just missed.

A sixty-year-old farmer, hard as the land he tills, with eyes colorless as quick lime, is questioned. After Herman finds that he reads the headlines and knows nothing in particular about

57

the case, Lynch begins asking if he would favor either side, the prosecution or the defense. "I would lean to the patriotic idea of supporting the U.S. government. I belong to the oldest patriotic organization in the country, the Patriotic Order Sons of America; I've been a member forty-four years and I don't know when I've ever missed a meeting." Lynch sees what they have on the stand, the personification of all the defense's fears: twelve Patriotic Order Sons of America. He makes a show of impartiality, saying that one of the greatest institutions in the country is trial by jury and would he be able to be fair. He reckons he would. He was never in the military service. Lynch stops questioning him; he lets him drop as quickly as a grenade after the pin is pulled.

Clark asks angrily, startling Herman, "Did you tell someone you thought the defendants should take a bath?" He had been overheard. "Well, did you?" Clark says when he gets no response. "In my opinion, the first day [meaning the first day he arrived for jury duty], they weren't properly tidied up," he says elaborately, pride-stung.

"Just what happens," Clark asks, "at meetings of the Patriotic Order Sons of America?"

"I don't know if you didn't hear, but this is a *secret* organization."

"What is its purpose?"

"To protect," he says, pride cracking apart the wall of secrecy, "the United States against attack."

"It always has stood with the government?"

"My question should be," he says, moved with fervor, "why shouldn't I stand with my government?"

He is excused; the courtroom is quiet; a balance has been imposed; it is as if everyone had just seen for the first time the defendants' exact opposite.

It begins to take all day to get through five candidates. Another batch is called. Sixty-two people appear. There were five blacks in the first group; there is one here. Herman gives his Magna Carta speech, "the king reluctantly and not with very good grace put his signature on it. . . . Judges are no longer subject to peremptory removal by executives, so there may not be as great a need for trial by jury as there was in those days. . . . In Japan trial is by three judges, learned in the law, usually an old one, a middle-aged one, and a young one . . ."

Twenty-seven are quickly excused for opinion.

"Well," a reporter says, "that takes care of everyone who can read."

"Are you sure," Herman says testily to a man who rose late with his announcement of prejudice, "that you have a definite opinion?"

"He has a definite opinion all right; he definitely doesn't like motels."

"Do your customers talk about Mylai," O'Dwyer asks a woman who runs a bar in Lewistown. "No sir," she says. "Do you know what I am referring to?" he asks. "No; I don't."

A large portion of the middle district of Pennsylvania shows an outbreak of amnesia that the rest of the country would like to contract.

Each prospective juror is asked: "Some of the witnesses will have long hair and beards and will be wearing unconventional clothing; would you give their testimony the same weight you would give to, say, a clean-cut, close-shaven FBI agent?"

"As long as they're *clean,*" has been the reply most often given. "If there was odor I'd be affected," a man said. One who had no convictions of any kind about the Vietnam war said, repeatedly, "I have convictions about FILTH!"

A retired Bethlehem Steel worker, who read only the "hunting and fishing columns, the funnies, and who died," when asked about watching TV, responded, "when I'm home I'm usually in my cubbyhole tying flies." Otherwise he'd be watching his dogs, fishing in the creek, or dressing deer. When asked the long-hair, unconventional-clothing question, he said he was not concerned about others, but that "I'll have a quarter-inch haircut when I leave for Canada this fall so the black flies and the gnats don't get in my hair."

O'Dwyer elicited the following: "I was going to go to this school to be a doctor, they had no scholarships in those days; business wasn't so good. There was six in the family and I had to leave in the first year to help out."

Boudin inquired about his National Guard service, which he had been in during 1931–33. "Why did you join the guard?" "They had football and basketball teams in those days." "Were you ever mobilized in the early thirties?" "Well, I remember there was a flood at Sunbury that we helped at . . ."

"The National Guard was sometimes called out when there were labor or farm disputes. Were you ever involved in any of that?"

The dry dust of decades is blown off in the courtroom. The thirties. National Guardsmen, picketing, labor unions forming. Boudin resuscitates withered history.

"No, sir," he replied with an alacrity that made his answer doubtful. "All I can remember is the flood at Sunbury."

"And the football," Boudin says.

viii

"I'm sorry for the delay, but we've sent one of our panelists to the wrong church." Arthur Waskow, radical Jew, has been mis-directed. "Which reminds me, that we Christians have been send-ing our Jewish brothers to the wrong church for centuries," says Paul Mayer to the fifty people who have convened at First Church of the Brethren, on Hummel Street in Harrisburg, this winter night. Mayer has been through various incarnations: he was born in Germany in 1931 and came to the United States as a Jewish refugee in 1938; a postwar convert at sixteen to Catholicism, he became a Benedictine monk and spent eighteen years at St. Paul's Abbey in Newton, New Jersey. Civil rights and the peace move-ment converted him once more and he left the abbey in 1967 and was married the next year. He has two children and is living in a commune in East Orange, New Jersey. I am amazed by people's histories for I have so little. In the first indictment he was labeled an unindicted coconspirator. That first indictment came down on 12 January 1971, less than a month after Hoover announced the "incipient plot" headed by the Berrigan brothers.

Count I, as in the second indictment, was the crux: they were charged with conspiring to "maliciously damage and destroy, by means of explosives, personal and real property owned and possessed by the U.S.," and "to unlawfully seize, confine, inveigle, decoy, kidnap, abduct, and carry away and transport in interstate commerce a person for ransom and reward . . ." Accusation by thesaurus. The first indictment had put that conspiracy under a provision—18 U.S.C. 1201 (c)—for which a conviction may be punished by life imprisonment.

Neil McLaughlin, Anthony Scoblick, and Joseph Wenderoth were arrested in Baltimore; six days later, on 18 January, they are each released on $25,000 bail and placed under the supervision of Lawrence Cardinal Shehan, Roman Catholic Archbishop of Baltimore. He does not provide the money for bail, but the cardinal's legal and political advisor, Francis X. Gallagher, is retained as counsel. Sister Elizabeth McAlister is released the day after her arrest on $50,000 bail in New York. Her travel is restricted. Two days after his arrest, Dr. Eqbal Ahmad was released on $60,000 bail in Chicago. His travel is restricted. Philip Berrigan is informed in Danbury prison where he is serving sentences for two previous convictions.

The first weeks are the worst. A possible life sentence spawns dark terrors. Fears multiply, reverberate off the fantastic possibility, unfounded or not, of life imprisonment. Capital crimes. Murderers. The macabre odds the corrupt bet with come to mind: five to ten, ten to twenty, life. Life. Neil, Tony, and Joe in a huddle through the damp January night in a Baltimore jail. The stain spreads; their own doubts their accusers. They all know their Matthew: "But I say unto you, that whosoever looketh on a woman to lust after her hath committed adultery with her already in his heart." And it is the sins of the heart with which they are concerned.

What have they imagined? Wished for? Even if nothing has come to fruition, even less—even if nothing has moved out of their private selves? Bad thoughts . . . Sins of omission. The examination of conscience on the cold floor of a Baltimore jail. Think upon hell and damnation, we were instructed as youngsters,

61

so we would leave no transgression unturned, no matter how small. Wrongs. Think upon life imprisonment. Is there anything else you want to tell me, son?

"It's about time we stopped sending Jews to the wrong churches," Mayer says again, redoubling his conviction by repeating the thought. "We'll have to start without him and hope he finds his way here in time to speak. I apologize for the delay and the snafu . . ."

On 30 April 1971 a new superseding indictment was handed down; two new defendants were added: John Theodore Glick and Tony's wife, Mary Cain Scoblick. The list of unindicted coconspirators changed. Daniel Berrigan, said by Hoover to be the coleader, was dropped entirely. So was Paul Mayer. The unindicted coconspirator list became the government's miscellaneous column to which they could add or subtract, pad or thin, in order to balance their ledgers.

Count I was changed drastically. Draft board raids became the most prominent part. The kidnap conspiracy charge now went under a general conspiracy statute (18 U.S.C. 371). The life imprisonment penalty disappeared like a midnight apparition. Five years became the maximum sentence under the conspiracy Count I. But the beast had been roused. The threat of life imprisonment receded like a swollen river, but in its wake, the same devastation remained.

The former pastor of this Church of the Brethren (Ted Glick is a member of the Church of the Brethren) begins. He strangely denigrates Martin Luther King, Jr. "When we compare him to Moses, King's acts seem pale indeed." The word pale is just the first of his infelicities. His speech is infantile Horatory: a children's dilution of the classics. "In ages to come when they ask who was Richard M. Nixon, they will be told he was the ruler during the time the Harrisburg Eight were being persecuted." He addressed himself to his former parishioners, about a dozen of them, who sat stiffly on folding chairs. The other seats were taken up by Defense Committee people and a handful of local supporters. The Defense Committee people are disappointed at the turnout; but the night's bitter and blustery, and the absent numbers are ascribed to the weather.

The former pastor takes his seat and we move about two thousand years forward to Dr. John Raines, assistant professor of theology at Temple University. Raines shambles up to the lectern; he has worried eyes, but has a talk prepared. He could deliver it to an audience at Yale or to this crowd of motleys at the Church of the Brethren's cafeteria-auditorium. It makes no difference; he could be on film.

His title is: Religion, Resistance, and the Curing of Souls. Before the main feature there is a newsreel that I'll paraphrase: We see the managerial mind that is in power, which considers the public too immature on matters of foreign policy. The public is frustrated not to be able to effectively affect foreign policy. The managerial élite considers itself to be acting in the national interest.

Out of the frustrated immature public called a community of common disillusionment there rises up a community of resistance. Its first order of business was to confront racism, to which Raines refers as "the basic stain of this country."

The sixties, according to Raines, examined racism, but the Vietnam war "came along," and the community of resistance found that there was not enough psychic energy to "do" race at home and war away. Besides selling tanks to Third World dictators. The abyss between the nation's preachments and practices becomes obvious. There starts a revolution of rising expectations. It is nipped in the bud by assassinations: Malcolm X, Martin Luther King, Jr., John F. Kennedy, Bobby Kennedy. "Well," Raines says, "Everyone then began to say, 'To heck with it all.'" To heck with it all?

The people become "privatized," and begin to perform random acts of violence. He mentions the Eleventh Street townhouse explosion. The Weatherpeople's "bomb factory." Leonard Boudin's daughter running naked from the ruins. Her disappearance into the undergound. Raines has touched down; the room smells of proximity. He mentions Diana Oughton (1942–1970), who was killed in the explosion. The graffiti on the fence put up in front of the hole it left appears before my eyes: "Too much money, not enough brains." Raines outlines Oughton's life, her social conscience, working in Guatemala, home to America, alienation, decadence, "down that slide." "Privatized." Sounds like lobotomized.

In opposition to this, these random acts of desperation, is the Catonsville tradition, Raines says. Direct nonviolent action. It, he proclaims, is the most patriotic of all. The Catonsville tradition struggles, pays its prices, resides in the public realm, is not privatized, and restarts the public conversation and the debate of vital public dialogue.

The speech is similar to a vitamin pill. The audience received its Adult Minimum Daily Requirement of history, social analysis; 125,000 USP units of moral purpose, and 0.05 mg. of uplift.

From theology in theory, we go to theology in practice: Father Tony Mullaney, a priest of the Benedictine order, currently serving an inner city parish in Roxbury, Massachusetts. Mullaney is medium height and build, black hair, an open Irish face and a patient voice that speaks slowly and clearly. In the early fall of 1968, after the Berrigan brothers had headed for Catonsville, Mullaney, with four other priests, a Protestant minister, and eight members of the "laity," removed about ten thousand 1-A draft files from a Milwaukee draft board and burned them with more homemade napalm. They were christened, by geographical baptism, the Milwaukee Fourteen. They burnt the records in a square near the board dedicated to war dead. Could each square foot of American soil be dedicated by now to a dead soldier? The Milwaukee Fourteen defended themselves in court; they received what some commentators referred to as "lenient" sentences. Mullaney served a year in Wisconsin State Prison. The judge cried when he sentenced him.

Ted Glick, the severed defendant, earlier in the week had recited to me the roll call of draft board actions. He said there had been over 270. He gave the body count of the imprisoned. Glick described the various kinds of draft board actions. There were "stand-by" actions. The deed was done; the participants waited for the authorities. Glick is three years younger than I am but the phrase "stand-by" comes from the same lode. Your television reception has been temporarily interrupted: PLEASE STAND BY. Your draft board has been temporarily disrupted . . . Glick had led off with the tale of Barry Bondhus, the Big Lake One, who accumulated a week's collection of his and his brothers' excrement and despoiled draft files in Big Lake, Minnesota. That had been in 1966 and Glick said with the relish of recounting a fondly re-membered fraternity prank, "We call that the movement which started the movement." That story is a principle staple of a re-sister's smoker. An excremental interpretation of draft board raids is within reach. The Catholic Left will not let itself be obscene, but being bawdy is *right on!*

Glick recited the list: The D.C. Nine, the Pasadena Three, the Chicago Fifteen, Women Against Daddy Warbucks (who in a piquant gesture removed the "1" and the "A" from the type-writers of a New York board), the Beaver Fifty-five, "We the People"; memorized like a scout's rendition of the presidents of the United States, he strove to keep them in proper chronological order. Glick had been part of the Flower City Conspiracy, which hit Selective Service, FBI, and the U.S. attorney's offices (all in the same building) in Rochester, N.Y. After serving ten months of his eighteen-month sentence for the Rochester raid (which, even though its perpetrators were caught, convicted, and jailed, is included as part of the overall "conspiracy" in the Harrisburg Seven indictment), Glick was released on bail and is awaiting the results of an appeal based on a "highly prejudicial" message sent by the judge to the jury during its deliberations, without Glick's knowledge—he served as his own attorney in Rochester, an action he wished to repeat here. One of the judges, hearing the appeal in the Southern District of New York, is Irving R. Kaufman, who presided at the atomic espionage conspiracy trial of Julius and Ethel Rosenberg.

"We decided to consider ours a stand-by, since the law arrived before we were out of the building. Boyd Douglas was on the scene by that time, so we've decided he must have tipped them off . . ."

Douglas, not seen or heard from or of since shortly after his testimony before grand jury; the name Boyd Douglas had become a password for a suspicion. Boyd. When his name is said it is always annexed by a question mark. There is only one picture of Boyd circulated. Standing in the sunlight on the Bucknell Uni-versity campus, wearing a pair of sunglasses that has a distinctive silver bar across the top, his left thumb hooked into his pocket, a hitchhiker's carrying-case, a cigarette pinched between two fingers; his other arm bent at a right angle away from his body, in the position of someone swearing to something, the fingers fixed in the V sign. Sign of what? Victory. Triumph. Peace. Man's separated Cartesian nature.

Mullaney's voice reclaims my attention. He, unlike Raines, is talking to the people here, for that is what these panels are for, to speak to the people of Harrisburg, even though they are not in attendance—at least their absence is to be addressed.

Mullaney is telling us that western religious tradition sees the public realm as good; but today the public has retreated into a world of dualisms and despondencies. He says that procedure is the most important thing to Americans. And it is true: process is our sanctioned amorosa. "They spent twenty-eight million dollars to get Nixon elected; and they spent that because they knew he was a good investment. We're number one and we're going to stay that way, that is Nixon's message . . ."

Waskow enters the room with two Defense Committee people. Big, billowing black hair, partially stuffed under an urban folkie's cap, a red sweater and blue jeans slit up one leg that is encased in plaster. The cast goes up beyond the knee. Waskow looks like the frenzied sea-captain, reeling on the stable floor of the Church of the Brethren, on his one plaster-peg. He lurches over to the speakers' table and claims the empty seat. The cold air his entrance let in rouses some of the sleepy audience.

Mullaney continues, "Man was not made for the Sabbath, the Sabbath was made for him." He chides the audience with a quote: "A political act must be effective, or you're dealing with magic."

Mullaney finishes with, "Faith and love are based on what you hope for, St. Paul tells us; our faith must be our resistance."

We began with introductions by a former monk, then heard from a fire-and-brimstone fundamentalist, then a professor of theology, a Catholic priest, and now a radical Jew, Arthur Waskow.

"It's a disgrace," a Defense Committee feminist says. "There are no women up there."

Waskow is a resident fellow at the Institute of Policy Studies, Washington, D.C. He participated in some of the actions that brought indictments for the "Boston Five."

He keeps his funky cap on, a radical yarmulke.

The Harrisburgians in the audience have become rigid in their seats since Waskow's arrival. Here he is: the certified wild man they have pictured in their troubled sleep. Here is the "revolutionary" waiting to steal their bread and ravish their daughters, use the flag for a snot rag and generally ruin their lives. Waskow, wiry black hair streaking from the side of his head like wrath's accusing fingers, red (red!) sweater, breastplate of godless communism, and jeans, torn at that, a broken leg, gotten, no doubt, during some riot.

Waskow has galvanized the tiny crowd; the Harrisburgians nudge their chairs closer to each other. What is a Ph.D. in American history doing looking like this?! A radical Jew. If he wore a different hat and a long black coat he could be a distracted Chassid on any street of New York's Lower East Side; but here!— and he has a booming voice.

He begins with a short historical survey of the FBI, which he says, could be called, "another wing of the Catholic Church." He marvels that but ten years ago there could have been no such expression as "Catholic radicals," that the FBI consolidated their power in 1918–20 when they eradicated the last indigenous radical movement in this country: the Wobblies. That there were thousands of draft resisters in World War I. But now there is a crisis in the FBI; they have been made to look dangerous and ridiculous, since they have become the political police of the USA. He mentions the revelations contained in the internal documents stolen from FBI offices in Media, Pennsylvania. Next to this, the evolution of the "Movement," from teach-ins of the spring of 1965 to May Day in the spring of 1971. The war machine broke down in 1965, he contends. It stopped fulfilling people's needs. Full employment went under; the cities began to break down. "You can do guns and butter, but not guns and bread—the basic services— food, clothing, shelter. Why they have to put down the new Catholic Left movement is because the Catholic Church has traditionally been in America the integrater of immigrant workers into our system. Not being owners of private property or capital, immigrants cause fears of possible uprising. The Catholic Church for its large share of its white immigrant population became the interpreter of private property. The Catholic Church assimilated

67

endless immigrants into the American system. But this system will not let you drop out of the traditional role. It is just because of that fact, and not in spite of it, that an upper-class Catholic nun, past president of an élite Catholic women's college, Jogues Egan is harassed. She had begun to drop out of her traditional role."

The audience is greatly depleted just by the exit of two couples.

"I'm intrigued by images of fire; Dachau, Hiroshima, napalm, the burning bush; we are what is burning and yet not consumed," Waskow says, the metaphor truly possessing him: his voice crackles.

"The atomic holocaust; and yet, that is why Catholics have moved into radical politics. There has been a religious upheaval in the last decade, which has touched us all; a religious upheaval against a system that smashes ecstasy!"

That's all they need to hear. Ecstasy. The numbers lessen.

"We are heading for the Messianic Age . . ."

Parishioners leave the cafeteria.

"I think that's what's going down," Waskow says, his voice quieting, a jet that is now merely taxiing from the runway, "We are confronted with total death; a new understanding of good and evil; we're wrestling with God and the political police of the death empire which carries on its own commitment."

"Before the question-and-answer period," Paul Mayer says, rising, a commercial interruption during a televised catastrophe, "I have some announcements of interest. Tomorrow at eight P.M. at the YMCA there will be a poetry reading and songfest with Father James Carroll, poet and lecturer; and the Medical Mission Sisters, a group of nun-singers from Philadelphia . . ."

A white-haired gentleman gets up, leans on a cane, body trembling. "I was right, you think the length of hair equals brains; Christians, we learn from the Bible, make good fighters, there should be no lack of courage; you misguided Catholics," he says, gesturing towards Waskow, "would be better to get off your duffs and get on with blowing up things, if that's what you think!" His challenge thrown down, he falls back on his seat.

A middle-aged woman, her features affixiated with ire, starts off, "What gives you the right to have all the answers? You're not as peaceful as you say you are, sitting up there; if someone pushes you too far you fight . . ."

"These people," a Defense Committee member says, "think we are violent and we aren't dissuading them . . ."

Anger's first wave abates. Raines has excused himself long before; the remaining panelists cannot erase the puzzlement from their faces, or the knot of worry from their brows. From the dozen local people left comes only vituperation; it is unexpected, so counter to the purpose for which these panels have been arranged. But they are the first representatives of the peace movement these people have seen and like absentee landlords just arrived to a dilapidated building the first greetings they receive are complaints.

"It's hard for me to stand up," an apparently frail woman says, "I'm not too well; I've been to Selma, all the marches, and I'm a pacifist; and I want Mr. Waskow to answer a few questions. First, how can he say things about America, call it a death empire, when we were the saviors of the Jewish people in World War II; and how come the Jewish church isn't involved in organized protest against the war; and just what can be done, anyway?"

"Well," Waskow says, "first off, I'm not sure that America did save the Jews during World War II; they beat the Germans and indirectly saved the Jews; they never bombed the railroad tracks to the concentration camps; the firebombing of Dresden was carried out as callously as any of the German holocausts; not particularly the act of a savior. But in answer to your second question, our rabbis, as an organized community, remember the oppression too well, the holocaust of European Jewry; that opened such a chasm that they are lying low and do not want to seem to be in too obvious opposition to the government, especially when it deals with policy questions about the Arab–Israeli conflict. There are exceptions, like the Jewish Defense League, but most, or a great deal, of early and late opposition to the Vietnam war has come from the intellectual Jewish community. Just look at the names who have signed endless petitions; and to your last question, the way we bring about what we want brought about is to act it out now, to create it, to be it; then it's here. We should not be in Harrisburg to celebrate this trial, or the Berrigans' as virtuosos of the Resistance. We have to de-Americanize the revolutionary scenario. There is no way to liberate the United States; it is too diverse, even though there is an attempt afoot to smash the ethnics, to homogenize them. One interesting event of late has been Congress's discovering its own powerlessness. That has turned most of them into permanent depressives, permanent junketers; but for a few it's awakened a new spirit, and there might be a lot of good yet to come out of that—when a body of our government realizes it is powerless, then there might be some real change."

The final minutes of the gathering take on the rhythm of lower-middle-class parties, where over bourbon and stale ginger ale, all the world's problems are theoretically solved.

"Well," Mayer says, in conclusion, "we have seen here tonight, that even though we hold divergent ideas we can still get together and talk about things civilly and think on and consider each side's view of things."

"*This* is winning their hearts and minds?" a Defense Committee member asks as we step out into the cold Harrisburg night.

ix

Jury selection drags on like a botched suicide.

"I'm beginning to think the Japanese are right," a bored reporter says.

Some of the press have been out examining the days and nights of typical Harrisburgians.

"They really have this thing for bingo," P. says, "a floating bingo game; it travels around the town and the same people show up night after night. One night it is at the Moose's, the next at the Democratic Club, and the next night at the Knights of Columbus . . ."

"Bingo hustlers, they bring their own special beans and boards . . ."

"There's a little money to win; they live to hear those numbers called out . . ."

"Yeah; F-111, B-52, M-16 . . ."

"You know, the defendants are clothed in the presumption of innocence," Herman says for the hundredth time to a venireman

70

who has just said, "There must be some evidence against them, or why would we be here?"

"The defendants should wear white robes that say 'INNOCENT' across the front," P. whispers.

"You're getting pretty far afield again, Mr. Boudin," Herman says once more in response to an objection from Lynch.

"Someday we're all going to meet in that pretty far afield . . ."

A pornographic novelty pen, looked through like a spyglass, occupies the press section for a while.

Herman would look up at the clock and ponder, as if the answer to how things had gotten away from him hung on its hands. The questioning now ran well over an hour for each prospective juror. Boudin would now have to make a juror announce the most flamboyant prejudice in order for Herman to excuse him for cause. When he managed this, the offensive remark out of the venireman's mouth, Herman would wince, knowing there was nothing to do but dismiss him. Boudin would execute a veronica away from the prospective juror as the damning admission came by.

The consensus reached in the middle district of Pennsylvania about the Vietnam war is, "If there's got to be a war, there's got to be a war." Everyman's tautology.

These are citizens; they are neither the heights nor the depths, the movers nor the makers; these are not doctors, lawyers, public officials, members of the armed forces, policemen and firemen, persons over seventy, clergy, women with children under ten, dentists, nurses, sole proprietors of a business. These are the people.

In order to get twelve, close to four hundred were summoned. The panel of forty-six resulted in seventeen males, twenty-nine females. Three blacks: two female, one male. Thirty-two Protestants, five Catholics, three no-church, and six unknown. Fifteen were urban, four suburban, and twenty-seven rural and small-town. Four single women are among them and one bachelor. From this selection came these twelve:

Juror No. One. A smiling black woman in her late forties who doesn't read newspapers. Her husband manages a State Store

71

(commonwealth-owned liquor store); an older son, once a medic in Vietnam, now works locally in a toy factory. Her smiles are not silly; they are black black humor.

Juror No. Two. A white man in his late forties, a fire-school instructor, once worked as a consultant (in fire-prevention procedure) at Lewisburg penitentiary. His wife is a Catholic, he a Lutheran. Had one year at Bucknell University. When asked if he had heard about the case he said, "When I first read about the conspiracy, I thought the whole thing was kind of funny—the idea of blowing up heating ducts and zipping off with Henry Kissinger."

Juror No. Three. A white woman in her late twenties, a redhead, who would be the most-sought-after waitress at a truckstop eatery. Husband is a welder. Chews gum slowly, a worked-over sexual cud. No opinions.

Juror No. Four. A white woman in her late forties, four older children, heard expressions of guilt expressed by other prospective jurors. Very dignified. Husband a plumbing and heating contractor. No church. Son-in-law served in Vietnam. Said about the war: "I wasn't opposed too much to it at first, but the last few years I've been against it."

Juror No. Five. A white woman about sixty. Brethren in Christ Church, diabetic, no Vietnam views. All four of her sons are church-sponsored conscientious objectors.

"My sons through their church affiliation took alternate service instead."

"Would that affect you?"

"No. I think that was their decision to make."

Lynch said, "The Vietnam War is not on trial here, nor is war in general."

O'Dwyer interjected, "That's just giving half the story," to which Herman replied, "You readily give more than the other half."

Juror No. Six. A white man, early forties, a Lutheran, went to business college, has five boys and a girl; owns Superthrift Stores in Dillsburg and Middletown. Sons help run them. Asked about clergy in antiwar movement and social involvement, he said: "Church people should do more of that." Asked if he was not sequestered, would he be able not to talk about the case with anyone, even on the golf course, where he said he spent a great deal of time. He made everyone laugh with his answer: "I'm usually so far in the rough I don't see anyone else to talk to."

Juror No. Seven. A white man in his late forties, early fifties, who became a pawn in the fight against sequestration. It would be an extreme financial hardship to him, he protested, but since he did not plead prejudice to get off, his honesty became apparent, and that he was a college graduate, possibly acceptable to the prosecution, made him desirable. Herman was inclined to let him off if he would claim the slightest prejudice; Boudin requested that Herman reconsider his order of sequestration. Herman would not let him off because of the sequestration hardship.

Juror No. Eight. A young white woman in her twenties, working for the Dauphin County Board of Assistance, lives with her nineteen-year-old brother. She said, "I feel in some ways it's a necessary war, in some ways, it's not a necessary war." She was a philosophy major in college but dropped out after the third year. Her examination was lengthy, the court lulled by her voice, temperate with her because she was pretty. Boudin made her seem hawkish on the war beyond her want, to make her more acceptable to the prosecution, by going on at length for explanations of her views, which could be arguments for either position.

Juror No. Nine. A middle-aged white woman from York, who read the Philadelphia *Inquirer*. She vaguely remembered reading about a plot to kidnap, "which seems years ago." Lynch kept calling her "Mrs. York." She graduated from the Philadelphia College of Pharmacy but had not worked as a pharmacist for the last eighteen years. Her husband is an interior decorator. "He will decorate anything anybody wants him to decorate."

Juror No. Ten. A white woman in her thirties, single, a Catholic, bookkeeper for a printing firm, high-school graduate, lives with aunt and uncle, thinks the war "a big waste."

"How long have you held that opinion?" O'Dwyer asked.

"How long has the war been going on?" was her reply.

Juror No. Eleven. A white woman in her early thirties has mulled over, in regard to the Pakistani defendant, Eqbal Ahmad, "whether an alien should express their feelings against a country they are living in." She thought it was "possibly bad manners." She and her husband lived in Thailand for three years, 1967–69. Her husband was a civilian civil engineer. She has a child six years old. Asked why she didn't request to be excused on those grounds, she said: "It concerns me, if all of us asked for excuses, what type jury it would be." About Vietnam and her time in Thailand she said, "When I was in Thailand I had the feeling that I was more remote from the war than when I am here in the United States."

The twelfth juror was a white woman in her early twenties, tiny, black hair pulled back from a center part so tight it shone smooth as shoe polish. Married just four months. Clark had asked: "I don't want to ask a question that'll get you in trouble at home, but would sequestration be a hardship for you?" She said, not at all, she'd prefer being sequestered. Lewd innuendos circulated in the press section. About Vietnam she said, "I'm not sure I'm for this half-and-half business; we should either give full support or full withdrawal."

The defendants and lawyers had argued over which jurors would be kept after the government eliminated their six. They squabbled like relatives claiming favorite pieces of furniture from a deceased kin's home.

At a press conference following the jury's swearing-in and the imposing of sequestration on the twelve, Sister Elizabeth said that what she had seen the past weeks during jury selection had altered her ideas about the women's movement. "I've never been an outspoken advocate of women's lib, but now I realize how much it's needed."

Eqbal says, "With all the cards stacked against us we are trying very hard to test the capacity of the judicial system to give us a fair trial."

Not entirely in jest, the prosecution had told the defense, "If you call off your investigators we'll call off ours." Both sides had done as much checking on each potential juror as possible.

Out of the rule of four hundred they had gotten as close as they could to twelve exceptions. Sequestration was still opposed but it had become a *fait accompli*.

The last sequestered jury for a federal case in Harrisburg was in early 1951. "It was a white slave case," the clerk of court from Scranton obligingly found out for me, "say it involved 'two prominent Scrantonians,' two guys who were running girls to Nevada. You know, whorehouses are legal there; they brought up a madame to testify, from one of the houses they tried to place them in. She said, looking at the defendants, that she wouldn't deal with them. 'We don't allow pimps in our house.' And then about the girls, 'They didn't have enough of the social graces; they could only talk about baseball . . .' "

Now the jury will be read daily like tea leaves, but the issue of sequestration is put to rest with one final motion. The trial proper is to begin; what previously seemed paramount is dropped as other matters arise that have to be dealt with, just as a doctor treating multiple patients of a disaster leaves the dead and moves on to that which still might be saved. Any powers of resurrection are assigned to the appellate courts.

Before Boyd

The business of America is business.
—CALVIN COOLIDGE
29th president of the United States

i

Spotlights are the farthest social extension of the interrogator's bare bulb and two of them are trained on the platform that awaits Joan Baez. Behind it is an exit that leads to the dressing rooms under the stands, but those are not outfitted with birdcage lights and many mirrors, for the acts this hall sees are usually booked not by agents, but by livestockers and tractor dealers; this is Harrisburg's Farm Show Arena, and that name is not the camp nomenclature of a Manhattan discothèque.

Baez is the queen of the Movement's USO adjunct, and she is here to give a benefit concert for the Defense Committee.

The packed dirt of the arena floor is as dark and dried as chewing tobacco and it is covered with a complete blot of people. Their faces are familiar as a picture dimly remembered; then comes the shock of recognition: adolescents. Eclipsed for a decade, they have returned intact from the far side of hype. Clots of boys staring at girls who are joined by the Siamese code of a rural night out. They travel in pairs as nuns used to and the FBI (when making house calls) still does. There is no haze of marijuana floating over the crowd like a cartoon character's blue-funk cloud. We are far from the city. Near eight thousand have come from area high schools and neighboring colleges.

The boys, like Lieutenant Calley, still roll up the bottoms of their jeans. A bra is no longer the emblem of a pubescent girl's emergence into womanhood. It is after eight and there begins the whine of impatient crowds: handclapping. The spotlights play back and forth, their operators continually knighting and re-knighting the shoulders of the microphones. They wait to dub Baez, whose first act of Resistance, the Defense Committee's bio supplies, was her boycott of the *Hootenanny* TV show, after they blacklisted Pete Seeger. The *Hootenanny* show! Time warps ripple across the Farm Show Arena. Nothing ages as quickly as the cover art of record jackets, but Baez's voice is perennial; hers is everyone's sister in each inner ear.

Baez arrives on stage, dressed in a Pucci mini, looking like an attractive thirtyish photographic-researcher for Time-Life.

"I've made a deal with the TV people; they can take pictures during the first two songs, then they have to pack up and go home." Applause. Film crews as new lepers, driven out with stony looks.

"This song isn't much good, so I'm going to dedicate it to the attorney general." Applause. The lights of the TV cameras move in like white-heat locusts.

Throughout the performance she makes only two references to the Harrisburg Seven. Baez announces, "It takes a lot to break out of the Catholic Church and do something brave," and later, before singing her "calypso version of the Lord's Prayer," something she hadn't "sung in eight years," she says, "It's a good one for Harrisburg." She is here to raise cash; and no one is going to drive out the moneychangers.

"I'm here," she says, "not to lecture, but to have fun."

She sings, "Oh, Happy Day," and during it her voice rises to a terrifying screech: black passion turning into white neurosis. Afterwards she mimicked girls who would come up to her and ask, leeringly, "What are you thinking when you sing about Jesus?"

The laughter is the solution to a riddle. This led to a song of her own, about "Snuggies," a word for someone, she explained,

77

that you can spend an enjoyable two or three days with, but not much longer. She said that the word *snuggies* originated on the Coast like a perfume dealer who points to the import tag. The lyric was titled "Love Song to a Stranger." She is lovely; a hedonistic mirage to the parched and chaste Catholic Leftists; singing of cares for which they are not free.

On the Farm Show Arena floor are the young of a species, part of an animal kingdom. Bidding from the bleachers for the best reproducers could commence. They loved it; a night free of politics and "other sad dreams." The Defense Committee didn't raise many consciousnesses, but they did raise ten thousand dollars.

Baez didn't seem ready to go, but the rising applause signaled a proper time to split; she sang "Swing Low, Sweet Chariot," *a cappella.* A young girl heads for an exit ahead of the crowd, with a concert poster in her hand, bedroom-wall bound. Baez finished:

> Amen
> Thank you
> Good night

As the happy crowd left, three members of the Defense Committee were at the arena's doors with cardboard buckets the size of top hats in their hands, asking if you could spare any change for the Revolution.

ii

On 21 February 1972, after a month of jury selection, the trial begins. Herman reads the indictment:

> The Grand Jury charges:
> That on or about January 1, 1970, the exact date being to the Grand Jury unknown, and continuing thereafter up to on or about January 7, 1971, in the Middle District of Pennsylvania and elsewhere, EQBAL AHMAD, PHILIP BERRIGAN, JOHN

THEODORE GLICK [who, Herman says, will not be tried here and now], ELIZABETH McALIS-TER, NEIL McLAUGHLIN, ANTHONY SCO-BLICK, MARY CAIN SCOBLICK, JOSEPH WENDEROTH, defendants herein did, unlawfully, willfully and knowingly combine, conspire, confeder-ate and agree together and with each other . . . and with divers other persons unknown to the Grand Jury, to commit offenses against the United States . . .

"Did they sequester a hairdresser along with the jurors?"

All the women jurors have their hair done in high style; in their box they all look new, like yellow No. two pencils at the beginning of a school year.

Herman reads the overt acts:

1. From on or about January 1, 1970, until Feb-ruary 6, 1970, Joseph Wenderoth, Anthony Scoblick, Mary Cain Scoblick, and John Theodore Glick did attend meetings at 3007 Susquehanna Avenue in Philadelphia, Pennsylvania, where they and others planned to vandalize Selective Service board offices located in the metropolitan area of Philadelphia, Pennsylvania.

And on to the last:

35. On or about November 12, 1970, Joseph Wenderoth made a telephone call to Lewisburg, Pennsylvania.

Conspiracy law requires not only proof that a conspiracy exists but proof that a defendant committed at least one overt act in the furtherance of said conspiracy. What Juror No. Nine said seemed years ago, and what a prospective juror thought had been taken care of some time before, sets off. It was so stale that comedians no longer joked about it. After Hoover's Novem-ber, 1970, statement, Bob Hope said on the *Tonight Show*, "They suspect three priests because the ransom note was written in Latin." At that time, if Kissinger gave a speech, the Secret Service

79

men would be jocularly informed, "The building is surrounded by nuns; and they're all after Henry's body."

William Sebastian Lynch was the chief of the Organized Crime Section of the Justice Department; he left that post to be promoted to deputy assistant attorney general in the Internal Security Division, and to be in charge of this prosecution.

"That promotion is what they twisted his arm with to take on this case," a journalist remarks, making a turn-of-the-screw gesture.

Lynch does not look like a prosecutor of radicals, clergy or otherwise. His suits are expensive, but he buys them off the rack, his weight goes up and down but they stay the same, shapeless. In a ludicrous and false show of complete fairness the government has arrived with four Catholic U.S. attorneys. Let the Catholics persecute the Catholics. Let Jews try the Rosenbergs. (Roy Cohn, a prosecutor in that case, in his book, *A Fool for a Client,* offers that fact as a rebuttal to charges of anti-Semitism.) Let the Indians decimate the Indians. Let blacks wipe out blacks. Let the Mafia gun down the Mafia. Let the Vietnamese kill the Vietnamese. It's Roman sport; a tyrant's sense of justice. *Le roi s'amuse.*

No, Lynch is not the expected guardian out to forestall the last word in subversion. He is not sleek, sinister; no Interpol figure, he. In the fifties, perhaps; Joe McCarthy and he might have shared the same haberdasher. Organized Crime at the Justice Department fit him well; stuff you could get your teeth into; you knew where people stood; you had the goods on them or you didn't. Mutual respect on some levels. Straight talk; an easily recognized world. The one William Lynch knows well and understands. Kickbacks, graft, extortion, contracts, gangland slayings, the Yablonski murders; good and evil, right and wrong. Studs Lonigan in the Justice Department. Esquire after his name. It would make his parents as proud as if he'd become a priest himself. He would have to restore the good name of the fathers in order to retain his own, for they, in his world, are mirror images. You can't tarnish one end of the continuum without dulling the other. Besides, there's the promotion. Deputy assistant attorney general. So many reasons to take on this case. And there's the chance he might prove something.

Lynch doesn't look upon himself as a ninth-inning relief pitcher called in with the bases loaded and no outs. He was sent here from Washington to replace an assistant U.S. attorney, Guy L. Goodwin, under whose direction the first indictment was drawn up. Goodwin, took a de Sade-like interest in his intimate pursuit of Catholic radicals. Guy Goodwin, of the unique voice, so high-pitched and effeminate, one wonders how it passed a security clearance. Lynch was the horse that was brought in and changed to in midstream; and he is now skittish, waiting to give his opening statement. He junked the first indictment and fathered the second. He shuffles through his index-card notes. The opening address to the jury is public and unappealing to him; even though the rest of the trial is carried out on an open stage the discourse between attorneys and judge carries a private air.

Lynch begins, with the obligatory Friends, Romans, Country-men salutations. He then tells the jury, "you don't check your Godgiven common sense at the courtroom door." He introduces the conspiracy, and Philip Berrigan as the "leader" who master-minded "a meticulous and carefully planned" plot. He divides the indictment into three parts, as he wants the jury to see it: Count I, the conspiracy; Counts II and III, threatening letters; Counts IV–X, the contraband counts. He scorns the "lofty purposes" the defendants might have had and he says if they had stuck to peace-ful protest we would not be here. "Had they taken the traditional role"—yes, if they had taken the traditional role, alas, there is no federal statute prohibiting that, though that was their first crime—"of dissent, peaceful protest, and political action, we would not all be here. Instead they banded together, conspired, and planned a series of illegal acts, the thrust"—Lynch keeps using this word, "the thrust of the argument is," he would say, begin-ning a rebuttal to earlier defense motions; Lynch, always thrust-ing at windmills—"of which was to disrupt governmental activities and attract media coverage . . ."

He invoked the name of Boyd F. Douglas; this is my informer with whom I'm well pleased. The proportions of his fifty-minute

81

opening remarks would serve for the trial, Boyd taking up most all of it. Father Berrigan arrives at Lewisburg penitentiary and meets Boyd, who is on a study-release program that allows him to attend nearby Bucknell University during the day, and "almost immediately Boyd F. Douglas was recruited as a courier for communications outside normal channels . . . Philip Berrigan kept his followers and these defendants advised of what was going on, and in turn his followers, including Sister Elizabeth McAlister, would tell him what was going on."

Lynch chooses his words from a dictionary of Red-baiting. Mail drops were set up. Communication networks established. Cell meetings, "so-called 'rap sessions,' subtle means to garner recruits, turning them from academic discussions into the politically active groups they wanted." Boyd, he said, pausing, trying to sum up Creation in a week, "got . . . apprehensive," and began to make copies of the letters. Then on a "routine search" of Father Berrigan's cell, "a letter he had prepared for transmission" (over a wireless to Moscow no doubt) was found. Berrigan was confronted by the associate warden, and later Boyd, who, from then on, supplied the FBI with copies of the letters, including ones sent before the time. Any lapses in the outline of guilt Lynch was tracing were passed over with the acceleration of voice. Ten letters went out, fourteen came in; these letters revealed the plot to raid draft boards throughout the land; Lynch pictures Berrigan from his cell orchestrating, by closed-circuit letters, draft board raids in Delaware, Philadelphia, Rochester. Speak the word and it shall be done, is Lynch's sense of the loyalty Berrigan's followers showed. Douglas was recruited to be the "explosives man" for the "D.C. action." Boyd Douglas had indicated [to the defendants] that he was familiar with explosive devices. That was not a fact but he acquired a couple of manuals on explosives to familiarize himself in case he ran into someone who knew more about explosives than he did. Joseph Wenderoth and Neil McLaughlin found out about these manuals and asked to have them in order to make copies. Plans were going ahead for the D.C. action, the blowing-up of the tunnels, and it was to have taken place one year ago today," Lynch says, referring to the fact that George Washington's birthday was being celebrated. The kidnapping plan was to be merged with the bombing of the tunnels, he said, dealing with the most sensational charge with but one sentence. Strenuously avoiding J. Edgar Hoover's name, "At this point [29 November 1970] further publicity took place and everybody, so to speak, headed for the woods. Wenderoth got in touch with Boyd Douglas and said he thought it would be best that nobody said anything to anybody."

The speech was a great exertion for Lynch. Whenever he has to speak at length it turns into a deathbed oration given in fits and starts, gaspings and wheezes. Flushed, pouring water down his throat to keep it open, he finished with an odd piece of advice: "Please keep an open mind till you hear all the evidence."

The prosecution's case has two heads: Boyd and the Letters. Lynch had outlined dark deeds afoot; they fouled the air unrebutted till afternoon, since court recessed for lunch.

Ramsey Clark, when he was attorney general, recommended William Lynch for an earlier promotion. It was a default recommendation, saying that there was no one better qualified for the position. Some of the distress on Clark's face came from the need to reprimand, to chastise someone under him; an unpleasant thing to do. Disciplining children. Many emotions tax Clark's face now. His face is expressive in a particular way: the look he has either recedes or extends, grows darker or lighter, but the movement is one of forward-and-backward and not side-to-side. That aspect pervades his whole person. Clark does not seem to sway, his lips never equivocate into half-smiles or even curl cynically. They darken or lighten; he is like a compass that has only two directions: a north and a south. Nothing in Clark seems to vacillate, bend, change in shape. It speaks of his enshrined ideals. You make some headway, you might have a setback or two, but you continue, straight on your sights fixed, you do not look for exits on either side. You do not look for a way out. This is all in his face. In the lightening or darkening of his expressions.

Except for the stern questions directed to the steadfast member of the Patriotic Order Sons of America, Clark was the perfect Southern gentleman during the *voir dire*. He shucked folksiness till it became corn. When a prospective juror lamented he had only girl children, Clark replied, "In my view of things, you can never have too many girls." And after a lengthy examination of a Catholic man, who had been an enlisted career man in the navy, and was now a supply clerk at a nearby naval supply depot, who expressed the most strained sincerity, who was sorely perplexed and injured by Catholic priests being involved, "to the extent to which they are alleged to be." He has a son who enlisted in the navy after trying hard to get into Annapolis and was now, he said proudly, studying Russian at a base in Monterey. The prospective juror had a "secret" security clearance. He acted out on the stand the most arduous dilemma, trying to square for himself, and finding it impossible, why priests and nuns would get mixed up in these things. Boudin got him excused for cause; and as he left there was a recess and Clark met him at the door, said a few words, shaking his hand, wishing his son well, because it was obvious that his dismissal from the jury panel had bothered him, in another way that he couldn't explain to himself.

In a courtroom the only sense that isn't starved or atrophied is the sense of hearing. Sight, what you see day by day, is so little altered, that when it is, it is more of a blur, just the familiar scene slightly out of focus. And what is there to touch? The courtroom is an aural world. The ears of the regular daily press are tuned towards the front like green leaves to the light.

And the voice heard from Clark now is new to this courtroom. In what other chambers, dealing with matters of consequence, had this tone been used? Clark's voice is of a man who expects to be obeyed. Who is used to having his directions followed. That is its trunk, but it has many branches: hurt, betrayal, righteousness, concern, respect, fervor. Some of the jurors are blown back in their seats with its force. Far from Lynch's aggravated rasp, Clark's voice is the mirror of its sense.

"There was no conspiracy. There was no agreement; there was no capacity, no ability to conspire or agree to do the things they are charged with conspiring to do. You will come to know these defendants as the gentlest of people, not capable of kidnapping or harming any human being. . . they could not do it. They could not do it, deeply distressed as they were about their government's ability to bomb, to drop millions of tons of bombs.

"Beyond any doubt draft board raids occurred, many over the years, but there was no conspiracy to raid draft boards. You will never find, the evidence will show, that these defendants conspired to perform any single act together. They did their own thing."

Nothing is supersubtle. It is public oratory, the stuff of addresses. Clark's world is being created; it is as if a successful experiment is just starting. People watch keenly, a display of smoke and electricity, bubbles and electrons. But an experiment nonetheless, in the controlled environment of the courtroom, during the opening argument for the defense. Each lawyer presents his own personal vision when he speaks; and for the time each would rule the courtroom. No sooner than he finishes it would be replaced. Layer upon layer, with this variety of lawyers, civilizations would rise up and disappear. The sediment of different philosophies in the courtroom would rival the Grand Canyon; impossible to sort out, it became a minor national wonder.

It is a particular mode of speech Clark uses. It is the poetry of laureates. Each country produces examples of it; it is the Lincoln not of the Gettysburg address, but of the "binding wounds" of the Second Inaugural. It is rhetoric enlivened only by needs, past or future. In some respects it gains power just as any man's last words take on meaning beyond the simple sense.

I didn't think it existed any more; but Clark is its heir. I thought it had become extinct, too often parodied and mocked to survive. But in this courtroom Clark rediscovered it.

The hurt Clark displayed seemed genuine at the fact that the government, his government, the one he served, beginning with the marines, would make its case on the testimony of Boyd Douglas, and the letters of Philip Berrigan and Elizabeth McAlister. He says, "these two things are the saddest part of this case.

"You have to watch Boyd Douglas," he said, after having referred to him as a "very sad person," again infusing simple adjectives with meaning that their frequent use has long lost. "I think you'll find he's been in trouble all his life. The government in its majesty didn't deign to tell you this." Clark began to discuss the beginnings of this case, why an indictment was handed down.

The jury would see, he said, that the reason this prosecution was brought about was "to stop a movement, to silence a people, and to support J. Edgar Hoover."

"Of course we know Henry Kissinger wasn't kidnapped," Clark said. "He is alive and well in Peking today."

At this moment Kissinger is shaking Mao Tse-tung's hand.

Clark returned to the subject of Douglas, labeled him "an agent provocateur—an unstable person, who tried to commit suicide a couple of times . . ."

Lynch rose up, objecting, "Your Honor, he is trying to tell the jury things they would never be able to introduce as evidence . . ."

Herman agrees. "Ladies and gentlemen, opening addresses by counsel are not evidence." Clark took exception to being interrupted; an unusual thing to happen during opening addresses; Lynch cares not a whit about this type of courtesy; he is more of a social anarchist than Clark.

He refers to Lynch's calling Philip Berrigan the leader of the highly organized movement that he ran from his prison cell. He recalled, telling the jury who was hearing it for the first time, that Philip Berrigan had waited to be arrested at Baltimore and Catonsville, and was in jail for a vindictive sentence of six years. "You cannot expect a man like Philip Berrigan to conceal anything," Clark says. "He's not built that way."

And Clark believes people are built one way or another. Some men born and raised to be incapable of certain failings and humiliations. Like the slogan of Clark's marines: we build men. *He's not built that way.*

He reaches the letters: "How many letters have you written where you wrote more than you knew? Perhaps when you were a kid at camp? Or, if you're a mother, to a son going off to Vietnam? Or to a loved one? Trying to help a friend in distress?

"You will hear that Boyd Douglas asked to carry those letters, and that many of them got to the FBI before they got to the persons they were intended for." And then with more scorn than anger: "What do you think of people that steal letters?"

Clark's features and his small head atop a tall bone of a body make comparisons to small animals easy; women do so, saying he looks like a chipmunk, an expensive Steiff toy creature. But the

86

astounding contradiction about Clark, the way he looks and the way he acts, is that his face, in repose, looks meek.

"These defendants are extraordinary people," he says, beginning to finish. "They cannot be violent; but they stand to end it, before it ends us. They do have a passion. If we cannot preserve freedom so that people in this country with such a passion can be heard, then this country will be destroyed. Their passion is peace."

It seemed more a summation than an opening.

Paul O'Dwyer has eyebrows that are a caricaturist's delight. He was born in County Mayo, in Ireland, and left it for the new country at eighteen; the O'Dwyer family has a history in Democratic New York City politics; an older brother was the only mayor of New York City who had to abdicate while still in office, fleeing the city and a lickerous scandal. If there needs to be another synonym for Irish charm it is Paul O'Dwyer. Of the lawyers on the defense team it naturally fell to O'Dwyer to be the scourge of prosecutor Lynch, his fellow Irish Catholic, on matters of theology and church doctrine and lore. While questioning a prospective juror, a middle-aged Catholic woman, he asked her views about clergy participating in "antiwar marches and the like." He said, in preface, "You know now there are Catholics," then turning towards Lynch, "and there are *Catholics*."

The defense lawyers sit at an L-shaped table, and the seating arrangement had been worked out with slightly less trouble than the shape of the Paris peace-talk table. Boudin was first, who is Jewish, Clark is next, who is Southern WASP, and then O'Dwyer.

O'Dwyer rose to follow Clark with a shorter set of opening remarks. A long trial becomes a jurodrama with five hundred intermissions, each one of which is spent discussing the merits of the previous half-hour's happenings. The rules of theater begin to take hold. "He broke the mood." "The buildup wasn't sustained." Such comments are heard.

The script of O'Dwyer's remarks followed the same outline as Clark's so that it seemed we are watching another audition for the same part Clark played. He would rewrite it a bit for the jury; and it was in reference to Boyd. O'Dwyer would be more lenient in his appraisal, having, unlike Clark, an Irishman's tolerance for and appreciation of failures. O'Dwyer says that "part of the reason for this [indictment] is sinister," whereupon Lynch rose to object. Herman says to O'Dwyer, with a show of incredulity, "You intend to prove that the government was acting sinisterly in bringing this indictment." "Yes, sir, Your Honor, most definitely," O'Dwyer responds. "Oh, now, Mr. O'Dwyer, 'sinister'? All right, you'll prove it," Herman says exasperatedly, as if O'Dwyer was holding that night was day and Herman would let the fool try to verify it.

No one as yet knew what Boyd's story would be; he eluded detection as well as Daniel Berrigan had eluded the FBI. It is not difficult to disappear in America. If Gestapo officers can lose themselves in South America, Boyd can stay hidden in the states. The FBI had been for the last year Boyd's shepherd and he did not want. It was still a theory that Boyd had been caught smuggling out a letter and then coerced, by the threatened loss of parole, into becoming an FBI informer. O'Dwyer was allowing for this possibility while also stating something that was true no matter what motives Boyd had. The government, O'Dwyer charged, "put the squeeze" on Boyd and "robbed him of the last piece of dignity the man had and made him an informer." And the Irish know about informers. Three years before O'Dwyer immigrated to America, Patrick Connor, who eluded the IRA's revenge-justice, was followed to Manhattan. Connor was supposed to have informed on a group of IRA guerrilla fighters. One Patrick Murray gunned him down in 1922 on St. Patrick's Day at the corner of Central Park West and Eighty-fourth Street after the luckless Connor was seen taking in the annual Fifth Avenue parade. Murray was quoted shortly before he died (after enjoying long life) about the shooting of Connor. "I was sorry after. We heard later that the poor devil had been tortured to make him talk. We didn't know that at the time."

Had Boyd been tortured to make him talk? They didn't know at this time. O'Dwyer, brogue waving the language like a flag, addressed the jury: "I hope you'll consider this a chance to do something important for your country, for justice, for truth, and in this case, for history. I pray to God you're equal to the task."

"All right," Herman said to the prosecution, coughing slightly, "Call your first witness."

iii

> Please allow me to introduce myself. I'm Philip Berrigan, a Roman Catholic priest, a member of the Society of St. Joseph, seventeen years ordained, in prison twenty-nine months of a six-year sentence for draft file destruction. I am the youngest of six boys— we grew up during the Depression on a farm, during a period of dire poverty and hopelessness. All my schooling has been Catholic—elementary, high school, college, seminary, graduate work.

That is from an opening statement that wasn't made to the jury; Berrigan had prepared an eighteen-page statement and when Herman refused to allow him to give it, he dismissed Clark as his attorney, declared himself to be his own counsel—but Herman denied that also. Berrigan, in the opening address, wrote about his experiences as a soldier for the first time:

> Neither our parents nor us questioned the war— we considered supporting it our duty. And we went to war freely, even eagerly.
>
> Consciously, I was an enthusiastic soldier; unconsciously I learned from the destruction and horror of war. Four experiences with war helped educate me, helped lead me to resistance, to nonviolent civil disobedience, to federal prison, to this dock.
>
> The first had to do with my second night in France during World War II. We were outside Brest, and the Germans began to shell us, lightly and intermittently—more of a nuisance than anything else. In any event, a light tank company in the next hedgerow panicked—they were green troops like ourselves— and began to fire at shadows, sounds, and eventually

one another. My introduction to war was the spectacle of Americans killing one another.

The four war experiences all focused on the sight of corpses: "I saw dead and wounded men the next morning, and blood spattered half-tracks. . . ."

"It was near New Year's, 1945, bitterly cold—the corpses frozen, rigid arms and legs bumping on tailgates as the trucks bounced over the cobblestones. . . ."

"What sickened me most, however, was not the unremitting, tedious destruction. It was the smell of the dead, the cloying, nauseous odor of those killed in the terrible hysteria of bombing. . . ."

"There they rotted in the warm summer sun—with no one to dig them out, no one to bury them. . . ."

In other centuries the scholar would be pictured in his study, a fleshless skull as his aid to contemplation; it bespoke mortality, gave serious cast to his thoughts. Then, since few pedants mixed with carnage, a skull would have to be procured. We have developed apace, Philip Berrigan got to muse upon, not just a white skull, but piles of corpses. What does one need to see to change a man? Is there a moral "Eureka" that is unexpectantly called out, when a new truth is realized?

Seventeen years pass and Philip Berrigan is a priest, teaching in a black high school in New Orleans.

> Suddenly, in October, 1962, the city went quietly rigid with fear, and people began to count up their sins. By an intuition I still cannot grasp, residents realized they were in mortal danger—within range of the Russian missiles in Cuba, and if nuclear war broke out, they would burn in the first wave of terror.
>
> The crisis passed—to Castro's chagrin, Khrushchev backed down, as Americans widely thought. But what if he hadn't? What if he had insisted on his missiles in Cuba, as we had insisted on ours in Turkey, over the Russian border. Thoughtful people in

that city, in Miami, Atlanta, Birmingham, and Gulf-port, realized two things: (1) Khrushchev probably saved them, and millions of others, by taking the saner course; (2) Kennedy bargained with their lives in a way reserved to God alone.

The fifties and the early sixties exist in my mind like relatives I knew nothing about until their deaths, when I began to discover a great deal about them. I was a junior in high school in 1962, and Kennedy's triumph was that a Catholic had become a president. Nuclear warfare had passed into me, by the osmosis of the time, aided by the TV screen that served as the thin membrane through which information and wonder were exchanged like oxygen into my system. But the possibility of nuclear war produced an eerie serenity; it seemed to void the likelihood of battle and war as I had come to apprehend it; movies of World War II appeared to be as archaic as a knight's armor. At twelve I had accepted the possibility of holocaust and Armageddon and discounted the chance of ever shooting at a German or a Pole, an Englishman or a Frenchman, a Swede or African, Australian, or even Japanese. But I was freed of that childhood misconception, founded upon a reality of extinction. I realized Total War was an idol to be wor-shiped, and the sacrifices to it, the Nuclear Deity, to its domi-nation of us all, would be small wars, grotesque in their contrasts, countries separated by eons of technology pitted (truly pitted, as are bears and the sorry fowl of cockfights) against one another.

Being raised Catholic, even at an earlier age, we would dream, not so much of martyrdom, but of the eccentric tortures that Christian martyrs endured. Sister Mary Sadist, along with particu-lars of how Christ was crucified ("not through the palms, they would rip right through, but through the bones at the wrists"), would detail what sufferings the Jesuits went through at the hands of the Iroquois. The most frequent example was that of the fingernails being torn off, the quick exposed to further torments. Many preadolescent hours were occupied lying awake wondering how we would withstand the test. A certain resolve was awakened: we too would endure. But we seemed safe from the primitive tortures of the Iroquois. It was with a certain amazement that I watched the Vietnam War develop; there were the Iroquois with their sharpened bamboo. History had its tail in its mouth; my childhood dreams were prophetic, just as the odd coincidence that the only geography book we had studied at St. Francis Xavier's grammar school dealt with the rain forests and tribal mountain people of what I later learned was Indochina. Were those textbooks supplied to the nuns in 1955 by some forward-thinking AID or CIA project? Who knows.

Catholics make good soldiers for a number of reasons; one is the Christian tenet with which we are imbued: no greater love hath a man than one who will lay down his life for his fellow man. We are willing to be sacrificed.

As Father Berrigan puts it in his opening statement that the jury never heard: "Without dwelling overmuch on my attitudes —I was an efficient young killer—expert with rifle, carbine, sidearms, bayonet—eager to imitate the exploits of my three older brothers."

The odyssey Berrigan describes in his statement is the same one the country took during the nineteen-sixties. "I was impressively ignorant then, in 1962, as the threat of Cuba diminished . . . I began to read furiously, to hear every available expert on the arms race, to talk to anyone with an idea and a concern. . . . The next year, my order reassigned me in the North. Assigned to teach at our college in Newburgh, I joined tentative, gentle efforts to widen the questioning of our Cold War position, then hotting up in Vietnam. . . . But the uproar generated was sufficient to transfer me to Baltimore and parish work. There, in 1965, after a period of enforced silence, I again joined others to work for peace, and against the Vietnam war. We prayed, demonstrated, called rallies, staged debates, supported draft resistance, traveled to the nation's capital for the mammoth demonstrations there . . . I pursued all constitutional channels; I believed in the system; I believed our leaders were honest, decent, and humble men. I believed that peace would take time, but that it would come.

"But I changed, as people must change, under stress of conscience and event."

Many changed. Young men were forced to act out the change first since they were faced with an immediate choice: conscription. The "draft riots" of the sixties all were private skirmishes with local draft boards, carried on by mail. The oxymoron, conscientious evasion, was coined. Draft resistance had its public face, draft-card burnings, jailed resisters, deportees to Canada; but thousands of others quietly evaded the draft; in turn, thousands of others did not.

The postwar generation was raised more by a TV nanny than their parents; and because of this—life in the media nursery—they felt betrayed by this country as by a parent. Those in exile were turned-out sons. America is spoken of, in rage or with frustration, but nonetheless, it is spoken of personally—personified, anthropomorphized—whoever is denouncing it is confirming that he has been hurt by a person, a thing, an entity that has nurtured and bred him who is spurning it now. There is none of the easy abandonment of the expatriates of the twenties, who left America as one checks out of a hotel; none of the distracted back-there-ness of the soldiers who remained in Europe after the war; no, America has stained every cell in our bodies and we are it to the extent that we are raging against ourselves, what we are, and what we have become.

For men of Berrigan's generation, the change is less molecular; he has turned into a political man who has abandoned personal interest, for what this country does, challenges him, and every time he does not act against an injustice, it affronts him personally, just as if he saw a thug beating someone helpless and had to do something to stop it. He identifies his country and himself till they are inseparable. Because of that, thinking if he acted properly it would too (the government a shell the people give movement to), he "committed civil disobedience and waited for arrest twice in Baltimore and at Catonsville, not because I hoped that destroying draft files would arrest the American war machine, but because it was the only convincing way of saying that if we didn't end war, it would end us."

None of the eighteen pages was ruled proper for the jury to hear; he and Clark went up to the sidebar the morning of opening statements and Herman ruled against Berrigan. He did not fight it. One paragraph dealt with Boyd Douglas, his fellow convict, courier.

In closing, let me say something of my relationship
to Boyd Douglas, a government witness in this case.
Douglas was [*is* has been scratched out] my friend—
he still is, as far as I am concerned. I bear him no
resentment or rancor; I would welcome him tomorrow, should events develop that way.

What also has been crossed out is this: "None of us, the defendants or me bear him any resentment or rancor. All of us would
welcome him tomorrow as friend and brother, should events develop that way."

Another change is under way, another decade has begun, and
Philip Berrigan in this one finds he can speak only for himself.

iv

The long procession of witnesses begins; a safari through the wilds
of this case. Each witness a porter bearing someone else's burden,
the weight of testimony. Lynch, the pampered white hunter, rests
for a while. He lets William Connelly, a younger U.S. attorney,
prod them along. It is doubtful that this is a career-making case.
William Connelly is not Roy Cohn, marked for advancement for
his head-hunting the Rosenbergs. Connelly looks like a second-
string college basketball center who doesn't get to play much. He
volunteered for this prosecution. He interrogates the sympathetic
witnesses: a lengthy line of FBI agents, members of various police
forces, other government agency personnel. The first is an officer
of the Philadelphia police force. His testimony concerns the vandalism of a draft board in that city. Government's Exhibit No.
One is introduced, found on a desk of the disturbed board:

Today, February 6, 1970, we have entered these
draft boards in Philadelphia, Pa. and out of love for
our fellow men, have destroyed draft files . . . at an
appropriate time we will reveal our identities to the
American people. We will do so with feelings of trust,
hope and faith that they will come to understand,

approve of, and continue these actions of non-violent disruption of the death system.

The first twelve witnesses all have something to do with the Philadelphia draft-board raid. It was Lynch who inserted the draft-board raids as the spine of the superseding indictment. In his opening statement he said he would show how they would "to use one of their words—escalate" the defendants' protests against the war in Vietnam and would also serve as "boot camps" to train cadres for more violent future disruptions of the federal government. The draft-board raids, to Lynch, are the black seeds that would lead inevitably into bombings and kidnapping. And so the method of his case is to plant the draft-board raids in the minds of the jury and let everything else grow out of them.

The raiding of draft boards can be credited as the sole invention of the Catholic Left, yet no more so than Benjamin Franklin and his kite can be said to have discovered electricity.

Draft-board raids, on any evolutionary chart of protest, will be shown to be a short-lived offshoot. A species that could not properly develop beyond a certain point—and that point was violence. Philip Berrigan, when looking for a method of protest that would jail him, went to a military installation, Fort Myer, Virginia, to demonstrate against the war. He and members of a Baltimore peace group went down on their knees, praying, surrounding a flagpole. Three times they went, just as Peter denied Christ thrice, and three times they were thrown off the base, but not arrested. Thereupon, in October 1967, followed the raid on a Baltimore draft board and the creation of the Baltimore Four and the birth of draft-board raids. The pouring of blood did not stem from the much-touted symbolic creativity of the Catholic clergy involved: it was suggested by a lawyer that they just deface the files with some liquid. At once, though, the implications were seen.

When any scientific experimentation occurs for the first time, other teams capable of the same thing, since these developments are parallel, begin to perform them; once done, the taboos are diminished, the magic fear of the unknown is lessened. Some reasons are exemplary, others venal, and others entirely neutral.

But draft-board raiding occupies a very specific limbo: it was

95

"escalated" protest, but it still existed in a shadow land that could be called "nonviolent." Catholics have the tradition of Limbo: the region on the border of Hell, the abode of the just who died before Christ's coming, and of unbaptized infants. For Catholic radicals, draft-board raids lived in the region on the border of violence, but a region where they could safely trespass.

A theological definition of "simple" that the Jesuits left with me, out of St. Augustine, is "without parts." The initial draft-board raids were theologically simple. Philip Berrigan and three comrades walked into the United States Customs House in Baltimore, pulled open the 1-A files in front of the startled matrons, the grandmotherly figures who work in Selective Service boards across the land, and poured blood on them. They then waited to be arrested.

Catonsville became less theologically simple. There were more parts to it. Homemade napalm; Ivory Snow and gasoline. The numbers increased, more parts had to be played. The press was alerted (as they had been in Baltimore) but this time the whole action was filmed. Lights! Camera! Action! One of the elderly draft-board harpies had her finger cut; though the wound did not become infected, there it was—the infection of possible violence. Bloodshed of the other kind. It is curious, but because of this—the chance of violence—these "stand-by" actions were decided to be too dangerous. Not to the raiders, but to the workers. Daylight raids, it was thought, could lead to possible human hurt.

So, the night was consulted. Ah, the night. Truly it was the road too often taken, and it did make all the difference. With the night, went out the idea of standing-by. The night is a cloak; the night ransomed them time. Haste and its necessary limitations gave way to time and its opportunities. They could take their prey into a cave, the cave of night, and do with it what they would.

Vertebrate animals can only grow so large; when the mass gets beyond a certain point the skeleton cannot support it. Even if the skeleton grew, the mass would in turn grow, so there is a mathematical limit that cannot be exceeded. A natural limit. As there was to the idea of draft-board raids as practiced by the

Catholic Left. In order to grow further it had to change into a different kind of beast. It first needed to become extinct and grow up entirely new elsewhere. But draft-board raiding was not abandoned: it just grew and grew, to the point where it became ludicrous and ominous.

They became dinosaurs. It was a fundamental mistake to think they could serve as a foundation from which new and better forms of protest could be built. Engorged with people, outfitted with the trappings of stake-outs, burglary tools, and stealth, they swelled till what originally motivated them was lost; symbolism was relegated to dorsal flippers. To ambulate they would need a new medium, and not the dry riverbed of nonviolence.

Draft-board raids were a dead end; some of their adherents chose not to see them as such. And Lynch chooses to see them as something else too: boot camps. Each man has his vision, and an alphabet where the "a" waits upon the "z," the alpha begets the omega.

Officers of the Philadelphia police department sketched out the raid. "Would you describe the condition of the Selective Service offices on the night you saw it," Connelly asks. An FBI agent intones, "I found the premises in great disarray, numerous papers strewn about and ripped and torn; numerous filing-cabinet doors strewn about and ripped open."

FBI personnel take a course in testifying. It produces a standard form, similar to a correspondence course in business letter writing. There are blanks to be filled in, different names are inserted, places, dates—but the form is the same. Connelly shows a man photographs and asks, "Do these accurately depict the scene as you saw it on the night you describe?"

The defense asks the same question of each of them: "Were you ever called before a grand jury in Philadelphia relating to this matter?"

"No sir."

"Were any of these defendants here today arrested in connection with any of this?"

"No sir."

97

Boudin objects to the photographic exhibits as irrelevant, immaterial, and having nothing to do with these defendants or this case. Herman admits them, "subject to connection."

The state director of Selective Service for Pennsylvania takes the stand. He identifies exhibits, memoranda for overtime pay dispersed to employees who reconstructed the draft-board files and offices that had been damaged. He is a young man, appointed to the post by the Democratic governor, Milton Shapp. He is unenthusiastic about testifying. The dollar amount of the overtime work, he says, is $2,384.50, which does not include an additional four hundred hours of regular work. The figure is about the cost of each single day of this trial.

Defense attorney Terry Lenzner asks, "At that time [of his appointment as director of Selective Service] did you make a public statement to the effect that the draft system was unfair and should be abolished?"

Connelly is up: "Objection, Your Honor, that is immaterial and irrelevant."

"Yes," Herman says, "you don't have to answer that." The director blushes.

"Yeah," a local reporter says, "there was a movement in the legislature to get him fired after he said that."

Thomas Menaker follows Lenzner and asks, "Could you tell us whether the Selective Service offices are located in areas where minority residents dominate?" Connelly: "Objection." Herman: "Overruled." He does not know; though he has visited the offices, he has never "surveyed" the neighborhood.

A burly policeman testifies about an incident concerning the severed defendant, Ted Glick: "At two fifty A.M., on January 9, 1970, I observed a car parked illegally on a sidewalk with the motor running . . ." The prosecution elicited that a building containing Selective Service offices could be viewed two blocks away. There were no arrests; but he filed an "incident" report.

"Objection," Boudin says, not bothering to rise, "irrelevant, not connected. It wasn't even a violation, just an incident."

Connelly says: "We will connect it beautifully."

"Did you hear," F. says, just arriving, "there was another

draft-board raid a week ago, the Yonkers I, a Christian brother . . ."

As the officer lumbered out of the courtroom another reporter mused aloud, "Officer, do you salivate when you hear a police siren?"

The story of 3007 Susquehanna Avenue in Philadelphia is told in fits and starts. It was a residence for an "experimental community center," which taught remedial programs. It was called "Shalom House," and it served the black community that surrounded it. A group of nuns and Temple University students made up its staff. 3007 Susquehanna was a way-station for many different journeys. Two women who testified concerning it were former nuns who made their decisions to leave their order while they lived and worked there. They bespoke one kind of transformation.

3007 Susquehanna housed white civil-rights workers while they watched themselves expunged from the black civil-rights movement. Their tutoring programs were considered sops; the black children playing about the house only made them seem more paternalistic. Black Power ascended; liberal white programs withered. 3007 was an hourglass for this time of change; when the sand had all passed to one side, they strove to tip it over, reverse the trend. The new Catholic Left would take action, incorporate, graft onto the raiding of draft boards, another element. Baltimore and Catonsville protested the war; the Philadelphia draft-board raid would expand; they would protest both war and racism. They tried to make a point by destroying draft records of the black poor.

Two streams merged at 3007 Susquehanna; war and racism. The draftees or draft-eligible did not raid draft boards; it was their elders' tack. Philip and Daniel Berrigan wanted to do something commensurate with the jailing of draft resisters; but they had no draft cards to burn or inductions to refuse. Draft-board raiding was left to "adults." And they came, not from any new political vanguard, but from veterans of a decade of civil-rights work and aspirations. They were similar to veterans of an unpopular war;

they were not proud, but vaguely guilty and bewildered, banished by a wave of black separatism. They looked for atonement in the way some veterans do when they recount what they know of atrocities they witnessed or participated in.

Each bit of testimony was a shard from which an anthropologist could reconstruct an entire civilization.

A fourth-grade teacher, a friend of one of the ex-nuns of 3007 Susquehanna, appeared; she was an eager witness and told of being called by her friend, the ex-nun who was then married to the owner of the building, to come over and bring a camera to take pictures of some diagrams she had seen.

"Objection," Boudin says. "Hearsay."

"I assumed," the witness started.

"Objection, that is a state of mind, Your Honor."

"Just actions," Herman says, "not what you assumed or were told. I'm going to let her answer. Just what you saw."

"I saw a black binder on a table and removed two papers from it . . ."

How did you get it, she was asked.

"My friend has *power of attorney*"—a magic term she kept reiterating—"from her husband, and a key. I brought a camera in my sewing basket . . ."

What were the premises at 3007 Susquehanna used for?

"A day-care center; some poverty-program project—whatever it was . . ."

"She's a junior G-man investigator; Polaroid camera in hand, out to trap a few commie-pinkos," a reporter interjects.

She talked about the empty premises excitedly, with the voyeurism of landlords.

"The diagram really made an impression on me."

After obtaining the diagram she arranged a meeting with the FBI; it appeared to be a diagram of the Selective Service offices that were raided.

"Did you ask permission to take the papers?"

"I didn't think I had to."

"Were you friends of the sisters and the students who worked at 3007 Susquehanna?"

"I don't know whether you would call it friendship. I have no antipathy for them."

The press corps chorus chuckles.

She could not positively identify the other paper when it was shown to her. She did not examine it very long when she first got it and gave it to the FBI; she didn't think it was as important as the diagram. Is that at variance with earlier testimony, Boudin asks, when she had said it was definitely the same paper. She replies as if instructing a class: "I'm not telling you it is at variance, no. I am not telling you that at all. What I'm saying is that, according to a principle of education, one remembers what one has delved into longer, that is all I said."

People are eager to help with the investigation of some kinds of crimes. Even previous to a crime, they will initiate investigations on their own; especially landlords, who like to have control over tenants. Today, in Cuba, there are block spies who report on anyone in the neighborhood they consider to be engaged in counterrevolutionary behavior.

There are low-grade urban informers: tipsters, bartenders, news vendors, doormen. Each looking for a way to tap the power nexus. The press corps gets tips, has informers, sources. Scoop mythology prevails. There is a Dow Jones average on information; it is high depending on how few people know it, the value nil when it becomes common currency. Currency; current; the electrical charge; the power glow, the invisible radiance that imbues *secret*. The fourth-grade teacher feels it. She goes to the FBI with an offering to placate stern gods. Be friendly; come forward with libations, offer sacrifices. Turn in 3007 Susquehanna. There are so many reasons. Pick one. Writing about the TV show *The FBI,* which has been on the air since 1965, J. Edgar Hoover touched on a reason for his encouragement and support of such ventures: it has "won additional friends and admirers for the Bureau, thereby causing more doors and additional channels of information to become available to our investigative staff." Who can be turned in during a commercial? It's a principle of education that you remember what you delve into.

When I was thirteen my father took me down to his business on a Saturday afternoon. This was not an ordinary trip, but something special. A stolen car had been found left in their parking lot. There was going to be somebody there he wanted me to meet.

It was an FBI agent; my father introduces me. The agent and I shake hands. A proud moment for all; to rival the day I got my Social Security card and my Ad Altare Dei medal from the Boy Scouts. In the FBI agent's other hand is a snapshot of the car-thief subject, a young black.

The Berrigans attract informers; from the purloined Media, Pennsylvania, FBI office's internal documents:

> MEMORANDUM
> TO: SAC, PHILADELPHIA
> FROM: SC, PAUL B. MURRY
> DATE: 3/2/71
>
> On 3/2/71 at approximately 10:15 A.M., Brother Patrick, Villanova Monastery, Villanova, Pa., called the Philadelphia office and advised that he may have information pertinent to the bombing of the Capitol building, Washington, D.C. 3/1/71. The brother stated that a Monastery car had been signed out for the entire weekend, prior to the bombing, to Father CASEY, who is an instructor and hall rector at Villanova University. PATRICK further advised that CASEY is a sympathizer with the BERIGAN'S [sic] in their recent court trial.
>
> PATRICK will be available for interview between the hours of 2:00 and 4:00 P.M. 3/2/71.
>
> SA MULDERIG advised 3/2/71

Brother Patrick's file subsequently carried this notation: "dim old priest." Father Casey had an alibi.

The government witnesses enter from a door near the press section. It is a parade of FBI agents.

"He's straight off a gum wrapper."

"Hey, they're not supposed to wear colored shirts."

The agents have another monitor; one of their own, sent down from Washington, who sits behind the prosecution on a pew along with a few federal marshals. He is grading their performance on the stand, and a report will be sent in on the deportment of each of them. The agents are not disturbed by the judge, the prosecution, or the defense, but they are made nervous by him, their brother.

Testimony about 3007 Susquehanna established this: a diagram of the Selective Service offices was found there. Mary Cain Scoblick had been seen arriving there with luggage. Philip Berrigan had been seen there. A van belonging to a frequenter of 3007 Susquehanna had been found near the vandalized SS offices; in it were a brown briefcase, tools such as crowbars, drills, gloves, and a taped flashlight. There was another bag containing Clorox bleach. Another box marked "powdered varnish." And what looked like a draft record that had Selective Service printing on the papers. A car identified as belonging to Joseph Wenderoth was seen parked out in front of 3007.

None of the witnesses testifying about the raid had been before a grand jury concerning it; nor had any prosecution been initiated. It was thought to declaw draft-board raids by paying them no attention. If they weren't prosecuted, brought to trial, there could be no more public forums like the trial of the Catonsville Nine. The government was practicing a form of Berkeleyism: material things exist only in so far as they are perceived. The authorities held the same notion: the raids did not exist unless they were publicized.

To circumvent this, the Catholic Left, tutored as everyone has been by the Free University of Advertising, invented their own promotion: "surfacings." These were public demonstrations where the perpetrators of the draft-board raids would come forward, take credit for them, shoulder public responsibility. The next group of witnesses testified about the first such surfacing, held at Independence Hall in Philadelphia on 14 February 1970. The idea of "surfacings" can be found in Catholic tradition. Christ, after being crucified and buried, "surfaced" a number of times: first, to Mary Magdalene and the other Mary, after they had gone to the sepulcher. He met them on a road, saying, "All Hail." Twice he surfaced for the apostles, the second time so doubtful Thomas could caress his wounds.

And so draft-board raiders of the Catholic Left surfaced after they liberated the Selective Service sepulcher.

A sergeant from the "civil-disobedience unit" of the Philadelphia police department testifies; he had been assigned to photograph the demonstration at Independence Square previous to the ceremonies inside the Hall. Photographs were shown to him: "Do these accurately depict the scene . . . ?"

Herman, a hobbyist of renown, showed himself to be a camera buff. A 35-mm. camera? How many shots to a roll? Did you print all of them? Earlier on, when a sound system was installed, Herman complained rhetorically, "I can't understand it. This is a new building! The acoustics shouldn't be bad." His faith in technology is implicit; newness equals good. He could not settle his dismay over the terrible acoustics of courtroom no. one: ". . . a new building!"

The sergeant, during cross-examination, stated that he took 140 photographs. He then said there were approximately three hundred people at the demonstration. Every other person got his picture taken, and everyone would turn up in group shots. "How does it come to pass that you photograph a peaceful demonstration?" the defense asked. Even Herman's face turned quizzical.

"We often photograph demonstrations when we think there's a possibility of problems, arrests . . . we never know . . . we're always prepared . . . we keep a record on file . . ."

When was his surveillance unit founded?

"We're not a surveillance unit," he says, insulted by the designation, refusing the label, denying the validity of synonyms. Protective reactions; incursions; the shield of language. "We try to stop demonstrations before they start." An intriguing objective. "We have many contacts within various groups." Contacts? Boyds?

The "civil-disobedience unit," we are told, was begun in 1963. A bastard of the birth of the civil-rights movement. It evolved, in the same pattern of the larger movement, from watching civil-rights marches and demonstrations, to watching antiwar demonstrations and marches. "We keep a record on file." How many photographs are in that file, he is asked. He will not hazard a guess. Lots.

104

The jury is shown the pictures; they are the first exhibits they have been given and they stir as eagerly as pups at feeding time. The tiny young girl, juror no. twelve, is wearing her newlywed husband's letter-sweater. It covers her like a huge quilt; her remembrance of their nuptial bed.

The defense objects: peaceful demonstration, detriment to First Amendment rights, no connection, just to appear at a meeting with a defendant or codefendant produces spurious coconspirators.

There is more testimony about those who surfaced. Among them are Father Joseph Wenderoth and the severed defendant Ted Glick. A special agent says that Wenderoth stated that in addition to breaking into draft boards in Philadelphia they also broke into General Electric offices in Washington, D.C., on 7 February 1970.

Boudin objects; Herman strikes the reference to GE and instructs the jury that Wenderoth's statement cannot be used against any other defendant.

Draft-board raids had developed another spore; raiding reached out to the offices of large corporations judged complicitous war profiteers. The D.C. Nine, another group of Catholic Left raiders made up partially of clergy, are named so, not just because the raid occurred on Washington draft boards, but also because they hit the offices of Dow Chemical.

Those taking responsibility for the Philadelphia draft raids called themselves The East Coast Conspiracy to Save Lives.

The special agent's testimony included this exchange:

> THE WITNESS: There was a demonstration in progress and a guerrilla-theater-type affair was going on.
> THE COURT: A what?
> THE WITNESS: A demonstration.
> THE COURT: I didn't get the other words. Did you say gorilla?
> THE WITNESS: A guerrilla-theater-type play was being performed on the steps of the U.S. courthouse.
> MR. BOUDIN: I hope that will be explained to Your Honor.
> THE COURT: Yes, I don't know what it is.

105

> MR. BOUDIN: I'm sure Mr. Connelly will agree that it is quite innocent—not gorillas.

And as the day drew to a close, Boudin was arguing the matter of First Amendment rights:

> MR. BOUDIN: I don't see why anybody has to do anything at a public meeting. If I went to a public meeting and then was to be blamed because I didn't get up and say 'Stop talking . . .' [Laughter]
> THE COURT: This isn't a funny trial, ladies and gentlemen, and if the press and other people think something funny is going on, I am going to have to curtail the press in here, and the public, too. There is nothing funny about this at all.

V

A week earlier I had attended a production of Daniel Berrigan's play, *The Trial of the Catonsville Nine*. It was given in a church, the insides of which were decorated like a mobile home of worship. The exterior resembled any number of subdivision churches that can be mistaken for dry-cleaning chalets, cathedral-ceiling restaurants, or motel year-round swimming pool annexes. The pews were blond wood, none of the cherry dourness of Bethel AME. Sin here is not dark and bloody, but thin and blond, a mere yellowing of the soul, not a blotching of it. Something akin to prosecutor Lynch's hair, sin being a linen tablecloth faded from the sun. St. Mark's Lutheran, at 4200 Londenberry, a street name that developers chose from a list of unoffensive nouns. There were no blacks in the audience; in this area integration means that the three-foot iron statues of footmen that are by their front doors have had their faces painted white. Mimeographed play programs are passed out. On the back, an advertisement reads: If you like *The Trial of the Catonsville Nine,* you'll like the Trial of the Harrisburg Seven. Political trials as Broadway seasons. The play begins, a succession of monologues taken from the trial transcript of the Nine.

The local actor playing Philip Berrigan has a lot of soft flesh on his body, whereas Berrigan possesses none. To see Philip Berrigan arrive in court each morning for the last month, his presence outside Dauphin County Prison and the courtroom bracketed by federal marshals, and to see tonight an actor assume his person, is to be mocked by time. The day before (24 February) Daniel Berrigan was paroled from Danbury Federal Correctional Institution in Connecticut after serving eighteen months of a three-year sentence he had been given for Catonsville. The actor portraying him has an easier task; Daniel Berrigan has created a costume, so any actor need just be measured for it. The black turtle neck jersey, the chain and medallion that changes shape often, though it never disappears, like the face of the moon.

It is difficult to listen to the earnest declamations of the actors parroting from Berrigan's transcript-play. It is like hearing the buoyant words of balloonists before they ascended, only to know that all hands eventually were lost. Over and over, a debt to history is being paid well in advance.

The residents of Colonial Park, where this church is located, fifteen minutes from Harrisburg, have gotten as close to the present trial as they care to; like the movies playing downtown, they'll wait till it comes to the nearby shopping-center houses.

It is opening night for the play, and as befits such an occasion, there is something special planned. When it comes time for the actor playing attorney William Kunstler to give the defense's summation, William Kunstler himself rises from the audience and delivers it. Sleight of hand; the real and the unreal, Plato's cave in the guise of St. Mark's Mobile Home of Worship.

The actor-Kunstler was a deflated version of the man-Kunstler. Whereas the production heretofore had all the faults endemic to "little theater" groups, Kunstler's takeover, the understudy of the study's study, utterly transformed it. Kunstler did not appear to be himself, but the consummate actor, the performance of the performance. Kunstler has propelled himself into a realm few men have occupied; he gets to play himself, be his own imitation. He vibrated in this unique stratosphere: a luminous substance emanated from his body; he was a presence. Ectoplasm.

At Green Street for dinner, before the journey to the church, he was still terrestrial. Asked where the Chicago conspiracy trial's case stood, he replied, "We presented oral arguments on the appeal last week; our side was terrific; for a while I thought it was so good that I wouldn't be going to jail [for the contempt sentence Judge Julius Hoffman gave him]. The prosecution was backing off so much from the whole case, literally and figuratively, that the judges couldn't even hear them; they kept asking the prosecution attorneys to speak up. Foran is gone; the man who replaced him said it was a disgrace to be associated with this case, it was so bad; that it was something the last administration started and they were stuck with mopping up . . ."

Talking to Ted Glick, in Green Street's tiny kitchen, he touched upon the thing that had been gnawing at Glick since his severance from the trial for wanting to defend himself. It had conflicted so much with the idea of the lawyers' defense that they were relieved when Herman jettisoned him. "You know, had Philip wanted to defend himself then, and had he teamed up with you, Herman would never had been able to sever you both. It would have altered the case radically. He would have been stuck, checkmated."

Glick nodded his head in a troubled affirmation, as he is doing now, when the fact is brought up again, early in the morning at another Defense Committee house, where the speakers from yet another panel have come to spend the night.

Harrisburg was having a series of snowstorms. The city under the snow was as white as a freshly washed corpse. The sidewalks were lethal with ice. Court had been delayed some mornings, the jury-van that brought them in from the Penn Harris Motor Inn had gotten stuck in traffic. Kunstler had come and gone, but was slated to return for the Holy Week demonstrations that had been planned. The remainder of the Chicago Seven legal team is here tonight: Leonard Weinglass and Arthur Kinoy. Yesterday they were both in Washington, where Kinoy argued before the Supreme Court. He and Justice Department attorney Robert C. Mardian debated the merits of the federal government's twenty-six-year-old practice of wiretapping, without first obtaining court approval, domestic radicals considered dangerous to the national security. Kinoy argued on behalf of three members of the White Panther party who were accused of plotting to bomb a Detroit Central Intelligence Agency office. Another attorney argued for the United

States district judge, a black appointed by President Lyndon B. Johnson in 1967, who ordered the Justice Department to reveal the transcripts of the defendants' conversations obtained by wiretaps initiated without a warrant. The U.S. Court of Appeals for the Seventh Circuit upheld his order. The Justice Department appealed.

Tom Hayden, one of the Chicago Seven, spoke also; the panel had been held at the Friends Meeting House. Kinoy, exhausted, but still held in thrall by what had occurred, launched into a long monologue: "Rehnquist [Nixon's newly appointed Supreme Court justice] didn't sit on the case, because he either wrote or masterminded our opponent's brief; and it would have been pushing it just a bit." Mardian, assistant attorney general in charge of the Internal Security Division, William Lynch's immediate superior, argued, Kinoy said, "for this rather extraordinary claim of power . . . that the president of the United States should be able in the sole judgment of his one representative, the attorney general, to set aside provisions of the Constitution of the United States anytime just because the attorney general, in his own head, unchallenged, unquestioned, unjudged by anyone, decides that the opinions, the associations, the ideas, the activities of an American citizen might at some time—and this is what was so fantastic," Kinoy said, his voice startled and excited, "these were his words— that these ideas and activities might *at some time* tend to subvert the existing structure of government."

At dinner a few nights before, at State Street, a member of the Defense Committee came into the kitchen where the dishes were being washed and announced that on every channel of the TV were trial programs; even Dick Van Dyke was in a courtroom. Yesterday, while Kinoy was arguing with Mardian, Mardian entered the courtroom here in Harrisburg in the form of a letter supporting the government's application for a grant of immunity to a former Bucknell University librarian, who was called as a government witness. Mardian had written S. John Cattone:

> . . . . This request is for the purpose of enabling the Government to elicit testimony during its case in chief in the case of United States versus Egbal [sic] Ahmad, et ALL No. 14950.
> Upon consideration of your request, I find that the

109

testimony of [the Bucknell librarian] is necessary and in the public interest. . . .

Accordingly, you are hereby authorized to seek a grant of immunity pursuant to the provisions of Title 18, United States Code, Section 2514 for [her] in the event she asserts her privilege against self-incrimination.

Sincerely,
s/ROBERT C. MARDIAN
Assistant Attorney General

There had been many hearings concerning these grants of immunity. Two former girlfriends of Boyd Douglas and the reference librarian still at Bucknell were being saddled with grants of immunity in order to "gain" their testimony. They all were represented by a young attorney whom Herman treated with none of the reserve with which he checked himself when confronted with Ramsey Clark, Leonard Boudin, and Paul O'Dwyer. The attorney made a point of wearing a tie to court that had an American flag motif. He argued against the propriety of the grants of immunity, and questioned the affidavits by the government covering whether or not his clients had been wiretapped. He had argued whether the government's immunity application was "legally sufficient." That brought the letter from Mardian. Mr. Lynch had responded, "If we allow [the attorney] to play his own game of tag with the court . . ." He replied to Lynch's fulminations with, "Mr. Lynch thinks that would be awful; the grants of immunity would not be able to continue to roll off the Justice Department's mimeograph machines . . ." He had been arguing that the immunity application was defective since it had not been personally approved by the then attorney general John Mitchell. Section 2514 requires that any application for immunity must have the "approval of the Attorney General." The argument was over the provisions of 28 USC 510 allowing the attorney general to delegate his authority in certain cases. He contended that the delegatory power did not extend in cases of grants of immunity and he told Herman that he was not free to rule "contrary to the precise language of the act." Herman considered himself quite free, though. Everyone eventually went through what the young attorney termed "immunity baths," and came out dripping with their dubious grants.

Kinoy continued his monologue, his excited speech never flagging, driven with the necessity of an awakened sleeper who has to record a fantastic dream. "And Mr. Mardian gave the reasons for it, this rather extraordinary claim of power, that it's necessary, that the future of the state, the safety of the state depends upon it. And suddenly I said to myself, sitting there—it's like a *déjà vu* —wait a second, I've heard these arguments before—those very words—those were the exact words which a very eloquent lawyer had made to a court on this continent, only he happened to be the lawyer, not for President Nixon, but for George III; these were the arguments made in 1761 in the Massachusetts court when John Wilkes was there arguing against certain things known as General Writs of Assistance—an argument that a well-known commentator on the American Rebellion known as John Adams, said, 'then and there the child Independence was born.' Out of the fight against the power of the executive in his own head to decide when an individual's ideas, opinions, thoughts, belongings could be ransacked. Why? Because the state needed it—those were the arguments that were rejected. Where? In the courtroom? No. They were rejected by guns. They were the guns of the American Revolution."

Kinoy is a small man, left with only a few tussocks of gray hair; he operates out of an aptly named organization in New York City, called the Center for Constitutional Rights. He didn't seem to be making a speech to the sparse crowd in attendance at the Friends Meeting House; his eyes focused inward, on the scene he still beheld in the Supreme Court. But the voice we heard here, ringing in the small Quaker room, was the same eloquent carillon that the justices of that august body had listened to. "This same question—that there's something wild going on here—was not only going through my head, because suddenly after about fifteen minutes of this stuff that was coming out, all of a sudden Mr. Justice Marshall sitting there stops Mardian, cuts him dead, and says, 'Just a minute, Mr. Mardian, where does the Constitution fit into all of this?'

"Just like that. Mardian was flustered; after all, that's not some radical lawyer up there, you know, who's raising the question. Mardian was not master totally here. He was flustered; he couldn't

111

just hand Mr. Justice Marshall a subpoena, or pull him before some grand jury, or grant him immunity, he couldn't do that; not one of his tools of his trade worked, you see; and he says, 'Well, I'll get to that at some point.'

"Justice Marshall didn't let him go, because two minutes later Mardian is back to dire necessity and the country's going to collapse unless the president has this power and not only the president, this one person, the attorney general. Two minutes later, Marshall is back again. He says, "Just a minute, Mr. Mardian, why don't you discuss the Fourth Amendment.'

"I had two emotions that surged through me as I sat there listening to Mardian. One was anger, but the other, now let me be just as honest as I can be, the other was fear. And it would be doing no service not to say that loud and clear to you here and to the people of the country. There is cause to be afraid. I'd like to know where everybody was when we were arguing on this question, because it wasn't just the fight of the three young people from Detroit whose case the government decided they'd make the test of this, because they thought nobody will support the White Panthers, they are pariahs to everyone. Where was the Harrisburg Defense Committee? Where was the Angela Davis Defense Committee?

"The government is shooting for the biggest possible stakes in the fight on this wiretapping issue. What did Mardian do when he was standing before that court, knowing full well he couldn't care less about that particular Detroit case. In the most incredible way, with an absolute straight face, he asked the court to put the stamp of legitimacy, the stamp of legality on the proposition, the theory, that the executive branch of this government has the power any time it decides in its own judgment that any activities, ideas, opinions, associations of any citizen of this country or organization of citizens can ultimately," he said, stretching out the word to reach to its farthest implications, "ul-ti-mate-ly, be a threat of any kind to the existing structure of the government, then the executive has the power to suspend the provisions of the Constitution. That's why this goes so far beyond the wiretapping question.

"Wiretapping has been held to be a search and seizure; never has been more effective search—a search of your conversation.

112

Do you know how big that search was that we were arguing about yesterday? James Otis of Massachusetts and John Adams must have spun a hundred thousand times in their graves when they heard that argument yesterday from the government. That search lasted fourteen months. It was one surveillance authorized for fourteen months during which nine hundred telephone calls took place. Imagine how many people were involved in those nine hundred telephone calls? Now, this kind of a search they say you don't have to follow any of the provisions of the Constitution—which would ban completely such a search—as long as the attorney general says in his sole opinion that the activities of this organization might tend ultimately, someday subvert the existing structure of the government.

"If that theory is sustained, what does that mean? All they have to do, if that theory of yesterday afternoon is sustained, is say, tomorrow morning we're going to have mass raids from one end of the country to the other because we decide that all of the following thirteen-hundred-and-forty-two people on our list constitutes a potential threat to the existing structure of the government, even though we can't prove they've done anything that violates a single criminal law. And that means the provisions of the Fourth Amendment are thrown away. If they can do that, what can they do? They can throw away the provisions of the jury trial. You know, they're getting so they don't like jury trials in this country. That old, old concept is beginning to work out in life, the jury being the champion of the people against the oppression of the crown. Sometimes a group of citizens take their courage in their hands and refuse to convict on laws they think are unjust.

"There's loads of people in this country who take seriously this question of liberties. Wiretapping frightens people, almost more than any other thing. My lord, if you think of the things you say on the telephone . . ."

Judge Herman, in a pretrial hearing on wiretapping, said to Paul O'Dwyer after O'Dwyer voiced a similar sentiment, "Speak for yourself, Mr. O'Dwyer; I don't think I'd be hurt if the government or anyone else listened to what I said on the phone. I have nothing to hide."

"The concept of privacy," Kinoy continued, "is a good concept;

113

American citizens want that, millions of them want that. What's the problem? They don't know it's going to be stolen from them. I put it to you, that it is possible, on the wiretapping issue—if it isn't treated as a dead dry legal technical question, but something that goes to the heart of the liberties of every single person in this country; it is possible to organize hundreds of thousands if not millions of people, more people I put to you, than just around the Harrisburg trial or even an Angela Davis trial; here is a unity of issue, affecting the defendants here in Harrisburg, in California [Daniel Ellsberg], and Chicago [the Seven], that touch on the liberties of millions of people. The people have not stood together on the simple, most elementary things. There ought to be inscribed in front of every single political defendant in this country, every political lawyer, every member of any kind of people's movement, a slogan from the American Revolution: IF WE DON'T HANG TOGETHER, WE WILL ALL HANG SEPARATELY."

Every room of this Defense Committee house has a bed; land-grant universities created communal living. The towering dormitories that rose on the wheat fields of Kansas, Oklahoma, Arkansas, Missouri, provided every generation after World War II with a taste of communal life. The domestic habits of college moved away from the campus; endless numbers of young people have been vaccinated with it. Kinoy, Weinglass, Hayden, Glick, and a couple of others talk about this trial, before retiring. Wine is drunk; the steam heat of this old row house does not dispel the cold.

"Either severing Eqbal or getting him a directed verdict of acquittal would be a big mistake," Weinglass says, with Kinoy and Hayden concurring.

That prospect had been discussed.

"They've got nothing on Eqbal, just Boyd's word about two phone calls he is supposed to have made to a laundromat. That's it, except for the hearsay in Liz's letters."

"Regardless, if there's the least evidence on Eqbal, that's more of a reason to keep him in; he's the nigger of the group. That jury, if it finds it can't convict the nigger, are never going to be able to convict the white folks."

"And the business about a directed verdict of acquittal; if there's just one, and it's for Eqbal, then it's like telling the jury there's to be a directed verdict of guilty for the rest of them. It's a bad idea; don't let your nigger go . . ."

"What do you think the wiretapping decision will be?" Kinoy is asked.

"We'll win; but that'll just be a temporary stay. Some of the justices were truly alarmed. But it will be the jury that will be attacked; they might uphold that Oregon case, which would absolve state juries of the burdens of unanimity. That will be the next tact; to get rid of juries entirely—to go to a three-judge panel . . ."

"They can't get convictions on anything heard by a jury these days; even in up-front murder cases. Hogan [the New York City D.A.] is distraught; there's always some fucker on the jury who won't convict."

"How is your jury?"

"Better than they hoped for; it took long enough to get them."

"Trying to psych out a jury is impossible," Hayden says. There had been no voir dire of the Chicago Seven jury. "There was one woman who was fingered as the real hangman, child-burner; she, it turned out, was one of the three who held out for a while."

"Everyone's uptight about the effects of sequestration."

"Yeah," Hayden says, "our jury served longer terms than any of us ever will. Five months."

The antics of long-sequestered juries are just beginning to be reported; but their plots rival those of dime novels. During arguments against sequestration, there was mention made of a local law-enforcement official who, during a sequestered state trial, had been dallying with the female jurors. Herman acknowledged he knew all about that. What tales would come out after the trial from the confines of the Penn Harris Motor Inn?

Hayden, founder of the Students for a Democratic Society, had cried while addressing Judge Julius Hoffman at the end of the Chicago Seven conspiracy trial; Hayden was tired of holding the large view and began at the beginning saying he was being prevented from having a child. He has glossy black hair pulled back like juror no. twelve, tied into a long pony tale. He is tan; strange to see amid the vigil-candle pale faces in Harrisburg; a dusty brown tan, the stain of southern California.

The Chicago Seven trial was Dionysian, but the trial of the

115

Harrisburg Seven is Apollonian. Bacchus does not leave the print of his cloven-hoof on the snot-green carpet of courtroom no. one, as he sometimes did in Chicago. No, the seven here do not promote the rites of any New Age; they are its chaperons invited last to the party.

Kinoy retires to an upstairs room; Weinglass is taken to another destination. Hayden asks Glick, "Do you have one lawyer like Lennie [Weinglass]? We wouldn't let anything go through—do anything—without checking with him first; he's the one we all went to. Kunstler is good on his feet, extemporaneously, but he doesn't do any research. Lennie was the workhorse."

"Yes," Glick says, "Terry Lenzner; he did all the investigating. He was the one we all talked to; after the second indictment came down he came to us and said, 'Hey, they might just have a case.' He's the one everyone goes to . . ."

Hayden had said earlier at the Friends Meeting House, "I'm very surprised how few people are attacking the Justice Department . . . as of 1968 the Arizona gang took over the U.S. government domesticly. There's a group of people who have Birch Society connections and ultramilitarist, rightwing connections, used to work on Goldwater campaigns, and are involved in the Mafia in the Southwest. They have taken over the Justice Department. This should be a scandal; these people have undertaken to alter the whole bourgeois structure of liberties which America supposedly holds so dear. This concept of clear and present danger— that's gone, according to them. They claim we're in a period of clear and present danger, and that we can't wait until such a period occurs. This guy, Kleindienst, is on record saying over and over that the real danger to America is the ideological criminal, that is, people who have the wrong ideas, and others of them go around publicly making speeches, writing articles, urging that people be rounded up and put away. They are more clear about their ambitions than Hitler in nineteen thirty-three. I think the liberals in this country agree that there should be some sort of repression; there's very few cases that they're standing up in the way that Ramsey Clark, who comes out of this tradition, is standing up."

Clark's own views about wiretapping have been well expressed (in his book *Crime in America*); he opposes it for two reasons. It is an unconscionable attack on privacy and because it is hugely inefficient. But, concerning the paranoia about the number of phones that are or have been tapped, Clark has said, privately, in the kind of language which must have been one of the strong bonds he had with Lyndon Baines Johnson, "Just because the grass is wet, doesn't mean ol' J. Edgar's been pissin'."

Hayden had concluded with, "I say unashamedly that we have to get rid of Nixon in seventy-two. I say that forthrightly after saying that Humphrey and Nixon were the same in sixty-eight."

The talk shifted on to Ramsey Clark. Hayden told of seeking his testimony for their defense during the Chicago Seven trial. "We went out to his house in Virginia on a weekend. He had told the Justice Department that we were coming—he said he did that to be fair—and they sent out a couple of boys. Two blue-suited dudes who just sat while we talked, didn't say a word. His wife was there and his daughter—I think Clark had just come back from the doctor's with her; she's retarded in some way and Clark takes her from doctor to doctor . . ."

The lunchroom in the Federal Building is run by the Department of Welfare, Office of the Blind, and a sightless man is its manager. Clark did not treat him in the ostentatious way most of the patrons did, elaborately counting out their change for him; there had been an ease that I did not understand till now.

"The guy's a very human cat; Kunstler left the room and the two Justice boys get him [Clark] literally up against the wall, telling Clark that *we* just want to *use* him, that he'd be doing a disservice to his country, really coming down on him, and the only thing Clark says to them is: 'I believe in telling the truth whatever the consequences.' So he came to testify and it was ruled inadmissible. That's one thing that didn't sit well with the court of appeals; they couldn't get over the fact that Hoffman wouldn't let the former attorney general testify . . ."

"Who knows, not being allowed to testify at your trial might have prepared him for being on the defense for this one."

"Hey, this might just be an ego thing, but where *are* the defendants? When we brought people in to speak, like we met with them, spent time with them . . ."

117

"Well, it's Friday; some have gone off to speak themselves to raise money; others just take off, to get away; it's hard on them, day after day . . ."

"You don't have to tell me, man; we had six months of it; taking pills just to get it on. It almost destroyed us, the grind, the pressure. You'd just think that when they get people here like Arthur Kinoy and Leonard Weinglass, that they'd come by and say hello."

The trial had been on for a month; the Defense Committee lost some of its original people. The resignations spoke of some larger break. They were not giving up a job, but announcing a diminished zeal. Their faith in what the defendants were doing and how it was being done, had grown cold. And late at night, pushed on by some further apprehended indifference, real or not, by one or any of the defendants, more bitterness would come out.

"If we hadn't been chasing the Berrigans up and down the East Coast this indictment would never have occurred . . ."

On these occasions it would be Elizabeth McAlister who would be singled out, the target of most of the invective.

The letters. The secret letters.

"To this very day there are people mentioned in the letters who haven't been *told* that they're in them. We didn't know they existed until just before the second indictment; and then, even then, Elizabeth didn't come up to us and tell us, explain in any way . . ."

Boyd was a pusher to McAlister; her connection to Philip Berrigan. The contact became an addiction; the paper and pen, spoon and needle, and Boyd the carrier, the source, the instrument.

"How she needed every day to use that pay phone on York Avenue. Her days that summer were built around those calls . . ."

". . . Elizabeth McAlister, the revolutionary who wears a girdle to court every day!" says an exasperated voice, made plaintive in the face of a folly left misunderstood.

What had been built up around the small band of draft-board raiders, what was sought after, was the sense of community. Religious houses call themselves "communities." The apolitical young refer to their groupings as communes. The criminal and lunatic call their bunchings "families," mimicking the Mafia. The radical young, the Weatherpeople, have dubbed theirs "collectives," a harsher, more abrupt word, out of socialist jargon. The Catholic Left would call it community. The Weatherpeople collectives turned nihilistic, Spartan, fraught with encounter-group interrogations. Thinking to destroy sexual inhibitions and the middle-class mores that prompted them, they replaced one kind with another, banned monogamy, then resumed it, instituted homosexuality, experimented with forms, but it was the shuffling of the current deck of cards. Radical Origeons, who instead of castrating themselves to be freed of sexual turmoil, debased it—to be free of it.

What the Manson families and Weatherpeople collectives profaned, the Catholic Left tried to make again sacred. They promoted fragile Christian communities; to be built on love and respect, kept chaste and full of the holy spirit. Stemming from the odd matrix of draft-board raids and resistance is their flower: community. By the time Catonsville occurred, the "support groups" that surrounded the nine were many more than that number. And the defense committees that the trials created were the horn of plenty for those to come.

Yet, previous to this trial, they were breaking up. Christian communities built around civil-disobedience have, for a center, a wound which will not heal.

The Defense Committee supporting the Harrisburg Seven was built out of the bits and pieces of the community that had begun to disintegrate. This indictment was an electric shock given to a heart temporarily stopped; it beats again, though less strong from the unnatural stimulus.

Arrangements were made for Hayden to get to the airport early in the morning; the small gathering broke up. Walking the couple of blocks down to my rooms on Second Street, I passed behind the YMCA, a large brick building, built in a Moorish style, arches, curves, half-circle clay-tile roof. On its uppermost peak they have erected an immense letter "Y." It can be seen far and wide on the Harrisburg night skyline. It is outlined in orange neon, which is bright enough to give the snowdrifts a pink cast. This gigantic neon "Y" seems to be, each evening I pass it, the unavoidable question that is asked each day of this trial. Why? The mill grinds exceeding slow. Robert C. Mardian's response to Justice Marshall's

119

questions about the Constitution keeps coming to me, an echo
skipping over the frozen street. Mardian had said: "The Constitution is not a suicide pact." The orange "Y" had changed this
night; it was as if the cold had come up the base of the letter,
rising water, snuffing out the neon. Now, the initial that dominated
the night, was not a question, but a premonition, an answer. The
"Y" had turned into a "V." But which side would claim the
Pyrrhic victory?

vi

FBI men have faces that are difficult to recollect. Small, usual features, nondescript hair; they are expressive as a stone. Perhaps
this is a qualification. One exception takes the stand. Only 145
of the FBI's 8,600 special agents are members of minority groups,
which are designated black, Spanish-surnamed, American Indian,
and Oriental employees. This agent is among the 145. When
asked how long he had been with the bureau he answered
proudly, three years and four months, breaking it down almost
to the day, as young children do when they give their ages.

The testimony had shifted to New York and the actual beginnings of this case: the search for Daniel Berrigan, S.J. After the
appeals of the Catonsville Nine were rejected in April 1970, Daniel
Berrigan and his brother Philip, along with a nun, went underground. Philip was apprehended within a matter of days. Daniel's
capture took months. The nun is still at large.

It is not necessary to burrow very deep to find the American
underground. There has always been one type: the ignored, the
disenfranchised, those living on the margin, outfitted with no
credentials. Boyd F. Douglas came from this underground. A
hobo milieu, single-room-occupancy hotels, bus-station habitués,
transients. The ex-anything—ex-cons, ex-employed, just ex-ed out.
The anonymous underground. Then there is a newer kind: any-
where the FBI cares to look.

On 21 April 1970 Philip Berrigan was caught in the closet
of St. Gregory's Church, in the West Nineties of New York City.
"Here Father Phil. Where are you Father Phil?" the agents called
out. He was taken, along with young David Eberhart (one of the

Baltimore Four) to the Federal House of Detention on West Street. That night there was a number of things happening at St. Gregory's. A rock band was playing. Parishioners were demonstrating in the aisles, carrying placards, denouncing the use to which their church was being put. A contingent of Lower East Side Yippies were hanging about, like crêpe paper decorations. Puerto Rican and Black Power groups were represented. St. Gregory's was having a liturgy of pandemonium. Special minority-surnamed agent was there, his face as picturesque as the pottery from the pueblo of San Ildefonso, beaming back and forth across the crowd. He was looking for the fugitive, Daniel Berrigan, S.J. Boudin and the agent have this colloquy:

> MR. BOUDIN: As a matter of fact, your visit to St. Gregory's was with a large number of other FBI agents, wasn't it, for the purpose of, I suppose, capturing Daniel Berrigan.
> THE WITNESS: Yes sir.
> MR. BOUDIN: How many agents did you have there?
> THE WITNESS: Approximately one hundred.
> MR. BOUDIN: Out of an audience of how many people?
> THE WITNESS: Approximately five hundred.
> MR. BOUDIN: You had 20 percent.

"He just got himself a one-way ticket to Butte, Montana," a reporter says, "for letting that out." Another comments: "It reminds me of the saying that if the FBI would remove its agents from the Communist party it would collapse after losing all its dues-paying members."

The Catonsville trial had been a public relations triumph. The Nine had the upper hand; they admitted their holy guilt. Daniel Berrigan said the clergy, all in black, played their role to the hilt. The government was the sack of guts their sword went through.

Then, to go underground and to show the FBI hamstrung by—as Daniel Berrigan has characterized himself—"a rather absent-minded cleric"! Would Hoover elevate Daniel's face to the Ten Most Wanted List? He was the most wanted. Two hundred agents were assigned to his search. The FBI can stand terror, pillage, bloodshed, but they can't stand being made to play the fool. A hundred agents encamp at St. Gregory's; that same night Daniel

121

Berrigan "surfaces" at a church in Germantown, Pennsylvania. Vengeance is mine, sayeth J. Edgar Hoover. He stewed, fumed. It is only seven months till he announces the incipient plot of bombing and kidnaping of which Daniel Berrigan is one of the leaders. Hoover's position in the government, besides that of chief law-enforcement official, was that of Archbishop of Canterbury. It is his morality, against the Berrigans', that is at stake, or, that is, to be burnt at the stake. A pious man, he would make a good Archbishop empaneled at a new Inquisition.

At St. Gregory's that night, so the testimony goes, Eqbal Ahmad read a speech that was to have been given by Philip Berrigan (on Berrigan's views of surrendering to the government on the Nine conviction) had he not been taken into custody. Eqbal was introduced as Phil Berrigan's "friend." There is some dispute as to that. Eqbal Ahmad had never met Philip Berrigan till this indictment brought them together. The defense held that he was introduced as "Daniel Berrigan's friend." Elizabeth McAlister is observed at the church.

Paul O'Dwyer asked an FBI man who took the stand if there appeared to be some sort of celebration going on. He described what he saw there ("Symbolic communion, as they call it; they passed a bottle of wine around and bread and flowers"). Because of his familiarity it seemed he was a Catholic and O'Dwyer asked: "Did you eat of the bread and drink of the wine?" "No, I did not," the FBI agent said, as if disowning a mortal sin. He had been deeply offended by what he saw going on at St. Gregory's ("hard rock coming from the *sacristy*"). Sacrilege is the crime he observed.

A surveillance of Elizabeth McAlister is reported by several hands. Day and night watching her residence, on East Eighty-first.

"At approximately noon on August 3, 1970, she and another woman, a gray-haired woman of about fifty, got into a blue 1963 Oldsmobile and proceeded to Brooklyn to the home of Eqbal Ahmad. We parked cars and went down to a position on the street where we could observe people in the apartment. On that occasion there was observed Eqbal Ahmad, Elizabeth McAlister, and the gray-haired woman [Sister Jogues Egan] talking together . . ." Such is the FBI's testimony. "Yes sir," an agent says to a question, "they were visible from the street. They were on the second story, not counting what you call a basement. But they were on the second story. They were visible through two open windows."

(Later, in the evening, Eqbal tells me, exasperation setting aside secrecy, that there is no way the interior of the apartment can be observed from the street. "Besides, there are plants hanging in the window and from that angle, if you could see anything, it would be them. That one agent almost give it away, mentioning the 'basement.' My apartment is on the third floor from the street level. Leonard doesn't want to stress this. But they did see us there. Of course they saw us there. From an apartment directly across the street, from which they had been watching my apartment for four months.")

So, the FBI fibs on the stand. Do you solemnly swear, blah, blah, blah. They do what they want; they have reasons.

Telephone records are produced. Numbers, times, places, and dates become for Lynch, the justice-astronomer, the stars of a constellation that makes the beast, guilt.

Eqbal's father-in-law appears on the stand, to verify heretofore-produced telephone records. He reports that in the summer of 1970 he and his wife were on a trip to Europe. During their absence their summer home in Weston, Connecticut, was occupied by his daughter and her husband, Eqbal Ahmad. He identifies government exhibits as billing stubs for the period of August 1970, the accurate bill being sixty-one dollars.

And you just paid the bill without asking your daughter who made all those calls? Lynch asks, the frugal prosecutor.

"I must have, they haven't disconnected our phone."

The prosecution also assumes it benefits from showing the jury Eqbal's is a "mixed marriage." A Pakistani marrying a nice Jewish schoolteacher, a traditional trick of foreign-espionage types.

Eqbal was a professor at Cornell University when Daniel Berrigan was teaching there. Berrigan performed the ceremony at his wedding. Eqbal, the Pakistani peril, became indicted through friendship, not international intrigue.

"After the second indictment came down Eqbal went to a reception at the UN for the Algerian delegation," a reporter says,

123

"and was humiliated by their questions of how he, an expert on counter-insurgency warfare, could get mixed up with this wacky group of nuns and priests . . ."

Except for the fourth-grade schoolteacher, the first eighteen witnesses were male. Now there follows, with a few exceptions, a procession of women to the stand, nuns, ex-nuns and four Bucknell University acquaintances of Boyd F. Douglas, Jr.

"I wonder how much pictures of Boyd's scars would bring on the black market," is asked in the press section.

This carpet of femininity is rolled out, leading to Boyd's entrance.

A sister takes the stand. Lynch questions. The "mail-drops" are established.

Catholic families are not only prepared to give up sons to foreign wars, but are willing to tithe part of their large broods to the church, for vocations. Priests and nuns to their parents are the blessed on this earth, the brides and brothers of Christ. When my oldest sister entered a convent, fast on the heels of her breakup with the high-school football star, wooed by a recruiter-priest who would squire carloads of Catholic girls to drive-in movies, she was seventeen and full of tears.

On the day she took her first set of vows, I (a high-school senior) wandered around the cathedral in St. Louis, up a spiral staircase leading to some unknown heights, only to be met by some of the novices coming down the stairs, who had been in a room changing from wedding gowns into the black robes of their new order. Their heads were bare, their hair had been crudely chopped back; they were startled by me as by an attacker. I retraced my steps; their fright had shut off their weeping for a moment. This nun testifying, had entered her order four years before my sister; she remained in it, my sister did not.

This vestal on the stand came out like the sun from behind the previous clouds of FBI men. So sweet she was spoiled. Tall, with boyish-cut blond hair, she would make her simple three-word answers to Lynch three musical notes. She received mail addressed to herself for Sister Elizabeth McAlister from Lewisburg, Pennsylvania. She would know it was for her because of the postmark. "Did Sister McAlister ever talk to you about Selective Service board raids?"

"She did not." Do-re-mi.

Lynch shows her a document that she identifies as a statement claiming responsibility for a draft-board action in Dover, Georgetown, and Wilmington, Delaware. She cannot remember if Sister Elizabeth had shown it to her though she knew she had one. "Did she ask you to sign this document?"

"She might have." Fa-sol-la.

The "surfacings" of draft-board raiders altered; planned obsolescence is at work here. They cannot just surface and surface. They need to change its design, add a tail fin, six headlights instead of four. This new method was hit upon; an offshoot of the thousands of petitions filed against the war. This petition would accept the moral responsibility for the draft-board raid. Lynch suggests this surfacing statement is meant to obstruct justice. The statement, with its 302 signatories, is put into evidence.

Paul O'Dwyer asks when she was professed and about her order, the Religious of the Sacred Heart of Mary, an international order, founded in 1849. They maintain Catholic women's colleges, where young women are bred for monogamy. The sixties fissured these, but they still stand. Catholic women's colleges are trade schools for Catholic mothers. Their standards are low, their curriculum faulty. They have their secular counterparts in the private girls' schools filled with daughters of the rich who lack degrees, if nothing else.

Terry Lenzner asks if the FBI had called before calling on her. "They just showed up." He also asks, after she was told she would be called before the grand jury in Harrisburg, if Sister Elizabeth had told her there was no reason to consult a lawyer. She replies, "Yes, she did."

"For the good of the Movement," a disgruntled reporter says, "they should give McAlister five years."

The cross finishes with Lenzner saying, "And finally, I believe it was also your birthday yesterday and congratulations."

"Thank you."

She seems so young, it is appropriate.

The Religious of the Sacred Heart of Mary must have been the nunnery Hamlet had in mind when he gave his advice to Ophelia.

Another ephemeral nun takes the stand. She is McAlister's other "mail-drop."

Lynch asks her how many letters she received for McAlister. "I don't know how many came," she says, with downcast eyes. Her lowered lids shield her from precise memory. "More than one, less than fifty, that's the best I can do," she replies to Lynch's pressing.

Lenzner questions her on her contact with the FBI. They had come by with her subpoena at 8:00 A.M. They showed her between fifty and one hundred photographs out of which she was able to identify only Philip Berrigan. During this part of Lenzner's cross, Boudin objects.

"I'm going to object. I can't see any point to his question. What difference does it make. I object. I don't see what difference it makes. I object on behalf of my clients, Father Wenderoth and Dr. Ahmad."

Lenzner turns with his hands spread apart as if he had just dropped something and stares at Boudin. His expression is a mixture of amazement and hurt. O'Dwyer, the day before, had also objected during his cocounsel's cross-examination. Lenzner, now, doesn't know if he should go on. The lawyers of the defense have disputes and differences, but they try to keep them unobserved, to give the impression they are a frictionless team. After this incident the defendants order that it not happen again, objecting to cocounsel.

"I'll do the admonishing," Herman says to Boudin.

Lenzner lurches on, asking whether Elizabeth had told her she needn't consult a lawyer when she was called for the grand jury. Yes, she did.

There was redirect of this nun, then recross, and an attempt to reredirect. She was dismissed when Boudin said, regaining his good disposition, "No rererecross, Your Honor."

A buxom ex-nun appears, equipped with transactional immunity, who testifies about 3007 West Susquehanna. She visited Shalom House ("What? Shalom? What does that mean?" Herman asked), returning to it in late December 1969 after she left the sisterhood. Mary Cain Scoblick opened the door; Philip Berrigan was there. "Mary and I went upstairs and had a social visit." She later returned for a New Year's party. Recalls no conversations, except that it was purely a "social gathering." At that time, Mary Cain Scoblick was the only defendant present.

During cross she spoke of her sentimental attachment to 3007 West Susquehanna. It had been set up as a residence for an experimental community center to serve the surrounding black neighborhood; it had been an important time in her life, the months she spent there. Many things happened to her, she explained. She knew Father Joseph Wenderoth in 1968. He was, she said, a curate at St. Vincent's parish in Baltimore, an inner-city parish that was "vibrant. . . . Good liturgy was occurring," she said. "There were active lay people."

She had first met Mary Cain Scoblick during the summer of 1964. They were both in Washington, D.C., at the convent of Notre Dame. Then "I lived with her for a year in Philadelphia." Joseph Wenderoth had helped her secure Church permission to marry after she left her order. How strange that seems, her needing–wanting–their approval. She looks upon Wenderoth from the stand the way a woman looks at the doctor who has helped deliver her child. These are all government witnesses, but they seem to be for the benefit of the defense.

A New York Telephone Company employee brings more records. Charges to a certain credit card: S5545481082. Two calls are made to seem important. One, from a pay phone on 19 August 1970 to (717) 524-0038 (Lewisburg laundromat) from 5:00 P.M. to 5:13, and another made on 20 August 1970 to the same number in Lewisburg from 12:17:59 to 12:23:24. The records are called "mark sense" cards. They are admitted, subject to connection.

It is discovered that these records were subpoenaed for a grand jury in the Southern District of New York. They were never turned over to the grand jury (which did not convene), but to the U.S. district attorney. "That is illegal," Terry Lenzner says. There is argument on the merits of the process. Herman and Boudin have this exchange:

> THE COURT: What bearing does it have. He is bringing records here of another case.
> MR. BOUDIN: I agree with Your Honor.
> THE COURT: The fact that he had them at some

127

other time in New York has no bearing on this at all.

MR. BOUDIN: I agree completely, the fact that they are here now—the fact that there may have been an abusive process has no bearing on their right to come here.

THE COURT: No bearing at all.

It is the style of Boudin's baited-trap argument; Herman steps into it with his agreement.

MR. BOUDIN: But it does seem to me it might be relevant if the government has engaged in an abusive process in connection with the investigation.

Lynch, ever-vigilant, rises:

MR. LYNCH: Your Honor, this isn't an objection, this is a speech. And I resent Mister Boudin making these remarks in front of the jury. It isn't proper.

A special agent appears bearing a cassette tape-recorder. The tape thereon is offered as a "voice exemplar" of Eqbal Ahmad. It is admitted over strenuous objections on First and Fourth Amendment grounds. It records a press conference given by the defendants (excepting Berrigan) after their arraignment. O'Dwyer interjects, during Boudin's argument, that this voice-exemplar is "a fraud upon the court, tantamount to legal trickery." The tape will be used to establish Boyd's identification of Ahmad's voice.

Boudin finishes: "Let me speak frankly to Your Honor. Mr. Lynch will hold that there were calls made between my client, Eqbal Ahmad, and Boyd F. Douglas. I say those calls were never made." He speaks of the expectation of privacy that the First Amendment protects, that the recording of the defendants' press conference falls under. Lynch responds:

It must even strike Mr. Boudin, who is an able enough attorney, to realize he is taking a tenuous position and taking a principle and reducing it to an absolute absurdity. I suggest, Your Honor, that what was done here was perfectly proper. They were holding a press conference. It was a public meeting. This agent was there to record what they were saying for the world to hear. This was a press conference that was announced, and everybody was invited to it.

And Boudin says quietly:

> For the world to hear; but not for use in a criminal prosecution.

Queasy sailors, long at sea, we finally sight land, the terra firma of prisons. We leave draft-board raids, FBI men, nuns and ex-nuns, and run aground at Lewisburg Federal Penitentiary, where Father Philip Berrigan arrived 1 May 1970 and met Boyd F. Douglas, Jr.

We meet the corrections officer (né guard) who shook down Berrigan's cell and discovered a letter tucked in *Time* magazine, which, according to the government, set the juggernaut of this case in motion.

"I started to look around for contraband," he says, while Berrigan was "outside" on a work detail. He then says, with the empiricism of a prowler, "You can tell a lot about a prisoner by shaking down his cell." The discovered letter goes to his superior, then to his superior's superior, an inadvertent chain-letter.

A discussion of what constitutes contraband ensues. Drugs. Weapons. He says a letter is contraband if it has to do with prison security or circumvents proper mail channels. He says he knows personally of two or three similar finds, and perhaps fifty to a hundred for the whole prison. Boudin presses:

> THE WITNESS: Oh, I really couldn't say for sure, but it must be fifty or one hundred.
> THE COURT: I thought I had one hundred someplace.
> MR. LYNCH: Is this a guess?
> MR. BOUDIN: This is a prison official. I will take his word.
> THE WITNESS: A minor prison official.
> MR. BOUDIN: I beg your pardon?
> THE WITNESS: A minor prison official.
> MR. BOUDIN: Oh, yes, you are a minor prison official. Well, we are all minor in a way. Let us just go back a bit . . .

He is followed to the stand by a not-so-minor prison official. The associate warden of Lewisburg during the time of Philip Berrigan's incarceration.

129

He ended his stay there two months after Berrigan was trans-ferred to Danbury that August, and two months before Boyd was sprung in late December. Going from one institutional world to another, he is now in Florida, at an Air Force base, superin-tendent of their disciplinary installation. He refers to prisoners by their first names. Boyd. Phil. He is a gray turnkey, ill-at-ease away from his domain, the petty bureaucrat who now has to ex-plain his actions to overlords. But the wings of the government shroud him. He has the assurance of a shopkeeper who has his protection paid up.

In this case, there is one span of time that is obscured. When did ape become man? The shadowy epoch of missing links. And Boyd's transformation, his ascent into informer, is likewise be-clouded. But the associate warden was present at the Creation.

His explanation uncovered by Lynch is this: The letter was eventually brought to him. He takes it to the warden and joins the captain of security for discussion of it. The warden also has departed from Lewisburg, shortly after these talks. Berrigan is called in by the associate warden; they have a forty-five-minute conversation. The contents of which are not disclosed, since Boudin objects, saying that as a prison official he could have arrested Berrigan there, and since no declaration of his rights was given, anything that he said cannot be used in court, under the famous *Miranda* decision of the Supreme Court. It is known Berrigan met the charges aggressively, with a bluffer's bravura. It is also known that the associate warden spent some time making locker-room banter out of the nature of Berrigan's endearments to Sister Elizabeth McAlister, to whom the letter was written. Guards after-wards would say to Berrigan, "Hey, Father, you've got something going on the outside, I hear."

McAlister is removed from the visitors' and correspondents' list. She had visited him, labeling herself his "cousin." In the letter discovered there is this: "Sunday, an inmate hit us with the rumor that Pete was a courier of contraband, and that they are looking to bust him. Naturally, caution followed." That last is to be doubted. "Pete" is Boyd. The next day, Boyd, out on his study release since January, speaks with the associate warden. That conversation lasts two hours. Afterward, he drove Boyd to Bucknell and received from him a manila envelope filled with Xerox copies of material previously secreted out of the penitentiary. That evening a meeting with FBI men occurs on the prison ground, in a picnic area. Boyd gains use of his opposing thumb; a new creature is born: *homo informans.*

"How could they have gone on with the letters after there were rumors? After he had been confronted by the associate warden? After Boyd had been questioned?" These inquiries carom around the press section.

Jonah, inside the whale, must have felt an overwhelming sense of security. The worst has happened, yet he has not been vanquished. In the jaws of adversity he began to feel especially safe. In the house of his captor he begins to feel free. In prison it is the same.

Clark, after his opening statement, had retired to the sidelines, hardly venturing forth, but he begins this crossexamination.

He names the last three heads of the Federal Bureau of Prisons, asking the associate warden if he knew them; the associate warden says he knows of them and had met them, and Clark gives the impression that they are all personal friends of his. He then asks, "During your years of knowing these men as you do, do you know that it has always been the firmest and most important Federal Bureau of Prisons policy never to permit any prisoner to act as a government agent or informant while he is in prison."

"Objection," Lynch calls out.

Angry, Clark rephrases the question and asks it again. Another sustained objection. Clark asks if he knows of any prosecutions or indictments on contraband charges because of letters? The associate warden thinks he recalls one case some twelve years ago.

Lynch objects. Irrelevant.

Clark is on his feet. "It is not irrelevant. It shows the motives of the government."

Clark questions on how Boyd got on the study-release program. Doesn't it require minimum custody? No disciplinary record? Doesn't it depend on his previous criminal record? No crimes of violence? He asks the associate warden what Boyd's criminal record was; the associate warden says he doesn't know. Clark is aghast.

> MR. CLARK: And you have no knowledge of his prior criminal record?
> THE WITNESS: I believe only what I read in the

131

paper that he had been committed a number of times
to—

MR. LYNCH: Objection to what he read in the paper.

MR. CLARK: We don't want to know what you read
in the paper. We want to know what you know as an
associate warden of that penitentiary. You don't know
what his prior criminal record was?

THE WITNESS: No sir.

MR. CLARK: You do know that he had a prior criminal record?

THE WITNESS: Yes sir, I do.

Clark's voice is pained and impatient. He judges this complete
incompetence or deliberate lies. It is hard to tell which of the two
troubles him more.

MR. CLARK: Work-release and study-release were
first authorized in the federal system in nineteen sixty-
five, is that correct?

THE WITNESS: I believe that is correct.

Authorized when Clark was Attorney General; two programs in
which he took great interest—and now he saw to what use they
were being put. This prosecution and indictment based on a program he fostered. His study-release program used to facilitate the
use of informers.

MR. CLARK: As a practical matter, there was close
scrutiny of it, wasn't there, because it was a test program and we wanted to be sure it worked well?

And "we" wanted to be sure it worked well; sweet liberal prison
reforms made noisome.

MR. LYNCH: Objection, Your Honor, he is testifying.

The associate warden answers lifelessly; his only sign of viability
is a set of facial tics, that flicker—a candle flame just before going
out—following his answers.

He admits to knowing that the letters continued to go in and
out ("after we intercepted the first one I knew"). He is asked,
each a separate question, whether he knew Douglas had liquor,
use of a phone, an apartment, a private car, trips to Williamsburg,
was paid by the FBI, all in violation of the study-release rules. No,
he did not know any of that.

After Herman sustains a number of objections to the defense's questions geared to the issue of discriminatory prosecution, Clark says, "We're being denied the right to confront this witness." He then asks the associate warden whether or not he knew that Douglas had been caught with a hypodermic needle.

Lynch is up, objecting, "If Your Honor would instruct the jury that the answer is the evidence, not the question." The answer was no.

A set of records that he had used to reacquaint himself with dates, here in Harrisburg, had been sent back to Danbury yesterday; Boudin refuses to crossexamine him without seeing those records. He wants them and the associate warden recalled. He leaves the stand and us with his version of Boyd's evolution.

The women in Boyd's Bucknell life take the stand. Bucknell University is on high ground overlooking the hamlet of Lewisburg. It has an array of three-story red-brick buildings, modeled after the architecture of Eastern Ivy League colleges; but Bucknell's walls are denuded of ivy. It is a private university, Judge Herman's alma mater, and the setting has been fictionalized in *Goodbye, Columbus,* by Philip Roth, one of its graduates. Bucknell University has the three-pronged crest of fifties college-life: fraternity row, small sports cars, and beer. Girls walk the campus hugging books to their breasts; clothes change with the seasons. The antiwar faction fared as well as any minority club.

Boyd Douglas began there as a special student in the spring of 1970. He pedaled a bicycle each weekday from the confines of Lewisburg penitentiary. One of the requirements for study-release that is often overlooked, but crucial, is that you have to be able to afford it. Douglas had the money; the ten-thousand-dollar settlement he had received from his civil suit against the government for the scars left by the NIH experiment for which he volunteered. Bucknell was not cheap; each course cost nearly three hundred dollars. Boyd began with two. Leaving the prison for the day was like a blind man regaining his sight, only to loose it again come nightfall. Was this taste an incentive to behave, or just another flogging?

Boyd took an apartment at 204 South Sixth Street, a block from the campus, the beginning of June. Boyd has a talent for capitalizing—a Robinson Crusoe of penitentiary islands—on what is within reach. He took on as girlfriends the young Bucknell students who had the apartment above him. They were handy, saved time; he could do two things at once.

Douglas stood out from the callow young men attending Bucknell. Older than most, a sullen patina of worldly experience covered his expressions. Initially he hid his convict status till he understood its advantages. Sympathy. Boyd knew its powers. He tapped it better than the FBI phones. Hardship became a virtue; suffering has its fascination. Hadn't an eminent philosopher called a convict a saint? Boyd has scars, a brand he shares with a few. The two young girls were the Lewisburg end of the McAlister-Berrigan mail-route; they also copied the letters into Boyd's notebook; better to get them into the prison, little girl, he explained. His handwriting was illegible, he told one; another, that he didn't have the time to copy them himself.

Lynch quizzed them on the "rap sessions" they attended. They refer to them as picnics. He meetings. One luncheon is an overt act, as is a picnic. Tony and Mary Scoblick are placed in Lewisburg; so are the Fathers Neil and Joe. As is Elizabeth. What was discussed during these intense rap sessions? Lynch wants to know. Sabotage of Selective Service offices?

Both of the girls Boyd dated worked that summer at Perkins Pancake House in Lewisburg. We hear they talked about the low wages paid there; they also talked about the destruction of property and the destruction of people—whether it was the same. "Property in general versus the killing of people," one of them puts it. It was academic discussion. They used to have nice roast-beef dinners prepared. Lynch is not happy. Nothing distinct or incriminating is coming forth. Picnics, dinners, luncheons. Neil and Joe talking about their ghetto experiences in Baltimore. Racism. Social problems. The jury does not know about the grants of immunity the girls have; they do not know these women are presumed to have something to hide. During cross, Terry Lenzner asks one if Boyd ever proposed to her. Yes, he did. Boyd told me he had terminal cancer and had six to twelve months to live. I was troubled by his proposal. He told me I should talk to Sister

Elizabeth. She would be a good person to talk to; she would understand.

The trip is made; she talks to Liz; the talk is devoted to the "personal problem." Boyd had told her he was a demolitions expert in the army; he urged them both to get more involved, to go further in their antiwar work (though neither had done much protesting previously). Lenzner ends his cross with a series of questions:

"Has Mary Cain Scoblick ever asked you to participate in draft-board actions?"

"No."

"Has Anthony Scoblick ever asked you to participate in draft-board actions?"

"No."

"Has Joseph Wenderoth ever asked you to participate in draft-board actions?"

"No."

"Has Neil McLaughlin ever asked you to participate in draft-board actions?"

"No."

"Has Elizabeth McAlister ever asked you to participate in draft-board actions?"

"No."

"Has Boyd F. Douglas?"

"Yes."

Two librarians take the stand. The first, a young woman, daughter of a career army officer, testifies to receiving a thank-you note from Sister Elizabeth McAlister, for her help at a dinner party held at the house of the other librarian. Enclosed with the thank-you note is an envelope for Boyd. The kidnap letter.

"I just found out that juror number eight," a reporter says, settling in her seat, referring to one of the youngest women jurors, "has read *Soul on Ice* and the *Autobiography of Malcolm X*. Her brother let me into their apartment. It might not mean anything, since those books are assigned in college courses these days." But it might mean something that the young white girl has lived with a young black man, as the defense had discovered.

She sits, second juror in the back row, biting at her cuticles, staring down at her lap, during the testimony of the three young women all her age. These possible accessories to the fact. Patient scribes transferring letters into Boyd's notebook. Doing his bidding. Terminal cancer. Her fingers fall from her mouth, saved for a time by a lunch recess.

vii

"Why don't you sit with us?"

"Us" are two gentlemen, two bizarre bookends at either side of an empty chair at a table in the basement cafeteria of the building which houses the Defense Committee.

"I'm expecting to be joined later," I say, setting my tray down at a nearby table. They have no plates in front of them. One, a tall pink albino, wears a reddish sport coat, gray-patterned trousers. He could be a sportscaster on color TV, just that the flesh tones are wrong, improperly tuned in. His companion has a jeweled American flag in one lapel and a thousand-dollar bill replica pinned on the other. Tinted rectangular sunglasses, a mod charcoal suit.

The other tables are filled with the regular clientele, grim businessmen. There are no Defense Committee people here at the moment. The couple are stranger than any of the young long-haired people, for their dress and manner is the same as the other businessmen, but raised to another level, surreal, sci-fi, the norm exploded. The two of them are beyond the larvae stage of the other businessmen; they have shed their dull cocoons and are resplendent examples of what the rest are yet but a colorless stage. Jungle plants amid the omnipresent pine trees. The jeweled American flag sparkles. The tall albino says to me, not unlewdly, "Would you like to make thirty thousand dollars a year?"

They both smile at me. I am not sure the other patrons can see them. At first I thought they were the next century's FBI looking to question me.

"Would you like to make thirty thousand dollars a year?" the albino asks again.

I return their smiles.

"Won't you join us?" I will not be moved. No Defense Committee people have come in. There is no way to avoid it; storm-clouds are amassing. I'm to be deluged by a spiel.

"We're from the Turner Corporation."

"Oh," I say, beginning to understand, "isn't that the man who financed Captain Medina's defense?" Ernest L. Medina, accused and acquitted of the charge of murder at Mylai.

"F. Lee Bailey . . ."

"F. Lee Bailey?"

"He's our lawyer . . . a great man; he's also the president of a helicopter firm." Where ex-Captain Medina is now employed.

Chinook helicopters land on the sugar cannisters. The Medina court-martial. After a prospective juror had given an especially obtuse answer the New York *Times* had remarked, "I heard West Pointers at the Medina trial who were less intelligent than these people." Dare to be great Turner. Is that Lieutenant Rusty Calley with a jeweled American flag and thousand-dollar lapel pin?

"Yes, Turner's a great man; rose out of poverty, borrowed five thousand dollars, and is now a millionaire. People are too negative, always looking at the bad side; we're going to put out a paper called *Good News* and that's all we're going to print in it . . ."

"Yes," the albino says, picking it up, "We're going to report all the news, but only the good side—say for instance, if there's a car wreck and three people die and three live, that's what we'll say, 'Three people survive wreck.' "

"Why," the other says, not letting a second stand to sour, "We have a man working for us now, earning fifteen thousand dollars a month, who used to be a riveter. All a person has to do," he says, rising from his chair as does the other, "is to think he's great."

The albino stands at my side. His hands are rough and chapped, but his fingernails are manicured and have a high sheen.

"How'd you like to make thirty thousand a year," he says again, as if he'd gotten back to the beginning of a short tape. "You know, we are what we think we are. Why tell ourselves we're nothing, when it would be just as good to tell ourselves we're great?"

"You know, if a man practices golf in his head, and never

practices for real, he still plays even better than a man who plays on a golf course . . . studies have shown that people can't tell the difference between what is real and what is imagined . . . so you are what you imagine yourself to be . . ."

"Now, we're having a meeting tonight at the Ramada Inn at Carlisle; we can show you how to be great by telling yourself you're great and how to make thirty thousand dollars a year. Do you know F. Lee Bailey?" he asks.

"No."

"Well, he's a great man . . ."

"You'll be hearing from us; even if you don't get to the meeting; because we're great!"

As they depart I can hear Lt. Calley muttering to Captain Medina: I ordered a million dollars' worth of bombs dropped today; oh, boy, a million dollars' worth of ammo.

viii

"Give us Douglas. Give us Douglas," the mob of the press begins to chant in its heart. The jury has not been called in. There is a sidebar conference. The other librarian is going to refuse to testify, even though she is shackled with transactional immunity. In order for there not to be prejudice against the defendants, the defense argues, the jury should be out. They are. A woman in her fifties is sworn in. She is no longer at Bucknell but now lives and works in California. Lynch asks a question and she replies:

"I cannot in my conscience lend myself to this black charade . . ."

Herman is thrown forward in his chair. This, from the most timid and gentle-looking of all the witnesses. A fifty-year-old matron calling my court a black charade!

"Just hold on a minute, we can't have anything like this . . ."

". . . spying in libraries and schools is something I must protest . . ." she goes on, and is stopped. "I may be flustered," she says pluckishly, her prepared statement fluttering in her hand.

"I submit the witness is in contempt of court; the sanction of the court should be imposed so we can persuade her to talk," Lynch says. Persuade her to talk? The chief marshal stands by the bar of the court, lifting one foot up and then the other, a trapped bull ready to burst into the arena.

The defense has risen, offering to stipulate to any testimony that she might give, making it unnecessary. The prosecution objects to that. Herman says that will not absolve her of the contempt.

He tells her, "I could impose, or send you with the marshals right now, but . . ." He is reluctant to send this tidy lady off to jail. Lynch is up: "She has been told to do something by the court and she hasn't done it."

The defense keeps saying, "We will stipulate." Herman calls her July 4th–tied lawyer up to sidebar. It is decided to give her a day to reconsider. Lynch says, "I would urge that the time be shorter."

He is upset. An act has failed to show, to perform, and now there is nothing left for him to do but to proceed with the star attraction. Boyd F. Douglas, Jr., untimely ripped, is thrust back into the world.

Boyd

I under fair pretence of friendly ends,
And well plac't words of glozing courtesie
Baited with reasons not unplausible
Wind· me into the easie-hearted man,
And hugg him into snares.

          —JOHN MILTON,
    A Mask Presented at Ludlow-Castle

i

Until the winter of 1970 Boyd F. Douglas, Jr., had never owned a car. He had commandeered a few. A red station-wagon had once caught his fancy. Leaving a bank in haste, the boundaries of private property dissolved and he leapt into one, then another, trying to start them. He wanted to disappear. Cars are magic. Boyd did not have the proper spell. A voodoo ring of FBI and Wisconsin sheriffs surrounded it with a hex. He was arrested.

Boyd is a child of a disposable culture. He conspicuously consumed rent-a-cars, motel rooms, airplane seats. Vague commercial space that is leased, rented, reserved, occupied, but then is gone without title. Boyd was leaving a legacy of receipts. An automobile nomad, Boyd had never owned a car, just as Oedipus was a motherless child.

Our car universe is burning out; Los Angeles is its Nirvana, junkyards its Hades, and the highways, the arteries of the last generation of bleeders. The dynasty is advised not to spawn. But it is October 1970 and Boyd writes, in a simple sentence, "I have never owned a car." It is forthright. And perhaps it is true. Boyd's veracity is not an unbroken chain.

Amid the totems of puberty a car is special. You get a car when you graduate from high school, or become sixteen, if your parents can afford one. You get one yourself if you are industrious. You sign up for your first stretch of parasitism if you borrow one, use the family car. You steal them if you are an urban hoodlum; you take one for joy rides if you're from the suburbs. Every region has its imperatives and the great distances of the Midwest demand a car. A back seat is an adolescent's nuptial bower. General Motors has had more to do with the varieties of sexual intercourse than the Kama Sutra.

Boyd had never owned one. Perhaps, one can speculate, a 1952 Ford might have been in his possession, legally, for a while; but that was a rundown car, too much the soul's mirror, and if we have anything to do with our shells we don't want to be burdened with chassis rust and no finish. So many things speak for us there is no quiet on the earth.

Each evening in Harrisburg, aristocratic Front Street, running beside the path of the Susquehanna, becomes a racetrack. Cars, reshaped in the search for individuality, to divest a Ford of its fordness, or a Chevrolet of its chevroletness, these raised and lowered, chopped and rechanneled mutations canter up Front Street, snorting and downshifting, the occupants bad-eyeing any passers-by. The laying of streaks of tire rubber is as important a remains, to them, as the faint wings fossilized in sandstone.

Let us not diminish cars, even though they are baled and on display in progressive museums. Detroit designers are true Darwinians and there is no Monkey Trial for them. Did Boyd lust after a car? Did he burn? Hardly; that he assaulted a few, ransacking their charms for a clandestine trip, is testament not to passion, but to need. The cars were acquiescent. No, Boyd waited for *the* car, and *the* time and place. Boyd has a sense of economy. What will do in a pinch will not do when the time is unconstrained.

I have never owned a car. He might as well have said, I have never felt the sun, never seen the color of the sky.

Before coming into what Leonard Boudin referred to as "the orbit of this trial" Boyd was drawn to our major epicenters of

hustle: Miami Beach, Las Vegas, Acapulco. Boyd's father, peering through the gray clouds of newsprint, said, this is my son
Boyd, in whom I am not well pleased. We are all prodigal sons;
Boyd sent his father home his .38. No note accompanied it. Consider Mr. Douglas's somber reflections as he examined that parcel.
Boyd's .38. "I like guns," Boyd says. Take away guns and only
criminals will have them. The federal marshals favor the Roy
Rogers Beef Restaurant for lunch down around the corner from
the Federal Building. They all observe the admonishment found
on a plaque by each booth: "Western Etiquette." Eat-it-quick.

> Please remove all
> Waste paper & trays
> When you leave. . . .
> Thanks Podner
> Roy & Dale

There are vacu-formed revolvers mounted on black velvet above
each of the tables. The marshals wear guns, curled onto the
bottom of their spines. Fast foods and fast draws. Cheeseburgers
and .38s. Boyd has been having his noonday meal on the floor
above the courtroom. Roy caters.

"Mr. Douglas."
Lynch says the name softly, like someone who wishes to intrude,
but not too rudely, upon a daydream. A marshal exits.
"Will someone suggest to Lynch that he remove himself from in
front of the lectern; he is blocking my view."
"Luckily we can see right through Lynch."
The elderly librarian has been left in the hallway, holding her
torn-sheet manifesto, which she read to the press in full, her black-
charade edict. The press had wound her up like a top, she had
spun out her story, and they left her to come to a stop alone.
Boyd was arriving.
"The defendants will hang on his every word."
"This isn't a capital case."
The doorways have become substantial with marshals. Three
block the courtroom's main entrance. A number of them back
up the side doors. Their new weight thickens the mass in the

room. A clot of marshals seems to divide, some amoebic division takes place, and from their indistinguishable form an individual emerges much like the rest. Boyd had not yet entered, it seemed, but one of the marshals was shambling up to the witness stand.

"That's him?!"

His hips sway flaccidly, to some unheard burlesque-hall beat. Da dump, da dump. The impression Boyd had left with everyone who knew him was the same: lean and mean. That one picture showed him so, giving the peace sign. The long-sleeved shirt rolled up to mid-forearm. When did the scars begin? How many notables have been pictured with that gesture? Churchill, Richard Nixon ("That's what they hate to see"). Daniel Berrigan, wrists linked by chain. That is a gesture priests use often, but the fingers are not flared, but ride side by side, above the chalice before consecration. The scope of gestures that the hands can make is limited; they are finite, like the alphabet.

Douglas bends to sit, holding a wide lavender tie flat on his stomach; it seems something will fall out when he tilts if he doesn't. He stares straight ahead. His eyes settle on Lynch like a suspended object that has been disturbed but is now coming back to rest. He does not look at the defendants. Philip Berrigan favors the left side of his face. He speaks out of the left side of his mouth, all his expressions pile up there like small stones at the foot of a hill. He looks at Douglas, trying to hook his attention like a burglar trying to trip a lock, a probe that seeks an unseen latch.

Lynch follows a biblical exegesis: In the beginning was the word. Creation has always seemed quick. Done in a week, but the telling of it is even faster. He launches Douglas at his last arrest and conviction: ". . . falsely made and forged securities." Ajax forging securities; they heat and crackle. Falsely made, an Elizabethan taunt. Falsely made, gentle lass. Lynch will see what he can do. He has no Adam's rib here, but perhaps this Douglas can be made out of his own spittle and elbow grease. Lynch understands effort. He might not have the savoir-faire of Leonard Boudin, the authority of Ramsey Clark, the elocution of Paul O'Dwyer, but he says he has the facts. Faith in facts and sweat. Douglas will be a man of letters; he is a vehicle. He is to be the panel truck at election time touring neighborhoods, mixing band music and campaign speeches from a rooftop loudspeaker. Lynch will be as detached as the driver who steers the talking machine through traffic. The word dies and how it dies is a golden equation: It diminishes from its source.

Lynch is diminished by his source. Can he see himself as a sideshow barker behind that podium? He needs a straw hat and thin cane. His three gray shills sit below him.

And if you think this is something, you should see what we have inside. You should see our files . . . we've got such files. Files we show to no one but you. For one thin dime we'll expose for you, right in this very room, the most appalling, misshapen, quizzical members of Creation, the most outlandish, repugnant, suggestive documents ever to tempt money out of the tight fist of a Senate Appropriations subcommittee. And as an extra-special treat, stag films of the Reverend M.L.K., Jr. . . .

Douglas is explaining how he was accepted into the study-release program at Bucknell. The flash of vision has worn off the reporters; one asks another:

"What color would you call that shirt he's wearing?"

"Fink-pink."

Boyd's uncle uses a back country form of genealogy when referring to Boyd that keeps the Douglas family tree straight. Boyd Junior. Boyd Junior did this. Boyd Junior did that. Why, ain't he just like daddy? It is likely Boyd Junior did not appreciate any of this. His mother, an itinerant Ophelia, drowned herself when Boyd was seven. In Creston, Iowa, a hard-knuckled small town, Boyd was born. There is no birth certificate on file; tradition has set the date as 10 September 1940. Boyd's early education was a not-so-grand tour; his uncle said he had been raised by traveling. Growing up on the sere plains of the Midwest, his father an hourly wage-earner, that one measure of a life, so much per hour, a time-clock brand. Boyd works on the pipelines. His mother kills herself with an abundance. She *drowns* herself. Death is the first luxury she knows. Boyd might have sensed this; he is sixteen when a freshman in high school. Being older than the rest of the kids is a kind of advantage. The kind that is easy to take.

What is freshman year at Indian Lake high school to Boyd? He has this natural edge; he is older. It puts him outside, gives him an angle. Putting aside the fulcrum, Boyd could recoil an old axiom: Give me an angle slick enough and I'll slide the world along.

Indian Lake High School in Lewistown, Ohio, in 1958. It has school colors. Orange and black? Blue and gold? A football team, baseball diamonds, bad lighting, blackboards, civics classes, three-o'clock dismissal. Small-town high-school. Boyd gets to be nineteen. Ducktails, Brylcreem, *American Bandstand*. Teenagedom is just about to be epochized and Boyd is just about to leave it. The high-school principal says Boyd stole forty dollars from a teacher, but that he returned the money. No charges. Boyd leaves without graduating. You did not "drop out" in 1959. Girls left because they "got caught"; boys because they were "bad." The army or worse waited for them. Turned out of high school turned you out of your tribe. Certified loner, ducktail pariah, banished from civics class. Forty bucks makes you lose your ticket. Boyd learns how to make a fire with the only stick he's got: break it in half.

On the stand, Boyd does not look like his, or anyone's, past. From a distance his face has the character of a mannequin's head that is supposed to stay in style for at least five years. Dark razor-cut hair. He looks like the "Draw Me" man on matchbook art-courses. His flesh looks soft, uncured. If touched, the indentation would fill back in slowly, like a hole in the sand. His face has sunlamp color that sits on it like make-up.

He stares ahead at Lynch; Lynch is his lodestone and north star. Boyd's voice is high, the monotone of rote recitation, the only variance is a slight Ozarkian slur. It is smooth except for the recurring potholes of bad grammar and mispronunciations. He explains the study-release requirements. He alludes to his civil suit. In January 1970 he was accepted as a special student by the dean of Bucknell University. His stepbrother Jack Weckman wrote to United States Senator Richard S. Schweiker (Republican of Pennsylvania) in behalf of Boyd. When serving his first prison term Boyd volunteered for a National Institute of Health experiment. Lifers usually are the volunteers for these guinea pig experiments. The doctor as shaman; Boyd wants to change. It is time to graduate with a hypodermic needle. Emulsion is injected into the muscles of his arms and legs. Boyd waits to be transformed. The unknown dream of being discovered, the lost being found, the living contemplate death. Man's common hope, that tomorrow will not find him what he is today. The eighth plague of Egypt was in that syringe and Boyd develops lingering and recurring sores. Boyd has actualized his leper status. NIH had distilled Boyd's life, mixed it with the water of his mother's grave, added the sweat from his father's pipelines, the thin oil of his jalopy wanderings, and gave it back to him, a silver bullet. Boyd was vaccinated against himself. Lingering sores. Boyd ruminates over his scabs, his fingers contemplate their edges. He becomes a mystic of crustation, a connoisseur of the healing process. He knows best when it can be frustrated, the time just before it succeeds. *They are going to pay for this.* The lower classes in America have one source of capital whispered into their ears since birth. I have heard it. A one-syllable admonition, the alchemy of the poor, when suffering can be turned into gold. It issues from their lips the other side of lament: sue. *Sue.* SUE! Sue the bastards, the rich. Get a lawyer. Old women startled on a street corner by a speeding limousine: I'll sue you.

Boyd wonders at the pustular oracle. From the broken tablets of scabs at his feet these words are pieced together: THOU SHALT SUE.

Boyd tells the court that he received over ten thousand dollars and his lawyer received over four thousand as a result of the settlement of his civil suit with the government. He got the same amount the survivors of a dead soldier receive from his service insurance. With this he was able to afford the courses at Bucknell. He takes Psychology and Political Science. He had received his high-school equivalency diploma when in the penitentiary.

He continues to stare at Lynch. It is as if an astronomer, his radar disc heavenward, had finally discovered a signal from far space. Move one millimeter and the tenuous connection would be lost.

"I advised Professor Drinnon the end of April that Philip Berrigan and David Eberhart would be coming to Lewisburg." Professor Richard Drinnon is chairman of the history department at Bucknell University. They had met shortly after beginning classes at Bucknell. Boyd considered Drinnon a radical, because he had walked out of a speech delivered by Hubert Humphrey.

"Yes, I never heard the name Philip Berrigan before April of 1970." Though Boyd had been in the Towson County jail when Philip Berrigan was there while the Catonsville Nine were on trial; Boyd was there to confer with his lawyer about the resolution of his civil suit. "I met Philip Berrigan outside of the church, inside the penitentiary; I started out the conversation and said I was attending Bucknell and said Professor Drinnon [who knew Philip Berrigan] asked me to get in contact with him . . . it was more of a friendly get-together, I told him the circumstances of why I was at Bucknell, that I had won a civil action, been left with numerous scars, that I had been turned down for parole, and I thought that I would get a parole when the civil action was settled. I asked him if there was anything I could do for him. I told him I could possibly get a letter out for him. I met him in the mess hall. He gave me two letters, one to an address he enclosed, the other for Professor Drinnon to send. I read the letters and then sent them on."

Referral, the security clearance of mutual friends. Boyd becomes a middle man, the place where you can play both ends. An interlocutor. Philip Berrigan knows the tradition. I am here to explain God's ways to man; to explain man's ways to God. The priesthood is a courier system; in the confessional the priest transmits absolution. It is easy to trust a medium one is so familiar with. He also believes in Providence, a dubious precedent. Boyd is a gift. Boyd, an angel of deliverance. Trust Boyd; he has shown you his scars.

Lynch asks Boyd for the subject matter of the conversations he had with Father Berrigan during the first part of May. "In reference to Professor Drinnon," Boyd says, "in our conversations he said Drinnon had been in New York prior to his incarceration. He had tried to recruit Drinnon for the East Coast Conspiracy to Save Lives, for draft-board actions. I told Father Berrigan I had been in the service. Berrigan visited Drinnon in his home prior to incarceration. Drinnon did not get into the action because he was writing a book on the American Indians; Berrigan didn't trust him completely so he wanted to set up a mail-drop through me. I had told Philip Berrigan that I wasn't completely satisfied with the settlement and they had given me a bad deal on the parole; I had become sympathetic with his whole philosophy of draft-board destruction. He said there were other projects around the country. The destruction of utility systems in Washington, D.C., complete utility systems, that carried conduits through the systems; he and Joseph Wenderoth had been posing as electricians for the Rob Electrical Company down in the tunnels; GSA gave them no trouble; to destroy those pipes in Washington itself would be the utmost impact upon the U.S. government, if they were destroyed right and at the right time. I told him I had experience with explosives. He said there was no trouble walking around in them. The tunnels were eight foot by ten foot. He was afraid of them erupting up through Pennsylvania Avenue."

Lynch then steered him to the "mail-drops." The third week in May. Again, Berrigan told Boyd he didn't trust Drinnon; he gave him Sister Elizabeth McAlister's phone number. "I called her on the phone in New York; gave her my name. She gave me a number where I could call her back. I'm not sure if it was this time or when she came she gave me the address."

He said McAlister came to Bucknell, met him at a fraternity house where he took noon meals. "She just came back from the penitentiary and she told me how well Philip Berrigan looked. She also told me, she added, 'Phil was telling me you have a very interesting trade.' "

"Was that trait or trade?" Boudin asks. It is his first crack of the door; the first shaft of the light he wants shed on Douglas. Trait.

"Trade."

Boyd had responded to her query: " 'Oh, you mean my experience in the army as a demolitions expert?' And she said, 'Yes.' " She further asks Boyd to get a list of pay phones on campus, tells him they need a mail-drop, a good line of communications. She will try to call once a week. He tells her about his civil suit, the compensation he had received; that they had given him study-release as compensation for turning down the parole. He showed her the scars on his arms. The code name "Pete" is established. It was very friendly. The mail-drop address, mark it personal, put another envelope inside . . .

The new testimony, the book of Boyd. Chapter and verse.

Lynch approaches Boyd with a document. Can you identify this? "This is a letter I received from Philip Berrigan to be sent to Sister McAlister v-i-a . . ."

V-i-a? Reporters confer.

"He can't pronounce it."

"He's just so used to saying a-k-a that he can't get out of the habit."

Herman asks, "Is this a copy?"

"Yes."

"Who made the copy?"

"I did."

"How did you come to make a copy?"

Yes, Boyd, how did you come to make a copy. A primordial urge for reproduction. Proof. Ah, proof. Of existence. I make copies, ergo sum.

"I became concerned . . . about the goals of these people and that they were all clerics; I'm Catholic and I've been brought up a very strict Catholic . . ."

The courtroom blinks. A python has just swallowed a small animal. Watch it go down. Boyd has been brought up a very strict Catholic. Incredulity peaks out from under its shell. Boyd scares it back.

". . . in the religious sense."

Boyd has just boxed the ears of logic. A buzzing sets in.

"I knew I'd be discovered; only a matter of time before I'd be discovered taking contraband out . . ."

"I object," Boudin says, catapulted out of his chair. "I object, Your Honor, to the word contraband; it's a legal term," he says, turning towards Lynch, "I don't know where he got it . . ."

Boyd is not to be interrupted.

"I knew that I would eventually be apprehended for this and I felt that if I had enough evidence to produce at the time, that the authorities would believe in what I was telling them in regards to my conversation [about the tunnels], and also in regards to the letters and if they would realize the threat of these people to the United States government."

149

"Objection, Your Honor, to his reference to 'these people,' his interpolating of remarks, his answers which are more than responsive, please have him confine his remarks to the questions." Boudin sits down again and Herman strikes "these people" from the record.

"Now, Mr. Douglas, I am sure it was inadvertently put, but at this point in your testimony try to refrain from referring to these defendants or anybody other than Berrigan or McAlister concerning the letter that you had received and so on from there. Do you understand what I mean? When you said there are seven defendants—"

"I made that mistake, Your Honor," Boyd says, "because I know the story."

Boudin launches himself on a direct trajectory to Boyd, right arm outstretched and rigid, the entire distance covered as he says, "I object to that, Your Honor," his face reddening, "that is provocation!"

Herman gestures to the bailiff.

"Court is recessed for ten minutes."

ii

I was seven when the Rosenbergs were electrocuted and had just reached, according to the tradition of the Catholic Church, the Age of Reason, when you are held accountable for your sins. At one end of a table this evening at Augsburn Luthern Church sits Sister Elizabeth McAlister; at the other, Morton Sobell. The arc that crackles between them is two decades come and gone; between them sits a Communist once convicted under the Smith Act of 1949 who, after going underground for five years, was imprisoned for six. He joined the Communist party when he was seventeen. Next to him is a young White Panther, an accused bomber; and sitting on his left is an ex-WAC, who had been court-martialed for participating in a peace demonstration while in uniform.

Sobell, convicted along with the Rosenbergs, was sentenced to thirty years; he was released in 1969. He has let his gray hair grow long, a hermit's unattended locks. He is wearing a new, ill-fitting dark pin-striped suit. He has on high-top black tennis shoes. Prison is a time capsule of sorts; a bad place to observe social change; you are likely to think the world is much the same as it was when you entered. Sobell had spent the weeks before the FBI took him out of Mexico going up and down that country like a man pacing a cell.

Julius and Ethel Rosenberg were executed with lewd haste. A young Jesuit in France at the time, Daniel Berrigan, as he has put it, "heatedly defended the execution of the Rosenbergs." Sobell recalls their defense as being "inept"; the Rosenbergs' two heads should have been stuck on pikes and waved over a wall, a lesson, an example. Atomic spies. Hardly human. The general population greeted the Bomb the way natives must have reacted to the first observed total eclipse, or the discovery of fire. Demons were at large. It was magic, evil incarnate, therefore holy, a treasure to be kept in the buried center of the temple of temples, the Pentagon. The Rosenbergs, so it was portrayed by judge, prosecution, and press, stole the secret of the atomic bomb and delivered it up to the Russians. Thereby dangling a Damocles sword of nuclear fission above every American head. Their death was an exorcism of guilt; America is the only country that has dropped an atomic bomb on anyone. A sacrifice had to be found; pillorying the scientists who created it was not enough. The Rosenbergs' death placated wrathful deities. Their "stealing" the atom bomb would supply the missing second proposition to a syllogism of exculpation. We are justified in dropping the bomb since *they* would have, had *they* had it. *They* have the bomb because the Rosenbergs stole it. Hence, we are justified.

The Rosenbergs' deaths were this country's felix culpa; their electric crucifixion reopened the gates that Hiroshima and Nagasaki closed. They stole the vile secret; the curse had been lifted.

How much blame two hapless Soviet agents took with them when they died!

The panel is called "crimes of repression." The trial of Julius and Ethel Rosenberg, plus Sobell, and the trial of Philip Berrigan and Elizabeth McAlister, plus five others is placed side-by-side, though most comparisons and contrasts are politely left unspoken. Their fists are gloved with generalizations. Abstract similarities are recounted. "There is always a Douglas," the Communist says, naming his own Smith Act trial informer with FBI connections (David Greenglass, Ethel Rosenberg's brother, dramatist of fratricide, is not mentioned). "And after he revealed his duplicity publicly the government then indicted him and he received a five-year sentence for perjury."

The panelists begin to squabble about which period is or was more repressive. The fifties or the seventies. Elizabeth says the seventies are more repressive, because there are subtler forms of repression and the government is much better at their techniques and applications. Sobell, trying not to be jingoistic for his decade, avers that the fifties still seem to him to be much more repressive. The forces of repression, Sobell says, "are tremendous, but not as bad as our generation; we were so afraid to deviate from the norm. In 1933–38 I was attending CCNY and was afraid of getting kicked out, because I needed that diploma—or I'd be a . . . a packing clerk." He says that today's young do not worry so much about such things; they are "freer." Elizabeth is tired and harried; her thoughts speed by behind her eyes, which are startled and alarmed. She says, "The working class should experience hunger so they will know that economic security is not the highest value." The Communist blinks. What is she saying?! "She must mean middle-class for working-class," a sympathizer in the audience says to a friend. The White Panther speaks in a voice of a subject coming out of a sodium pentothal trance: "I found it disturbing that people were afraid to have me visit them in their homes; just me being there made them full of fear." It took about two minutes for the words to trail out of his mouth; he filled the silences with a display of Zen gestures.

The ex-WAC says: "Would I have had the courage to do what they [referring to Sobell and the Communist] did in the fifties?" What did they do? Would she have the courage to do what? Join the Communist party at seventeen? Be prosecuted under the Smith Act? Take a 35-mm. film can to the Lower East Side of New York and deliver it to Julius Rosenberg? The ex-WAC is wearing civilian clothes in the same style as her departed uniform, even to the shoulder bag. Did she join the WACs because she liked the cut of the clothes? What had she done? Dropped antiwar leaflets on military bases in the San Francisco Bay area from a private plane she chartered; disobeyed an order and wore her uniform at a peace demonstration.

Sobell says, "You don't fight repression per se; Nixon obviously plans to atom-bomb the North, to make the earth radioactive; make it unlivable for twenty years, a hundred mile strip of land along the DMZ, sowing it with radioactivity; they are going to deny it, but they deny today what they do tomorrow . . ." Some children have been playing at the doorway by the stage; they have now found the light switches. The church dims for a minute; the Rosenbergs have just been electrocuted. Morton Sobell is wearing high-top black tennis shoes. Elizabeth thinks the working class should suffer hunger. The White Panther is surprised people are afraid to have him in their homes. The WAC doesn't know if she could have been a Communist at seventeen in 1950. Is Sobell trying to make an atomic bomb in his basement from David Greenglass's drawings of snowflakes?

"This is where the movement should center; we should look forward and try to outguess him," Sobell says. Everyone is tired; the hall is full of static electricity. The Communist says, "We should be one for all and all for one; there is no such thing as instant revolution; there is too much talk of lifestyle, it is too often confined to culture; it should be a political style . . ." He looks like an extra from the original production of Odets's *Waiting for Lefty*. The five panelists are a Mad Hatter's tea party. Elizabeth replies to an earlier assertion of Sobell's: "We can't outguess them; what they always come up with is worse than we ever could imagine."

iii

There is an eerie silence in the courtroom; a sick-watch sound when the patient no longer breathes: the jury has never heard any of the defendants' voices. The defendants take notes, observe, act in their own fashion as judges, but of a higher court. Mary Cain Scoblick has a chair unlike the others since her feet do not touch the floor in the leather chairs provided for the defendants. Elizabeth

153

McAlister and Philip Berrigan are side by side at times; and they are now, during Lynch's recitations of their letters. His voice is a hand on the side of her head, forcing it to bend towards her right shoulder till her neck must hurt. Berrigan sits with his chin raised, his jaw set to resist an impending blow; he has the curiosity of a man listening to someone else's letters. Surprise darkens his eyes. McAlister averts hers. Both women, Mary Cain Scoblick and Elizabeth, feel sullied by the public display; this inspection of teeth before the sale of the goods. The men do not seem as offended by the public scrutiny; at times they even strut.

During the reading of the letters Douglas thickens on the stand. For the last thirteen months he has been the ward of the FBI. Living in the greenhouse atmosphere of government protection has given him the pulpy look of hothouse vegetables; he's turned into a plant.

Douglas was the medium for the letters, and they have the effect of a séance; he truly was a spiritualist, being able to go (on his study-release) from the dead out among the living, connect the nether world of the penitentiary with life beyond. Though Philip Berrigan pursued a prison sentence, his desire wasn't instantly fulfilled. There was a trial, conviction, then appeals, another trial, more appeals. The Baltimore Four raid took place back in October 1967. Catonsville in May 1968. He spent the summer of 1968 in Allenwood Federal Penitentiary, then was taken to Towson County Jail in Baltimore for the Catonsville trial; after which he was again released on bail during its appeals. Then on 21 April 1970 he was taken into custody at St. Gregory's Church in Manhattan. Between October 1967 and April 1970 he had not spent a full year in jail. With the postponements and intermittent gaps of freedom the zeal for committing yourself to the lockup abates. It is the same for the draft resister. If there were two doors to choose between—one marked ARMY and the other PRISON—and all that needed to be done was to walk into one, there might have been more jailed draft-resisters than the small numbers there are. It is not easy and simple for a white middle-class youth to go to jail: There are lawyers to arrange, court dates to be set, appeals to be made. Depending on your wants and the complications of the bureaucracy, you can be due-processed to death. What started as a passionate act of conscience, decisive and spontaneous, is bitterly dragged out, till resolve weakens, effects vanish. It is not a blow to a system, but more grist for one set of its mills.

Previous to October 1967 Philip Berrigan was eager to be the first American priest jailed as a political prisoner. But it is not till April 1970 that he began to serve the six-year sentence in earnest; the times have altered. The training he has put himself through to be able to withstand prison has been abandoned long ago; it is worse than he has imagined. His brother Daniel is "underground," but reported almost weekly in the news are his carnival-spirited surfacings. Boyd becomes the equivocation of his resolve. He is imprisoned, but yet partly free; his will can travel out beyond the cell; but the spirit he has chosen is the dark side of Philip Berrigan. It is a Faustian bargain he has made to let him be partly free: his pact with Boyd is in service of darkness. A disturbing triangle forms. Philip and Elizabeth meeting clandestinely in the shabby roadside lodging which is Boyd F. Douglas, Jr. Through him they exchange a love at once hesitant and expectant. "Call Peter [Boyd] once a week, and have him take notes," Berrigan writes. He refuses to examine Boyd, fearing that to look too hard will cause the vision to disappear. This blindness, which passes for trust, is shown in the letters: In them he writes about Boyd in a way that shows he actually believes that Boyd *does not read the letters* he takes out. "As for our Peter [Boyd], he is more and more immersed with the idea of being of service." As it continues he refers to Boyd as if what he is saying is being kept from him.

The correspondence covers the entire summer of 1970. In New York City the letters are deposited in a mailbox on York Avenue. That summer the police in New York City had taped to the bubble-top lights of their patrol cars, sticks from which flew small American flags. When a country must put its own flag on top of their official vehicles, it only announces to the population that they consider themselves to be an occupying power. All these tiny American flags fluttering in the torpid air of the city summer as if the country the cars belonged to had to be identified! The hound of hell chased the people down the side streets; J. Edgar Hoover dreamt of catching the new radical bombers. They had come out: in the fifties the "Mad Bomber" only brought to mind an individual

who wrapped his chest with sticks of dynamite and then threatened
to blow himself up, opening a trench coat to reveal the red tubes
like a sexual exhibitionist. But the fifties were a private, selfish
time, and in the sixties bombing acquired a social conscience. A
southern church blows up; three black girls perish. Only apocalypse
suffices to give life meaning; each searches for his own. So often
chided as cowards, the peace movement and its people no longer
stood the insult. Some of them had to show they didn't value their
lives any more or less than an average soldier. Tired of retreating
they attacked. One transcendental strain in American philosophers
is overlooked: the transcendence of violence. It elevated. It
detrivializes a banal life. Violence has legitimized itself beyond
eradication; violence creates; we must create violence.

This is the dead-end circuit of dualisms. Stretched on a rack of
absolutes, we are still tortured by them. Church and state. Light
and dark. Right and wrong. Success and failure. It serves, like the
calendar. Our culture is wired with it; it cannot adapt to another
current. A little Catholicism is a dangerous thing, for it is a
principal symbol-maker for this world.

The radical Left gnawed at the womb that bred it; its pleas
received simple scorn. They were denounced as weaklings, pla-
caters, unmanly and soft. They responded with bombs and capriciously sacrificed their and others' lives. Their creators denounced
them once more, as practitioners of the violence they opposed.
Justifications, they observe, lurk in every corner.

Father Berrigan writes to Sister Elizabeth, "Plus some of the
young guys here—who more and more, sit in on the raps—car
thieves, bank robbers, old and experienced cons, for all of their
young ages. They are creative, personable, funny, violent, racist.
But what an injection they'll add to our movement." But the
"movement" is not a bloodstream to which antibiotics can be
injected. What he means is clear, though. They have valuable
attributes—if some of us had their qualities, and if some of them
had ours! And Boyd was to be the first offspring of this union.
Boyd. A perfect specimen. Whose very first name is an anagram
for an interchangeable nonentity: Boyd—body.

The Catholic Left's hubris is the same as a lion tamer's. Surround
yourself with teeth and still you can withdraw unscratched. Steeped

in a tradition of Holy Wars, the draft-board raiders became militaristic, but with a difference. They *were* on God's side. Catholic support of the war in Vietnam has been a string of tin cans radical clergy have been unable to get off their tails. Diem and Madame Nhu were Catholic; she joked about the immolations of the Buddhist monks as "barbecues." LBJ would understand. There had been the hegira of Catholics from the North to the South after Dienbienphu. Cardinal Spellman had been in Haiphong while the French still occupied it. Vietnam was advertised as a struggle against godless communism. The French had brought Catholicism to Indochina along with colonialism. And now Catholic radicals were in 1970, by the fact they were latecomers and because of the successive abdications of various protest cliques, at the vanguard of antiwar protest. They had been left with it; the last shall be first. Right on.

The Catholic Church, in answer to its history, was an ardent supporter of the Cold War. President Nixon can feel justifiably indebted to a priest, Father John Cronin, who led him, then a first-term congressman, to fame over the body of Alger Hiss. Bishop Fulton J. Sheen, the clerical Lawrence Welk, was on television dispensing Poor Richard axioms and penning books on communism, its causes and cures. And it was the first Catholic president in history who picked the rakish green berets for the "special advisors" he sent to Vietnam.

With the excessive enthusiasm of converts, the Catholic radicals set out on their program of bigger and better draft-board raids.

> It would seem that one learns how to organize a community by reflection on the errors one has made through that process. What is needed is the willingness to review the errors and apply the lessons.

The good sisters who taught Maureen (her preconvent name) McAlister "English" at Marymount College did not stress brevity; she still wears language as cumbersome and redundant as the starched white linen wimples of the habits her order lately discarded. "We learn from our mistakes," is the cliché she is aggrandizing. The bulk of the government's "evidence" is the correspondence; what it proves is many things, none of which are charged in the indictment. The third McAlister letter provides a travel guide to the raiding of Delaware draft boards.

> So the story of the scene: the errors should be apparent. But first—forgive the silence from this end. From Sunday until last night i.e. Friday it was an ongoing quickly developing scene. There was not a minute to write much less to really grasp what was happening. Then the scene changed so drastically with every minute that it was impossible at any moment to say where it was at. Even the promised calls became impossible to fulfill. Those hours Thurs. & Fri. were both crucial. Never, since we began this, have I left this much time go by without a word to you. I'm sorry but beg you to understand & know that you do.

Duty can be more compelling than love and McAlister felt it a responsibility, a duty, to keep Philip Berrigan informed. It was a practical necessity, she felt, as much as the observance of Easter Duty or the keeping of a novena.

> (New Paragraph) Sunday return to the scene. All were at a picnic. Davidon [an unindicted co-conspirator] entered as soon as they returned & a cloak & dagger scene outside with Frank, then a message to take Tom Davidson [an unindicted co-conspirator in the 1st indictment, but dropped in the second] and Joan deNado and drive to a motel & rent a room under such & such a name. The exit of the rest did not go so smoothly. Everyone knew but no one knew what was taking place & security lead to misunderstanding & bad feelings.

Security—who can be trusted and who cannot; the rotten apple in the barrel of "community." The opposite of an open society, darting eyes, who is in the room? In Harrisburg it has become a conditioned reflex. Who can hear you? A splitting wedge driving people apart. But it is needed. Like the CIA.

> Particularly Joe Gilchrist who, out of some logic of his own, had his mother, his girl friend, a black boy friend & girl friends dog already on a very complex scene.

When this sentence happened to be quoted in newsweeklies and daily papers, all of them dropped "a black boy friend" from the list, not wanting to isolate any racial implications.

> Through the weekend there had been some bad feeling expressed about their presence there & he was angry & hurt & feeling that these people mean more to me than those in the group or this action. Sun. night it came to a head when his 3 were not invited to come for the session. He started out then just took off for a silent drive & went home. We sent someone after him which delayed the arrival process & forced our visitor to drive in circles for a couple of hours.

The visitor was Daniel Berrigan, S.J., erstwhile fugitive-felon from the FBI.

> The session was good. We discussed the guard & our decision to confront him & the man agreed. We discussed i.e. fought about the surfacing & he listened & said to get each one to publically burn or destroy a file & put their names down saying they did it. This was more or less received but with some reservations. The final phase was the new kind of relationships we have to begin living—along the lines that we have already agreed upon. But beautiful. The kind of trust that must exist without a lot of communication. . . .

The slings and arrows of outrageous irony that fill the letters!

> . . . a trust that frees each party in a relationship to be concerned about & responsive to the community immediately before him/her. This as opposed to the weakness that demands togetherness such as his [Daniel Berrigan's] appearing at the hospital where Frida [Berrigan's mother] lay ill with the FBI patrolling the corridors. [Berrigan did not go there.]

Noam Chomsky, at a panel at the YWCA a few nights before, had said that in reading the Pentagon Papers there are hundreds of pages devoted to the question of whether or not the North should be bombed; but there are only a half-dozen references that discuss at all whether the South should be bombed, though he considers that the more momentous decision. And in the letters, one thing never discussed is whether this community of trust can live in an amniotic fluid of civil disobedience.

(New Paragraph) Afterwards a listing of what remained to be done with Jolly Roger. Then return
home. An attempt to review this with Joe & a silence.
In the A.M. a trip to the State place to hang the platforms for the hide-in. [Above false ceilings in the
ladies room they suspended wood platforms where
they waited for the close of business hours.] On return a group was hashing it out with Joe & we had
had a visit from seminary officials with another evic-
tion notice. So Judy & I went up to the seminary to
explain our presence there while not explaining it.

The Catholic Church, with its seminaries, nunneries, schools, rest
homes, hospitals, provides a structure that can be easily inhabited,
a network that can be borrowed, a blueprint that can be incor-
porated into plans. The Church is feudal and autocratic and such
a kingdom needs only a *coup d'état* to overthrow it. The Church
can still be reformed the clergy of the Seven believe. Since it is a
country within a country, they believe—strangely echoing religious
persecutors—that if properly run it could worry the secular government the way, centuries past, the Vatican states troubled the rulers
of Italy. At its most utopian, the Catholic Left thinks it has the
answer to the taunt of radical detractors: What is your alternative?
In their most fanatical dreams they see the outline of the Church
as their model for restructuring society: and it is there—but not
properly tenanted. It is the vision of the Reformation, yet the
clergy of the 7 do not want to be expelled as heretics. Communities. Christian communities.

The forces called auxiliaries began arriving en masse
& the place was surrounded by cars from every state
in the union. Joe meanwhile had sent away mother,
girl friend, black friend & dog. Some of us began
working on a statement & at the same time I on cars
etc. Monday night amid the melee, a meeting of the
8 remaining. Joe has cut out can the rest of us work
together. Overriding personality differences, we want
to do this job, O.K. this ain't the way to operate. As
soon as this is over we cut out to a place known to
no one—security (& applying some of the man's advice, I might add, to a situation totally out of proportion). What appeared at that moment to be together-
ness was a gestapo organization received well because

there was so much chaos & so much to be done. But
the spirit was somewhat out of keeping. The agenda
had been prepared by a few & the rest of us really
welcomed it. But it was or I was uncomfortable with
it. Seems like an exclusion tactic. (New Paragraph)
Afterwards the 2 sections each had sessions on plans
& approaches to their own target. Tues A.M. typed
statements, met Peggy at the plane with Anne Walsh
who was just dizzy over what was going on. Called
about a lawyer & cars & went to reserve cars for rental. Tues. afternoon can't remember what happened.
I went to Wilmington (to rent a van) but went with
Grady who wanted to do timings. All the while uncomfortable with not being back working on plans for
the schoolhouse. Got the Van & drove home. Did
some stuff with Tony [Scoblick—defendant] on cars,
on where people wanted to go afterwards. In the
meantime there are police outside the house watching
this mad scene & paranoia grows. (New Paragraph)
Then someone returns with a report that the marshal
(armed) as well as guard is in the bldg. We are certain the whole plan has been known the epitaph being:
"how could it not be when about 500 people know
what's happening, where & when".

The raids took place. Delaware is a small state and the object was
to wipe out every board in it; there were four, three were hit. There
is nothing like a previous failure of nerve, to strengthen future
resolve. The Catonsville Nine was almost the Catonsville 10, but
Sister Elizabeth McAlister dropped out shortly before it took place.
To revenge her own wavering, to staunch any earlier flow of fear,
she required another test, though one with higher stakes, more risk,
increased jeopardy. Had she let Philip Berrigan down when she
dropped out of Catonsville? Had she failed him? The past is a
debt the present can never repay. You can whittle away at the
interest and never reach the principal. The farther we get away
from it the more we have to leave behind to cover it. Berrigan in
jail and McAlister free was an imbalance she strove to correct;
in mourning she copied his style and put on the widow's weeds
of civil disobedience. The letters were posthumous pleas of forgiveness.

Gone were the solemn ceremonial trappings of the draft-board

161

raids. The murmurs of prayers around a pyre of smoldering documents. They had progressed to the wild dances around the golden calf. If Philip Berrigan could have left the mountaintop of Lewisburg penitentiary and seen what the raids had become, would he have thrown down his inscribed tablets?

The destruction of the draft boards had the look of lunatic rampages. The frenzied throwing and tearing that usually accompanies a berserk fit. A child's demolishment of a room. For a war that is married to the adjective "insane" has produced a country of demented offspring. The destruction of the boards still remained a symbol, but of an unexpectedly darker kind: We are being driven mad.

Lynch reads the letters in a strangled monotone; his consumption of Camel cigarettes has left him short of breath, which has developed into a curt manner of expression. When he thought he was reading a damaging sentence he raised his voice and threw down each word like a dramatic turn of the cards: [from McAlister] ". . . the 4 of us also thought (& this is jist fer yer ears) of hitting the remaining eagle [the last unraided board in Delaware] a day or 2 later *in an explosive manner* without letting anyone know before or after . . ." And when he reached Berrigan's replay, he does the same: ". . . So two factors need stress, first, that circuses [draft-board raids] go on, even *with the introduction of fine and loud bang effects . . .*"

But, draft-board raids are just a small part of the charges against them.

Yes, draft-board raids took place, Ramsey Clark had said in his opening statement, but there was no conspiracy, "they did their own thing." Well. The conspiracy charge reads:

> It was further a part of said conspiracy that, in order to further disrupt governmental activities and to call their anti-war and anti-government views to the attention of the public, the defendants and co-conspirators would obtain maps and diagrams of the underground tunnels in Washington, D.C., containing the heating systems for government buildings of the United States. The defendants and co-conspirators

would learn the locations of the heating pipes within the tunnels and would enter these tunnels for the purpose of locating the heating pipes; that the defendants and their co-conspirators would obtain dynamite and other explosive devices; that on George Washington's birthday in 1971 the defendants and other co-conspirators would enter the aforesaid underground tunnel system in Washington, D.C., and detonate explosive devices in approximately five locations in order to damage and destroy heating pipes belonging to the United States and thereby rendering inoperative the heating system in government buildings of the United States.

It was further a part of said conspiracy that on the following day, the defendants and co-conspirators would seize, kidnap, abduct, and carry away Presidential Advisor Henry Kissinger and issue a statement that his safety depended upon the satisfaction of certain demands to be made by the defendants and their co-conspirators.

The government in framing Count I wanted to give the jury and the defendants a Hobson's choice: all or nothing. The defendants were put in the position of having admitted to some of it, but disowning all of it. Though the government in the person of William Lynch was trying to salvage a case by the introduction in the second indictment of draft-board raids, it unwittingly presented the defendants with a crisis. The first indictment did that—but it was a clean stroke; but the second one tore, left a ragged wound. There was talk of kidnapping; there was talk of bombing. The government precipitated a crisis by forcing them to defend their thoughts, not their deeds. They weren't prepared. The government accomplished its ends just by indicting. A conviction is secondary; they are after short-term results. They wanted to implicate, smear: the conspiracy trials of the late sixties and early seventies have been our McCarthy hearings, a judicial HUAC. The Chicago Seven, the Harrisburg Seven, Angela Davis, the Panther Twenty-one, have all been protective-reaction strikes. Due process is refugee control, New Life hamlets, resettling, systematic prolonged withdrawal, leaving behind residual forces. If by trial there is vindication, time has moved on so that this key has no door to unlock, except if the defendants are behind bars—ten months for Angela Davis, and two years for the Panther Twenty-one—unable to pay excessive bail.

Here, let us listen to an entire letter. We shall line up behind Boyd. He read them first. Next, the FBI. Then those to whom they were written. Now us.

McAlister IX: REFLECTIONS ON TECHNOLOG-
ICAL ADVANCEMENT—ON THE ANNIVER-
SARY OF MAN'S FIRST LANDING ON THE
MOON:

Is it possible to reverse the trend of technological advancement—of any advancement? Seems we all have the tendency (& in difficult circumstances almost the need) to look back to days when life was better, air was cleaner, and, with their difficulties, human relationships were easier & more "beautiful". Confession —I do that a lot. But it seems clear that it's not possible to reverse it, to go back. Despite the dangers & difficulties, one must apply a moral consciousness to here & now & all that means & commit one's life to shaping out a future of hope & life. Without knowing what that may mean in terms of proximity to loved ones one still tries to say "yes" at times more weakly than others. (New paragraph) What were our thoughts last year as man first walked the moon? It seemed equally interminable then; it is more so now. Today drove up to Amema, N.Y. Simply because a little boyfriend wanted me to come to his 1st communion. In the light of the amount of running this past week it was silly to go but in view of what it meant to him & his parents—a good thing. I had not been up there since the Christmas tree excursion which I probably told you about. We were to have left the city at noon & I was off with 2 nieces in Penn. trying to get back through snow storm & failing car. It just went dead on the road to the sheer frustration of its driver. All this came back today & I wondered if & when such a scene would be repeated. A little nostalgic & prayed for strength to accept the present & make the future. On the strength of the prayers, eucharists, & communions of the past it's possible. We'll make it! Won't we? (New paragraph) Where are we? This once a week business won't really work. Must develop some other way—diary perhaps—jutted-out once a week. Weeks become like months. Was it only last Monday we were working to finalize the delegation to the Federal Bureau in the midst of which a call from Agent Walsh who wanted to see me. I could think of about 5 things he might like to see me about & I wanted to discuss none of them. So told him I didn't want to see him & didn't trust him. ½ hr. later Mr. O'Toole (Agent) came looking for Jogues & she wasn't in. Later still they went to 85th St. Dan had been reported seen in N.Y. in bl. sedan & one was parked in front of the house with a clergy sign on it. Even Michael had to laugh at them for that absurdity. Meanwhile a contact with Tom Buck who came over & outlined some elaborate plans on your behalf. Some of them still in the works & maybe good. A session with Eqbal that night—very good. (New paragraph) Tues. down to D.C. for meeting with Norman A. Carlson & Richard Haney—Director & Assistant Director. We could have been Jane & Joe & they would have been equally intimidated. They agreed to investigate the case & send us a report. They had been swamped with letters, phone calls, telegrams & wanted to get rid of this. Stopped in Balt. en route back for session with 2 young turks & arrived home about 3:00 A.M. (New paragraph) Wed. phone calls re: Thurs., a session with Doug Dowd on the surfacing & obvious growing interest on his part in all we're about here. Sandwiched between was an effort to find an apartment & I think we succeeded. Ned came in that night & we left for Lewisburg in the early a.m. Hope you got some word about that scene. There were about 80 in all & we talked with Hendricks (i.e. after listening to Dan's tape—he described you as hostages of war). There were 2 obvious, serious contradictions between his report & that of the bureau: 1) Bureau claimed there was no interaction between the F.B.I. & the prisons. The former had nothing to do with your remaining in max. sec. Hendricks said that you were sent to Lewisburg with instructions "from outside prison authorities" to keep you there for a while. We said like F.B.I.; he wouldn't say yes i.e. clearly identify them but nor did he deny it. How could he when they were so obviously present there behind, beside & in front of him! 2) Bureau claimed that Dan's absence would never be a consideration in your transfer. Hendricks said that certainly it would be. He retracted a little when we put that remark in clear focus & said that that would be his opinion. Otherwise it seemed that a certain letter found in your quarters was the determining factor & that a promise from you to desist this communications system was essential to his recommending your transfer. (If you want to do that—O.K. by me—that sounds flip but I mean it. We can work something out). He had the advantage of having seen you & told us you had agreed that it was not harassment. (New paragraph) But . . . Sat. Judy & I had some work to do. Went to Haverford for a brief session with Bill Davidon. An effort to clear up confusion between himself & Doug Dowd as to what this surfacing was about. There had been many phone calls & they added to the confusion & we did manage, in short order, to get the thing cleared up. On to Newark, Delaware for a session with some of the peace community there to get the rally end of it cleared up. Again, a brief meeting was very productive. Delaware has to be the most up-tight state in the Union. This should be quite a show for them. Then on to Balt. for a meeting with Buchman, Neil, Judy & I. Don't know how productive that was. Maybe the only thing we accomplished was to help him understand better what you did & why. We also urged him to go & see you & maybe you could push that. He did suggest that we exert some pressure on the parole board & we'll find out who is on that & do so. Seems that after this furor, it may be timely to raise one about the sentence thing! He also told us that you had written to about 20 congressmen. If we could get their names, we could follow through on them & keep literature going their way. (Tom Buck is interested in that angle). You've been busy, yourself, there friend! Good show! Goodell's office has called me & wants to keep this going. He had also been in touch with Buchman. Re: the latter, maintaining contact there also seemed important. (New para.) Tonight a regional meeting here in N.Y., was a confrontation with the S.J.'s McGowan is away. Forty was impenetrable. [Another S.J.] received it well, anyway, & will reflect on it. Murphy is not an organizer & is torn up by the whole scene. The challenge—do we want to make N.Y. an area or not? If yes, then we must do it. Rochester wants, needs help. It was unresolved but they'll reflect on it. Geddes & co. were asked & didn't come. Genevieve was there & said nothing. Crain is handling her divorce proceedings & she's living with Paul Fleming in N.Y.—an un-good scene to say the least. We may finally have to work without them e.g. get something going & then call them in but not depend on them. Judy was astonished by them. (New paragraph) Jogues came back last night (late plane) & we're at the beginning of a new week—uncertain of your situation but with some arnaro & directions to pursue. Courage, friend & much love. It's still & more strongly yours.

And Father Berrigan's reply. Boyd. The FBI. Sister Elizabeth. Us.

I. Reflections on the anti-Communist drive and the efforts at countervail from Peace and Freedom Parties (informal) A. Knowledge now available implying that public manifestation in offing at DuPont city. (New paragraph) (a) If marginal people (signataries) show up in strength then activists might appear with them. Am afraid of frozen feet at last moment by the marginals, which may unduly expose those who have already chopped at the barren tree. If it is true that the heat in the kitchen is up, and that the Beantown eight have law and order counts against them. Then new legal manipulations might be awaiting the axe people (cf. above) I dunno, these are just considerations, and am far from having the total picture in my head. The alibi thing for the marginals I find solid—it should cause the para-military confusion and consternation. (New paragraph) (b) Eventually, I think the 'justice' boys will find ways to clip the surfacers. So two factors need stress, first, that circuses go on, even with the introduction of fine and loud bang effects, secondly, that people coming up for air be other than circus performers. So as to get them aligned to the real. The last comment presupposes a certain attitude toward consequences, so that one's personal bubble—or sanity—doesn't suffer a twisting at a bust. (New

167

paragraph) (c) Don't know how you're going to have
any startling success with organization, friend, at least
until the mid-month passes. Even after that, it's gorna
be a scramble. How about Eq or Mayer or the blood
line on this? Since people have agreed on a liason—
how about drumming it into the liason people first,
and then asking them forcefully to carry the ball with
the constituency? (Incidentally, who's the feminine
side kick you mention, J——?) (New paragraph)
Haven't told you what a profound impression recent
events have made on me, particularly the brains, guts,
devotion, savvy and drive of one ea. nee Maureen.
Figger if the movement had ten like her strategically
placed around this fair nation, we wouldn't be fishing
for 4th Party politics a'la Jack Newfield. Came across
a great quote from Huxley recently—he says, 'every
gain in revolution comes despite the violence.' So tell
the gal Maureen that she has emerged as 'main
woman." Among convicts, there is no higher compliment than "main man." (New paragraph) You can do
what is best about penmanship. Grateful for the note
to the main mandarin here, but afraid it's of no avail.
Moreover, he's taking another post far, far away, and
we'll get more of the same, if not most. But, as for
penmanship, if'n you got one solid commiqué here
weekly, it'd effect a shedding of years at each arrival.
(New paragraph) The local minister with portfolio
[Boyd] has emerged as the best thing hereabouts since
polio vaccine. His ministrations have been no less
than providential—and given the setting here, very
nearly heroic. Later on, I consider he'll be a burr in the
saddle for many of our people, for already he's paid
up the price tag, and kept the taxes in proper shape.
As he might have told you, there are guys here with
comparable potential. Somehow, one must break
through Little Brother's net of informers, spy glass
and omnipresence to get them looking beyond themselves. To feed a regular influx of ingenious and reli-
able ex-cons into the ranks would make a resounding
blow for public integrity. Some would have a bit of
bad education to shuck off, but they would help with
some of the bad education of our people. And they
do know the law and order people like we'll never
know them. (New paragraph) You're wise in taking
the whole bloody fiasco day by day. Personally, I feel
confident that some cards up some sleeves will drop

into the game and change it. The history of trust and fidelity—with higher powers—ain't been perfect from this yokel, and yet He ain't been greedy so far. So if the Master Design calls for a premature separation from this tender existence—and I think it will—it'll be because He wants another element of confusion among our people. And I think He does, if for no other reason than to plague you all. (New paragraph) Meanwhile, this yokel will take it day by day like you, trying to see a higher purpose in the daily wrenching of guts. For thus it is, and thus it is for one reason. But if perchance, we must go the whole term, it'll be chiefly to rid myself of some personal demons, and to pick up something better than the seven who found the house empty, swept and garnished—making the last state of this man worse than the first. Whew! long sentence. (New paragraph) Wrote your erstwhile boss, that may have some implications. She's getting better and better—how else, with you around? (New paragraph) Otherwise, no news. The two months have deepened convictions, strengthened loyalties and appreciations. Have come to a deeper grasp of what I have going for me. The hundred fold is more reality, and there is one embodiment of 94% of that. Later, it may be 95%, or higher. Am I in any sense, making sense? Am trusting you to cleave through the obfuscations, and the necessity of verbal garbage. That person at Happy Rockefeller's epitomizes meaning, direction, the whole package. Will add a word to this tomorrow. (New paragraph) Want to mention once again the necessity for new turf (further west, or south?) And the apparent need for more people to get out of the womb (embattled) that the East has become. Maybe I'm making too much of this, but it strikes me that more and more, the law and order people will see Eastern work as the work of one gang and this will lead to more strenuous attempts to pick off gurus already known. But in other areas, much more bafflement for them—security for you will result. (New paragraph) Thousand items else to mention, but had better let matters rest. Hope you had a chance to linger a bit in the Upper regions of the Empire State, and to meet everyone. We'll make it—or if we don't, we'll take a few shreds of honor with us. And the Kingdom will live.

The Angela Davis trial in San Jose, California, has begun. The prosecutor there announces that a great deal of his case will rest in love-letters between her and the deceased George Jackson. They are not called "love-letters" here. The government is a Romantic; they attest that crime originates in the heart.

McAlister's letters stay true to the actual desires of someone who is separated from friends and loved ones; they are full of facts, lists, names, dates, places, the particulars upon which the imagination can build; they never meant to speak to anyone but to whom they were written. It is the world of Big Brother when we are held accountable for every sentence we write, every word we say.

Two types of excisions were made in the letters before they were read in court. Sentences of only a personal nature: here the rule applied was modified Supreme Court on obscenity: if it only appeals to prurient interests and has no redeeming criminal value, out it goes. Also cut out was anything relating to possible offenses not charged in the indictment. One other thing the defense wanted removed, but wasn't, were the instances of sibling rivalry displayed in Philip Berrigan's letters towards his brother, Daniel.

"But getting back to the bruv thing—that's an essentially different scene, you know. He's trying to radicalize a wide range of liberals. Whereas you're working with hard core radicals. Most of the time, they don't mix. I remember how we operated with him—always happy to have him in a rap, but un-disturbed when he couldn't make it. His talents grab on a different level than ours, and are most effective there."

The Berrigan brothers, Dan and Phil, are a debate on when thought should turn into action. Philip is the thesis and Daniel the antithesis; they personify the ancient dialectic. Catonsville united them, but it was more the dark overlapping of where two lines cross. Philip could have quoted a nineteenth-century American educator to his brother: "I have never heard anything about the resolutions of the apostles, but a great deal about their acts." The boundary that Daniel crossed at Catonsville is not easy to locate, even for him. At that trial he said, "I suddenly saw and it struck with the force of lightning that my position was false. I was threatened with verbalizing my moral substance out of existence." The predicate "verbalizing" is a shroud thrown over an idea. A dilapidated bridge joining two modes of thinking. When I was younger, Daniel Berrigan, S.J., was pointed out often to me as an example of "See you can be both a priest and a poet." He, along with Thomas Merton and Brother Antoninis, were exceptions used to prove their rules. Reading Berrigan's verse as a teenager I considered him one of America's contemporary minor poets, who keep a career alive forever on one prize (in his case, the Lamont, 1957).

The Catholic Left formed itself from the few cells in the Church that were still able to change, split. The blastoderm, the fertilized portion that gave rise to the germinal developments within the Church. The attempts at "Modernization." They were not a lunatic fringe, or even far out; indeed, they were far in, deeply surrounded by a dry husk. They came from the last bit of quick. William Lynch and his Catholic colleagues of previous generations in the Justice Department sit around during their lunches grousing about the Mass being changed from Latin into the vernacular; they resent their youthful recollections being jettisoned. Ties cut. Daniel Berrigan, S.J., was one of the first priests to turn the altar around and face his congregation. The Catholic Church practiced a perfect form of population control; it did not reproduce; its children disappeared. Berrigan and other young clerics noticed this and in a long-followed tradition began to adopt; it adopted and adapted the culture which surrounded it. They saw that they were being left behind; the Church elders, great believers in cycles, said, "Hush, they will return." Daniel Berrigan was sent to South America.

The Department of Justice did not indict Daniel Berrigan for his months as a federal fugitive; it is said Hoover was upset at this flaunting of the law and accepted it with the stipulation that they might get him on something larger in the near future. The letters were coming in; all of Boyd's material had originally gone into the Daniel Berrigan file.

Dan Berrigan arrived in Harrisburg's courtroom on Boyd's eighth day of testimony. This Berrigan has a prelapsarian face; creatures of an enchanted forest come to mind. He wasn't wearing a beret, but a cap that sports-car enthusiasts used to wear. It was an updated biretta. His faces-of-the-moon medallion had phased by this time into a cross, made by a fellow convict at Danbury Federal Correctional Institution, fashioned out of two screws. During a recess he commented that the courtroom was the liveliest mortuary he had ever seen; Boyd had struck him as a sorrowful figure, a straw-doll. On the terms of his parole he needed to check each day with an officer in the Federal Building. All travel had to be cleared. In a peculiar way the state forces its detractors and reformers to be even more dependent on them.

He wears a blue nylon ski parka; and had been released for only two weeks. They had spoken of his bad health at the parole hearing; the bad prison diet. Dan and Phil were reunited (though that is a misnomer; separated as brothers, it took the Vietnam war to rejoin them) at Danbury. The information that lead to his capture provided by Sister Elizabeth. After that particular letter was read by Lynch, F. said, during a recess, "That's two things we were taught in the French Resistance. Never go to an island [Dan Berrigan was captured on Block Island off the coast of Rhode Island] and never, but never, write anything to a political prisoner."

Immediately upon his arrival at Danbury, Philip Berrigan had reinstated on his list of approved visitors and correspondents: Sister Elizabeth McAlister, Eqbal Ahmad, and Paul Mayer. The authorities waited for the kidnap plot to hatch, conspiracy to take its first steps. It didn't. Nothing moved. They held the egg up to a candle's flame: Nothing fertilized. Then, J. Edgar Hoover cracked open the rotten one they had: ". . . an incipient plot . . ."

iv

"And that's where you should place the plastic explosives," Tony Scoblick says, pointing up as we pass under an overhead bridge. He is driving to Washington, D.C., for a fund-raising party, which has been billed as a "Cocktail Conspiracy," and then to a benefit concert given by the folksinger Judy Collins. Tony chuckles; Mary, his wife, and codefendant, turns back to her book.

We were all met on the first floor of the Federal Building immediately after court by two Defense Committee women, who handed Tony keys to a rent-a-car and a set of directions to a townhouse in northeast Washington, and Mary a bag of cookies and candies, and two yellow roses. Then to a parking lot to find the car. "It's a Charger; is that a Charger?" Then to the Beltway to Washington, mingled with the five o'clock traffic fleeing Harrisburg. Tony flicked on the radio: ". . . today in the trial of the Harrisburg Seven, where the Reverend Philip Berrigan and six others stand accused of conspiracy . . ." The D.J.'s voice had the careening pace of an auctioneer repeating bids on the news.

Tony had long since grown tired of the trial being referred to as "the trial of Philip Berrigan and six others," and he had begun to introduce himself and his wife as Tony Other and Mary Cain Other. Tony is thirty-one and an "inactive" priest, the word most often chosen to depict a priest who is no longer sanctioned to perform his sacramental duties, such as saying mass, hearing confessions. Tony does not consider himself dormant, though; he is the youngest son of a former United States congressman, who served his first term with the freshman congressman Richard M. Nixon. Tony contends that Nixon owes his father a fifty-dollar loan never repaid. During a showing of the "Checkers" speech in Harrisburg he had wanted to add his father's fifty to a list of debts Nixon had read off. The two congressmen's careers diverged; Tony's father had scandalized Scranton with money-misdealings and had been jailed for three years.

Both relief and haste weight Tony's foot as we speed toward Washington. The weekend! Harrisburg Too-de-loo! The exaltation is momentary; the brief rush that comes from quitting a drudge machine. Tony and Philip Berrigan belong to the same order: the Society of St. Joseph, founded in a missionary spirit, to work among American Negroes. Mary had worked with the Defense Committee that surrounded the Catonsville Nine. She had received a dispensation from her vows as a Sister of Notre Dame de Namur and on 27 June 1970 she and Tony were married. Resistance work has never been said to impede romance. The courtroom heard about the wedding when Lynch read that particular letter. The FBI attended looking for Daniel Berrigan; a balloon had popped and an agent had unfurled his revolver. Mary had not even been mentioned in the first indictment but was charged in

173

the second. It was then that severed Ted Glick had been added. Except for her presence at 3007 Susquehanna, the only testimony concerning her had come from Boyd. He related a picnic at a Bucknell professor's home where she had said she was a member of the Boston Eight and had raided draft boards. Mary, with her nun's meticulousness, was one of the Catholic Left's best "casers." Who could better observe the midnight vigils outside federal office buildings than prayer-disciplined religious? Boyd also had recounted that after he and Tony had spent an afternoon talking about blowing up the underground tunnels, they had come up to the room where Mary lay ill and Tony introduced Douglas as their "demolitions man." Mary, according to Boyd, then replied, raising her sickly self on one arm, "Good, I'm glad we have somebody who knows about that stuff, so we won't all blow ourselves up."

There is a sense of the stock market about the daily proceedings in the courtroom. Today had been a "good day." Boyd had finally been caught in what appeared to be an outright lie. Up till today, Boyd had been as evasive as an oracle, framing his answers so that they could be interpreted two ways. He would say, "It was either in the day or in the night." "Possibly-maybe," was a favorite phrase; he had said, "There's a lot of testimony I'm giving in this courtroom that refreshes my memory when I testify." Boyd would try not to lie; he skirted troublesome questions. There had been this exchange with Terry Lenzner today:

> MR. LENZNER: Did you give information to Father Berrigan that you wanted him to write in his letters?
> THE COURT: Do you understand what he means? Are you talking about letters to Sister McAlister?
> MR. LENZNER: Yes, Your Honor.
> THE WITNESS: I did ask Philip Berrigan to do some of my studies, help me with my studies on Bucknell University. He did write some things on a prison system in that for me, yes.

It was a juggling act and the defense would try to introduce more things for him to keep aloft at once, so finally his dexterity would be taxed beyond his limits.

It happened once, and that was today, under questioning by

J. Thomas Menaker. He asked Douglas about Berrigan's views on nonviolence, which Boyd had said were not absolute, and to point this out he said that—for example—he and Berrigan had been talking about the University of Wisconsin bombing in which a physicist had been killed. Boyd said Berrigan was neither shocked nor horrified by the death. He said Berrigan had commented, "What is one life in Wisconsin when they are killing many every day in Vietnam?"

B., from the Washington *Post,* looked up from her notes and said, "That bombing happened on a Monday morning; the last time Boyd talked to Berrigan was the Sunday before; they couldn't have had that conversation." A lunch recess followed; the defense was informed of the contradiction, and in the afternoon Menaker pursued the matter.

"Was your last meeting with Father Berrigan on Sunday in the library?"

"Yes, it was on a Sunday."

"Did you see him after that?"

"Not that I recall."

"Was it at that meeting he talked to you about Wisconsin?"

"I believe it was before that."

On Monday, 24 August 1971, at 3:45 A.M. a bomb exploded in the Mathematics Building of the University of Wisconsin. Philip Berrigan was transferred from Lewisburg to Danbury the following day.

The defense was not going to make a point of this until closing arguments; it is a strange joy that comes from catching someone in a falsehood; the lips curl into a questionable smile.

To most of the defendants Boyd was a paschal lamb: slaughtered for the sacrifice. He had to be discredited, for he stitched the tatters of Elizabeth McAlister's letters into the garment of conspiracy. He filled in gaps, made connections, by reciting conversations, real or imagined, meetings, phone calls. He was the source of evidence pertaining to the tunnels. His testimony concerning the tunnels is telling. All the conversation he had about them with Philip Berrigan, Joseph Wenderoth, Neil McLaughlin, and Tony Scoblick only amounts to around a hundred words. He retold this paragraph over and over.

175

The tunnels are eight by ten. There was no problem walking around in them; no problem going into the tunnels in the daylight; Philip Berrigan and Joseph Wenderoth had been in the tunnels posing as ROB electricians; Berrigan was worried about Pennsylvania Avenue blowing up; the day of their destruction was Washington's birthday.

It seemed improbable, nay, impossible, to have the type of ongoing discussions Boyd testified about and not use more words than that. To believe Boyd, would be to believe they said the same paragraph over and over. What can be believed is that the words were said once to Boyd. By Philip Berrigan. And when Boyd talked to Joseph Wenderoth, he would parrot Berrigan, but with a difference. What he had been told, he would *tell*. The tenses would change; it would go from the past into the present. The tunnel plan? In Wenderoth's words: "We were never serious about it."

Serious. They were trying to be ingenious. Weren't the draft-board raids ingenious? They were trying to find another type of nonviolent-to-persons action they could pull off. Tunnels. Underground. Away from people. Buried. Draft-board vandalism was not the beginning of something, but the end; yet their imaginations persisted. Underground heating systems. The idea burned with that one coal: that they were underground. That seemed to imply safety to all creatures who lived above. Not much effort was spent. Eight by ten. You can walk around in them. Accessible in the daylight. From the fourth Berrigan letter: "Since resources appear to be available for the subterranean project in the District, this should have priority for the winter of '70–71." Be sure William Lynch made much of that sentence. Yet, in it is the clinker, the defective sprocket: "Since *resources* appear to be available . . ." The resources were Boyd. He had announced to Berrigan that he was an expert in demolitions. Boyd became Berrigan's Demiurge. The maker of Berrigan's underground world, his subaltern, the author of the sequel to the scuttled tunnel project. Berrigan referred to it in another letter as "the elusive golden fleece." He then entrusted it to his sleepless dragon, Boyd.

Today, in cross-examination, it was brought out that Boyd

wrote to McAlister in November, just two weeks before Hoover's announcement, asking, "I was wondering where Phil saw the D.C. project and if further thoughts concerning the 'K' thing was feasible at this time . . ." In the same letter of 11 November 1971 he admitted, "I really have not talked much to Joe [Wenderoth] about the tunnel project."

Of all the various uses of an informer, this situation wreaked havoc, not because of his disclosures, but because of how the defendants, in turn, had to *use* him. They would inform on Boyd, over and over, dredge up every distasteful bit of information they could. The defendants were aware of this position they found themselves in; they did want to save his soul. The government, in perhaps only this case, the prosecution of Catholic radicals, found a method of checkmating a defense. To gain acquittal they would have to sacrifice Boyd; it was being done, but at a dear price. It was, finally, the compromise of their spirits and consciences, which heretofore they had resisted with all their acts. The government was winning battles, if not the war.

I am certain Boyd heard the Wisconsin remark from someone; it is the kind of thing people say; it was just a bad slip of interpolating on his part.

J. is also in the car. He is the Catholic Left's one and only chapter of Gay Liberation. Homosexuality will be accepted by the Church long before birth control and abortion, for it entails neither. J. comes out of the kitsch-glamour world of New York City pathic culture: epicene film stars, grandness, banality raised to the level of art appreciation. He entertains the women of the Defense Committee with his burlesque of their male chauvinist pig coworkers; predilection saves him from that title. One of the skits has to do with "The Resister," any male whose acts of civil disobedience have elevated him into some arrogant stratosphere: "The RESISTER. Dum-de-dum-dum." (This is sung, followed by tap steps.) "Here, bay-ay-bee, type this stencil. Here bay-ay-bee, get me the Revolution on the phone. Hello, Revolution, this is—dum-de-dum-dum—the RESISTER." His mock-shows are appreciated; to all the straining for the sublime he brings a bit of the theater of the ridiculous.

The sun lingers on the horizon behind housing developments

that are uniform as tombstones between Harrisburg and Washington. Who pays that price of uniformity but themselves? Who calls the poor courageous for the suffering they endure? The bent backs of the houses supplicate themselves in front of the orange sun that flattens out as it begins to disappear, squatting like a balloon from which air is escaping.

In all the living rooms the six o'clock news is bringing them twenty seconds of the trial of the Harrisburg Seven. The network commentators film their "spots" in front of the Federal Building. When the camera rolls, a bell jar of concentration descends over the newsman; he looks into the snout of the camera; his irises focus tightly on a hundred million eyes. In the Xenophobia Bar & Grill down the street from the Federal Building they show the news in color. A map of America hovers behind the anchorman; his measured voice parcels out the world in seconds. Out of the bluish map of the United States a white dot appears, above it the word: HARRISBURG. Twenty seconds. The car that brings Boyd Douglas to court is filmed speeding down the ramp to the basement of the Federal Building; it is a Keystone Kops chase scene. "Today, in Harrisburg, Pennsylvania, at the trial of the Reverend Philip Berrigan and six others . . ." Twenty seconds. In the houses between Washington and Harrisburg the defendants burn for twenty seconds. A twenty-second burn, ignition. The injection into the daily orbit accomplished. The apogee of concern and the perigee of disinterest.

Washington, D.C., glows in a saucer of sepia light. Anticrime brightness. They think fire will scare off the beasts; very advanced. Washington, a city that is divided into the quadrants of the compass, a city that wants to navigate the world.

Arriving at the "Cocktail Conspiracy," Tony spies Ted Glick through the front window. "If Glick is here why the fuck did we have to come?!" The townhouse occupants call themselves the Third Street commune. A photojournalist had wanted to take a picture of the government attorneys standing out in front of the Holiday Inn Town where they stayed; then he wanted to take Ramsey Clark and Leonard Boudin, with the defendants, in front of the scared façade of Mulberry Street, where they live, and publish them side-by-side on the cover of the national newsmagazine he works for. A great contrast he thought. What do we learn from contrast now? It is all there is; soon, nothing that is said or written will be called a non sequitur; everything will follow.

The Third Street communards aren't your back-to-the-soil lot; young Washingtonian professionals, they gleam as do their parquet floors. A bar has been set up in the living room; a college student tends it. It is a twenty-five-dollar-a-person benefit for the D.C. Harrisburg Defense Committee.

These are the liberals about whom we have heard so many of Philip Berrigan's stern complaints read out by Lynch in the courtroom. "They want scenes where conditions are posh, where floodlights are on and the publicity secure, and there's no danger. All of them have been through surgery [here a reference to castration has been excised], getting a hose-pipe for a backbone when they were kids. Helps flexibility—bobbing and weaving with the issues." Liberals, Berrigan comments in the letters, are good for raising money and for providing hide-outs, because of the availability of vacation homes tucked off in woodsey places. Daniel Berrigan's underground was made up of these "liberals." One of its members described it as "middle-class, liberal and intellectual families, predominantly Jewish." Phil Berrigan's scorn for liberals is the same shared by hardhats for students, hawks for doves, wealthy for the poor. It's a common cup most anyone can drink from. Berrigan is a taskmaster, but he will allow for the failings of his people, if they share the *basics*. If they are *real,* a word he uses continually for the good. It is a blood allowance, which permits whites to condone whites, blacks blacks, believers believers. Forgiveness of others, the unreals, the nonbelievers, is as difficult as breeding two animals not of the same species. Catholics have a long tradition of forgiveness. Seven times seventy. To forgive is to acknowledge someone's return to a common absolute. This tribal nostalgia persists; race ease.

The powers invested in conversion are amongst the greatest. The Jesuits were founded by a soldier-convert. St. Ignatius Loyola, while convalescing from a wound, turned toward spiritual experience. He wrote a tract that came to be known as the *Book of Spiritual Exercises* which, still in the parlance of the author's former self, is most often described as a "field manual" for one who wishes to "enlist recruits" for the cause of Christian holiness. Berrigan is far from the first to talk of saintliness in paramilitary cant. Phil Berrigan is a convert himself, once having partaken in war, having seen the corpses like the apostle Thomas's necessity, to view the wounds. It is much easier to denounce, but there is a special pleasure, knowledge, in renouncing—giving up what one has had. A true convert is a unique individual; he has sat down with warring factions. It endows him with an unquestionable allure. He has a certitude founded on completeness for he has been there and returned, an Ishmael who has survived to tell the tale. He is greeted with the reception afforded an adventurer who has survived perils. Do not make my trip, he counsels; heed my words, taste not the forbidden fruit, but the fruit of my experience. He pares the dark from his life, his disciples clothe themselves with his discards. They will not become leaders; no one trusts men with only half of the world's experience. We will let our successes fail, even desire it, for it is the stuff of our fables; but we will not allow failures to fail—it gains us nothing.

As we leave the "Cocktail Conspiracy," Tony says, "It was great seeing Mische [one of the Catonsville Nine]; he's just the same as he was before he went into prison; just like he'd only interrupted a conversation, picked it up right where he left off. That's the way to come out of prison . . ."

We head off for the University of Maryland, for the concert. We pass through Washington and Mary points out early landmarks of her life as we go by them. "That's where I taught," she says, pointing toward a school building, "that very window there." Mary tugs on the cloth ring dangling from its green shade, the loop of memory. She is standing at the window about to turn to face her students; Mary, in a black habit, teaching languages. We pass Catholic University and she indicates another building in which she lived. "And Tony, that's where George comes from and he's going to come and testify and lie about you . . ." "He won't lie," Tony says. "He'll tell them you advocated violent protests; that'll be a lie . . ." A witness yet to be called. We pass the shrine of the Immaculate Conception, another stupendous house of God. Tony had been distressed enough by the riches of Catholic churches that he had taken antiques from them, to sell and finance activities of Resistance. It was like stealing from parents, though, not rewarding in any way. Tony had told a reporter at the fund-raising party: "This case is being handled by the government much the way they are handling the Vietnam war. Once they found they had been misinformed, rather than admitting they were wrong and putting an end to it they just changed their tactics. What they are doing now is confusing the issues so that the public will be confused, switching the indictments."

Boyd's spirit reentered the car. They had never trusted him, they had said, especially Mary. Phil's friend from prison. And that is how the groups would be enlarged; they would be seeded through mutual friends, the initial requirement for inclusion: You had to be somebody's friend. "And they didn't trust Boyd in prison, either," Tony said, naming two other members of the Catholic Resistance who had served time with Philip Berrigan. "Well," Mary says, "they are both married; and that made a lot of difference; they didn't have to be dependent on Boyd for anything to do with that type of thing." Tony and Mary (all the defendants were yoked in twos, except for Eqbal; Tony and Mary, Neil and Joe, Phil and Elizabeth) were incensed by the tearing of Boyd's flesh. They endured it by blaming the government for its cause. Tony said, as we reached the University of Maryland for the concert, "Boyd Douglas is Saigon."

V

William S. Lynch said at a sidebar conference, "Your Honor, they have been talking about Boyd Douglas now for months. The newspapers have been talking about him for a year, and how he was to be the central part of the government's case, and how they were going to destroy him on cross-examination. And I submit they should be made to proceed with the destruction."

Before the cross-examination had begun the defense wanted it delayed till certain records were produced. Boudin had questioned whether the skimpy files they had received from the FBI on Boyd were all that were extant. Boudin said, "If you just consider the size of the files the FBI keeps on a common citizen, that alone indicates that the file they have on a paid government informer with a long criminal record must stretch between here and Washington." On the last day of direct examination of Boyd by the government they introduced the matter of the "Molly letter." The day after Boyd took the stand, the government gave to the defense some material they had "overlooked, misplaced," when, earlier, they had complied with the disclosure requirements of the court's discovery order. Three items were given to the defense. Two were inconsequential. The third was the Molly letter. In it, Boyd asked for a "minimum reward of $50,000 (tax-free)," from his "handler," special agent Delmar "Molly" Mayfield. The adversary system is one of contrasts: The defense keeps saying black is white and the prosecution reiterates that white is black. Diminish the most important things and maximize the least important. On the last day of direct examination Lynch asked Boyd whether he had requested a reward of some amount and whether he had gotten it. Douglas said that "Absolutely, no," was the answer to his request and further that agent Mayfield had told him, ". . . if I had any thoughts along those lines, I might just as well forget it." Challenged by the defense to read the entire letter into the record, Lynch did, rather than let the defense do it later. He prefaced his reading with his one and only literary allusion: "This is much to-do about nothing," Lynch said, not without bravado. "I will read it."

October 3, 1970

Molly,
Thank the Bureau for the reward and thank you. This will be used for a new car soon. I have never owned a car. Can you get me some more expense money this month. After my cover is gone, I will need an honorable discharge from the army so that I can settle out West and it will look as though I just returned from Asia, etc. I will obtain a transcript of my grades here at Bucknell at the end of the semester, should I wish to continue at some University out West. I may either continue at a University or go into a small business out West. Considering what I will go through before and after the trial or trials, I request a minimum reward of $50,000 (tax-free) . . .

(Juror no. seven, the reluctant juror who asked to be excused for hardship since his tax-account business would suffer, flinched at the words "tax-free.")

> . . . Five thousand be paid me the first week in December, and the rest at the start of trial or when things are blown wide open. With this I could start a small business or continue at college. This figure may sound a little high, but considering everything, I feel it is worth it to the government and it will make a life for me. I will do all I can to help the government obtain enough evidence to prosecute these people concerned. However, I don't want to feel that I am just being used. I know these people may not bother me, but the only way I will be able to be comfortable, is to take some precautions as they are the cream of the Catholic Left. This figure doesn't account for expenses between now and the time for trial. I can have "no" ties with my family for at least a year and possibly I would never feel safe. At the present time we know only some of the Catholic people that are involved, but it may even involve other types of people in the movement. It will be much easier to work if I was free of supervision at the end of January. It would be necessary when my cover is gone because only you should know where I am at. Can the Bureau do something about that?? Would you please give me something concrete on this letter as soon as possible? ??? (Signed) Pete

Boyd never considered himself an informer. He thought of himself as a "double agent." The associate warden, according to Boyd, had told him during that first interview after Berrigan's letter had been discovered, "So, you want to be a double agent."

Another ex-con, involved at the same time as Boyd in the mixture of radical and criminal politics—Stanley Bond—appeared on a university campus—not Bucknell, but Brandeis, in Waltham, Massachusetts. He shared some of Boyd's qualities. One was his success with women. Bond (who subsequently lost his life in an explosion of questioned origin inside Walpole State Prison) and two young female students, along with two other men, robbed a Brighton, Massachusetts, bank, leaving a patrolman killed. All the men were apprehended, including Bond, but the two women in their fugitive status were catapulted to Hoover's Ten Most Wanted list. Bond was handsome, hard, daring, quick to act, and had served time for a number of bank robberies—and it was when he was on parole he enrolled as a special student at Brandeis, the very same term Boyd registered as a special student at Bucknell on his study-release program. Boyd sought out the "peace people" at Bucknell, because, he said, he could have more "freedom" around them; and so did Stan Bond. He became a leader of what was called The National Student Strike Center, which had been established at Brandeis. Its function was to be a clearing house of radical intelligence for college campuses around the country.

They both shared a fascination: the FBI. Bond, according to an ex-FBI agent who knew him at Brandeis, was more the puritan than Boyd. He avoided liquor and spurned drugs. The ex-agent said that Bond would "devour" any of the stories he would tell of the FBI's past exploits and history.

Boyd's latest sentence was for, among other things, assault upon an FBI agent; and, it is told, he had, some time before, had a brawl with four agents in a western saloon. This intimacy began to produce a strong identification. As the Molly letter and testimony revealed, Boyd was beginning to picture himself as an actual agent himself. Paul O'Dwyer questioned him about whether the business of informing on a more professional level interested him.

> MR. O'DWYER: And did you have in mind at that point that you might make a career of that?
> MR. LYNCH: Objection.
> THE COURT: Overruled.
> THE WITNESS: It is a possibility, yes.

Boyd was ready for a new shell. His scars hidden by his new agent-styled Dorian Grey suits, he had assumed the expressionless poise of the special agent of the FBI. There are many fantasy planets spinning in the universe of courtroom no. one, and Boyd's seemed to have the best chance of sustaining life. He had gotten one thousand five hundred dollars for information supplied concerning an upcoming draft-board raid in Rochester, New York. Sister Elizabeth was his Sugar Daddy bankroller. Molly had asked "the bureau" for two thousand dollars, but the fiscal-minded director trimmed it down. After he received the money—which came, he says, as a surprise—Boyd said, "I knew at that time, as I explained before, that my life would not be quite the same, yes." Shortly thereafter, Boyd purchased his first car, a sporty Javelin.

Boyd, cross-examination brought out, had received almost ten thousand dollars that the FBI admitted to paying him. He received about the same exact figure for his civil suit against the government that left his body scarred. This was Boyd's second civil suit. And here there was no five thousand he needed to pay to a shylocking lawyer.

Boyd spent the last year in the protective custody of the FBI. During this trial and before, Molly Mayfield and other agents would come to visit Boyd and his newlywed wife for dinner; they wouldn't discuss the case or testimony, Boyd testified, for that wouldn't be proper. So, we can imagine the conversation. Boyd with his new friends; a new set—gone are the Catholic Left idealists that fixed him so many meals, talked about civil disobedience, nonviolence, against the war, against the government, against property, against social injustice. Their interminable "raps." What a bunch of downers! Negative people. Stifling anti-this, antithat. Here, at a dinner table with Molly and other jovial agents, finally an uplift. Up with America. Not negative at all. Adventure, exploits, always getting their man. Positive thinking. Judge Herman believes in the power of positive thinking too. When he visited New York City he went to Sunday services at the Fifth Avenue church of the Reverend Norman Vincent Peale.

Boyd said they talked about hunting. The excitement of blood sports. Boyd, the modern Odysseus, always searching for a new self, finds it at last. Feeling at home with the FBI and the hag Penelope, in the person of Molly Mayfield. Boyd had wrapped himself in the colors of a patriot and jumped from the Catholic Left's sinking ship. There is a radio promo heard often over the local Harrisburg rock station: "If you're tired of being a loser, join up with a winning team, the outfit with the longest record of crimebusting in law enforcement, *The FBI* . . ."

Boyd did not suffer many hurt looks on the stand. As the days went on, he settled into a surly funk. Questioned by the defense,

Boyd said the only thing Lynch would ever tell him, outside of court, was "Stay calm." Stay calm, Boyd. More cigarette-cough laconicism on the part of Lynch. But, once he did look wounded, and that was at the hands of his protector, Lynch himself. Boudin was questioning: "And at that time you were acting as an agent or informer for the FBI?"

> MR. LYNCH: Objection on the agency.
> THE COURT: Yes. That is right. I would sustain that.

Lynch snatched the crown away, just as Boudin was putting it on Boyd's head: an agent. Objection to the agency. Boyd could not mask his disappointment. After the direct was over and all the letters were read into the record, the prosecution began to dump Boyd. He had served his purpose; the letters were in. "And I submit they should be made to proceed with the destruction."

Lynch was asked in the hall if he was planning on getting a superseding informer. He replied, "What did you expect, that we had a bishop?" Lynch was content to let Boyd be thrown to the Christians.

vi

Boyd. The enclosed is dynamite and I mean it . . .

The kidnap letters are the omega of the correspondence. The last one in and the last one out. Daniel Berrigan had been captured and retired to Danbury and Philip was to follow him there. Previous to this, Philip got himself placed in the "hole," as segregation is called, in order to initiate a protest against the harassment of which he was being made the brunt. According to the associate warden, Berrigan "bucked" the chow line; once in segregation he then went on a fast. Philip Berrigan's logic is implied: in order to accomplish something you must first do its opposite. You get ahead of someone in the chow line so you might eventually go on a fast. There was a subsequent protest in front of Lewisburg prison that included Sister Elizabeth as spokeswoman, and Little Shane and Big Joe German (as Neil McLaughlin and Joseph Wenderoth are termed in the letters). A meeting with the associate warden was arranged. Elizabeth sent "thank you" notes to him, which were then used as handwriting exemplars. Upon Daniel Berrigan's capture it was agreed to transfer Philip out of Lewisburg; that there was any causal connection was adamantly denied. The obvious is the first to be denied. When Eqbal Ahmad read Sister Elizabeth's "kidnap letter" that was attached to the second indictment as Exhibit A, it has been reported he responded, "It is insane!" In fact, a defense plea of insanity had been considered, though not at length. The defense had been at a disadvantage after the first indictment; the existence of the letters was known only by the principles and in fact, for them, did not physically exist. Elizabeth McAlister, possessor of a tenacious memory, was able to reconstruct hers. The government provided an assist when they began to leak complete sets of the letters to various publications before the second superseding indictment came down.

The summer of 1970 still reverberated with the violent spring's previous bombings. One estimate in a counterculture journal puts the number of bombings during 1970 at five thousand. In one week during March 1970 the courtroom scheduled for the trial of H. Rap Brown was bombed, an associate of his was killed when a bomb exploded in a car in which he was riding; the Eleventh Street Weatherpeople townhouse blew up, from which Leonard Boudin's daughter escaped, and shortly thereafter three large New York corporations were damaged by bombs. The air of that New York August tasted of saltpeter, sulphur, and charcoal.

The killings at Kent State that May of 1970 seemed an ominous prefiguration. The photographs of National Guardsmen and students resembled nothing so much as the Civil War daguerreotypes of Mathew B. Brady. Kent State gave new meaning to the words "civil war"; it need not be black against white, old against young. The National Guardsmen who fired into the students on Blanket Hill were the same green youths of Charlie Company at Mylai 4. They were young whites, sharing the same long sideburns and wire-rimmed granny-glasses of the generation they sprung from and shot. Kent State signaled a reversal not because it was white middle-class children who were killed— —but because it was white middle-class children who were killing

187

white middle-class children. The terror that that mirror image gave back was a memory this country could no longer hide from or deny. It was capable of even this again. Not racial war, or war raised against emerging Third World populations, but what had been buried as a real possibility, brother against brother, with no distinctions necessary. Ramsey Clark in his cross-examination of Boyd referred to it as a "massacre"; it was worse than that: It was the horror of reawakened national fratricide.

Daniel Berrigan was a fugitive from the spring of 1970 through its summer, an *ignis fatuus* flitting over the decaying matter of this country, eluding the FBI. Philip Berrigan was disquieted by some of the actions of his will-o'-the-wisp brother. But he would be seeing him—and others, for (he could rightly think for the wrong reasons) the visiting and mail regulations, different at every institution, would be relaxed at Danbury. Sister Elizabeth knew this too, and I think one thing that governed the writing of the kidnap letter was her haste to tell him, introduce to him, even if just a mention, that there had been a discussion, as she put it, which would "give you some confidence that people are thinking seriously of escalating resistance." She wanted to be the first to tell him. Primary experience is etched on the heart like no other. Berrigan had written her (in an excised portion) that she was the "first" woman to have "enkindled" him. Even with reporting this bit of after-dinner, cordial-oiled loose talk, she wanted to be first. To be important to him, as if she or he needed additional proof of that. After the letter was read in court, G. said, "Loose talk sinks ships. You're probably too young to have heard that. It was a slogan during World War II. It helped the FBI implant the idea that there was a spy lurking on every corner."

Berrigan, with all his vituperation against liberals, should have known from just the setting alone, a summer cottage in Weston, Connecticut, that the conversation that Elizabeth related was aimless chitchat, fired by frustration, anger, helplessness. His reply to her letter reads like an older gallant's equivocations to a young maid's pleas for matrimony. (Indeed, even that inchoate idea was taken up by both parties to the kidnap letters.) He does not want to hurt her; some aspects indulge his ego and to these he permits elaborations; but, all in all, he will beg off with an indifferent and ambiguous invitation to try again.

The intellectual left, at times, has the air of deposed court advisors; they are without power, stuck with theory. Those who cannot implement their ideas are like machines in a land without electricity. A verb much used by the activists of the Catholic Left is "plug in." What is envisioned if not some bank of power, some source that fuels great designs? Elizabeth uses it in a letter about the Delaware raids: "But Davidson, rather than plugging into this, came in with the only other walkie talkie & blasted us."

There has been a lot of discussion of entrapment during the trial: Boyd, entrapping the defendants, the agent-provocateur. They were entrapped, but not by Boyd. They were caught in a net of language, flux, style, culture, that they were adapting piecemeal. Walkie-talkies for draft-board raids! Even their technology raced beyond their comprehension. A little of this, a little of that, appliquéed onto a fabric still whole with Mother Church. They were as resplendent and foolish as Joseph in his coat of many colors.

Excised in court, but intact in Exhibit A is another proposal as thought-out and concrete as the kidnap plan. It was taken out as a crime not charged in the indictment: "The second is the proposal that half jokingly I opened to you in the corridor." Just read that sentence again to understand the doubts and hesitancies that crib her pen. It is a written stammer. She refers to the meeting they had after her talk with the associate warden arranged at the "hole" protest. "If you would like it—now or some time later—we we can do it." She wants to please. "See bruv talk to him about it if you wish & think it over seriously & we'll work it out. En route to Danbury might be too soon at this point to do anything. Either while there or later passage is subject to discussion. We can also arrange it 'non-violently.' I say this not to exert pressure one way or another." She is talking about an escape plan, another fantasy encouragement. Though at a minimum-security work-farm, a month later, 15 September 1970, in San Luis Obispo, California, Timothy Leary, priest of acid, aided by Weatherpeople, took off only to land in Algeria.

BOYD

The kidnapping letters also feature in Counts II and III of the indictment. Lynch added these to his superseding indictment—blood out of a turnip, that Lynch. These were the "threatening letter" counts, and in Count II, Sister Elizabeth was not alone. Eqbal Ahmad was charged also with "willfully and knowingly causing to be delivered. . . . a threat to kidnap Henry Kissinger."

The reasoning that called for the inclusion of Ahmad is not obscure. One person can write a simple letter; if two people write it, it is a plan. By adding the threatening-letter counts, Lynch also found a way to expose the letters as exhibits, besides publishing excerpts in the body of the indictment. The objection in law is that it is surplusage: any part of a pleading or proceeding not necessary or relevant to the case. Though it was essential to the government's extrajudicial pleading. After Hoover's November statement, Representative William B. Anderson (Democrat of Tennessee), the former commander of the U.S.S. *Nautilus,* raised objections to his statement in Congress. The first indictment, with its possible life sentences, did not completely quell the criticism. The second indictment with its Exhibits A and B and excerpts was evidence *ad hominem,* for the jury of press and public. The microfilm held up by Nixon taken from the pumpkin. Proof. It served its purpose. Reading the letters turned most vocal supporters and silent sympathizers into pillars of salt. A hush fell. The inclusion of the letters was the long-awaited result of a biopsy: diseased.

Lynch served as Hoover's champion; his reworked indictment strutted out the source of Hoover's allegations, much the way the North Vietnamese parade captured American pilots. In the words of Paul O'Dwyer in a pretrial motion for mistrial: "I must conclude that as a move to rehabilitate Mr. Hoover, the maneuver cannot be surpassed."

In Hoover's original prepared statement before the subcommittee, his charges follow immediately upon a paragraph about the Weatherpeople: "The Weatherman group is now completely underground and in May, 1970 Bernardine Dohrn, one of its leaders, declared a state of war against the United States on behalf of the group. Over 20 Weatherman militants are currently fugitives, including Dohrn who is one of the FBI's 'Ten Most

190

Wanted Fugitives,' arising out of indictments on antiriot charges and violations of Federal Bombing and gun control statutes during the past year.

"Willingness to employ any type of terrorist tactics is becoming increasingly apparent among extremist elements. One example has recently come to light involving an incipient plot on the part of an anarchist group of the east coast, and so-called 'East Coast Conspiracy to Save Lives.' "

Hoover believed America was in a state of war; all opponents to the status quo were in the same army. Empty-handed when it came to the Weatherpeople, confessing that twenty of them were still eluding "the outfit with the longest record of crimebusting in law enforcement," one of whom (and for what undivined popularity poll reasons), B. Dohrn, was raised to the Ten Most Wanted. The Ten Best lists. Hoover transformed crime, and placed criminals squarely in the free-enterprise system where they could compete, like all other Americans, to get to the top of one heap or another. The Catholic Left found itself playing second banana to the Weatherpeople. Hoover used them as an *example*. (One example has . . .) And it might have gone no farther. The tough would have backed off if ignored; but the Berrigans challenged him from their cells in Danbury. Outcries began. This trial came to pass. Now, as the indictment reads, "part of which communication was of the following tenor and description to wit":

> . . . Which leads me to #3 & this in utter confidence & should not be committed to paper & I would want you not even to say a word of it to Dan until we have a fuller grasp of it.

Don't tell it to Dan; it is our secret, our baby.

> I say it to you for 2 reasons. The first obviously is to get your thinking on it, the second to give you some confidence that people are thinking seriously of escallating resistance. Eq called us up to Conn. last night along with Bill Davidon who, in case people have not told you, has become one of our better people. Parenthetically someone with a knowledge of the scene, a keen sense for tactic & detail & little fear of risk for himself. He's the most central fig. in the

191

Phila. scene & went into the Boards in Georgetown
with those kids.

In generations, Elizabeth is closer by age to those "kids"
than to Philip Berrigan. She compensates, placing herself somewhere in the middle distance.

> Eq outline a plan for an action which would say—
> escallated seriousness—we discussed pros & cons for
> several hours. It needs much more thought & careful
> selection of personnel. To kidnap—in our terminology
> make a citizens arrest of—someone like Henry Kiss-
> inger. Him because of his influence as policy maker
> yet sans cabinet status, he would therefore not be as
> much protected as one of the bigger wigs; he is a
> bachelor which would mean if he were so guarded, he
> would be anxious to have unguarded moments where
> he could carry on his private affairs—literally & fig-
> uratively. To issue a set of demands, e.g. cessation of
> use of B 52s over N. Vietnam, Laos, Cambodia, &
> release of political prisoners. Hold him for about a
> week during which time big wigs of the liberal ilk
> would be brought to him—also kidnapped if necessary
> (which, for the most part it would be)—& hold a trial
> or grand jury affair out of which an indictment would
> be brought. There is no pretence of these demands
> being met & he would be released after this time with
> a word that we're non-violent as opposed to you who
> would let a man be killed—one of your own—so that
> you can go on killing. The liberals would also be re-
> leased as would a film of the whole proceedings in
> which, hopefully, he would be far more honest than
> he is on his own territory. The impact of such a thing
> would be phenomenal. Reasons for wanting to do it:
> it will ultimately be done by someone here & end in
> fiasco or violence & killing.

William Lynch interviewed a potential witness at Catholic University. Unbeknownst to Lynch, he was being filmed. Midway,
he realized that the awful turnabout had occurred: he was the subject of hidden surveillance. He broke out into a characteristic rage.
There were a few private screenings in Harrisburg of this blue
movie of Lynch.

Eq. wants to do it & do it well before anyone else
does it badly & I believe he has the know how to
direct such an escapade. The major problem, as I see
it, is the severe consequences for something that is
largely 'drama' with little lasting effect. Second problem I envision is position of something like this in a
movement context i.e. what next. Some thought would
have to be given to that. It seems at least possible to
have 2 fairly distinct groups on the one hand the
felons who have a scant chance but a chance of remaining anonymous & the big wigs, who will provide
the "public" aspect of the action who are preserved
by their own position as "captives" also. The concept
of a film of the trial to be released to TV etc is phenomenal. Then, his aspect of the war will be at least
impeded by his absence & the involvement of all
close to him in an investigate of his whereabouts.
Think about it . . .

Think about it.

. . . & maybe when I see you in Danbury I can get
your thoughts as well as fill you in on where the plan
lies.

"& *maybe* when I see you . . ." There is such insecurity in that
"maybe." It is the insecurity of a daughter after she has just
played her first piano piece for her father. Waiting for praise.
What is he going to say?
And what did he say? "To wit":

(New Par.) Now we come to #3. Just between you
and me, I have never been overmuch impressed w/Eq.
He's dear friend, very helpful in the last months . . .

Playing an organizational role in Dan Berrigan's underground;
intellectual confessor for Sister Elizabeth.

. . . lovely guy, good ideologue, but still to produce.
I think the role of man from Missouri is the safest
one with him. (I have this terrible suspicion regarding academics). With few exceptions, the b-stards
will let others go to the gallows without a *serious*
murmur. They did it in Germany and they're doing it
here. And E is from that strain. You see love, the
belief isn't there—

193

The belief isn't there. Eqbal had told Joseph Wenderoth: "I am not a moral man." Belief is the irrational bedrock that cannot be shaken. Berrigan is sure that anyone without that bedrock will waver, fall, give out with unserious murmurs. "But still to produce." It is easy to see how Boyd appealed to Berrigan. An ex-con, totally unconnected with the Catholic Left, said of Boyd, "In prison you get to know which guys had any morals and which guys didn't. Ol' Boyd was in the latter category." A man without scruples can appear to be a man who possesses them to a rare degree; he will act without hesitation, decisively. In Berrigan's eyes Boyd was beginning to do things for the right reasons; in Boyd's position it was just as easy to do things for good reasons as for bad. Boyd had "produced."

> Stringfellow at least believes in something. But these are mere reservations—I'd be delighted to be wrong. (New Par.) About the plan—the first time opens the door to murder—the Tupamaros are finding that out in Uruguay—I hope you're following them (last 2 issues of the Guardian). When I refer to murder it is not to prohibit it absolutely . . .

Berrigan used to put forth as one argument against the Vietnam war the Catholic Church's definition of a "Just War," and show that Vietnam violated the rules. If Berrigan can reason to a just war, he can reason to a just murder. Who would gainsay him?

> (violence against nonviolence bag) it is merely to observe that one has set the precedent, and that later on, when govm't resistance to this sort of thing stiffens, men will be killed. More to the point, the project as you outlined it is brilliant, but grandiose. I've found, with bitter experience, that when people opt for too much, they're either stupid or egotistical (another red light for our friend E.) Which is to say that grabbing the gentleman will take a force of perhaps 10 of your best people—guarding him, getting communications out, perhaps moving him 2 or 3 times within the week. Now, in addition, to grab a prosecution of liberals would take dozens more, making the network too wide. But even if that were possible, how can it be guaranteed that they would indict him in any sort of real fashion? Then too, the

common view is that K. is the architect of honorable withdrawal from S.E. Asia, and even some of the liberals believe that. How to get the truth out, ie, that the economy needs war, and it mind [sic] as well be there as elsewhere, and that we intend to stay. That might mean a Korean type answer, but then we'd have to hot it up elsewhere. Or go into the dilemma of more serious recession rising unemployment at home. This is what should be gotten from K., but can the liberals do it? (New Par.) Nonetheless, I like the plan and am just trying to weave elements of modesty into it.

What did Berrigan really think of the plan? What thoughts passed through, what reactions that he would never put to paper and address to "Maureen." With all the honesty that was being professed, it could be forsaken in behalf of her feelings. The dissembling heart. In private—such as this was before it was made more public than a pissoir. Here is an element he weaves into the plan: "Why not coordinate it with the one against capitol utilities?—You see, I really do like it and to show you I will top it."

> You should talk more thoroughly with the *chargé* [Boyd] about this, or with Little Shane or Big Joe German. To disrupt them. . . .

(Like his government that hides in euphemisms, "protective reaction, interdiction, etc," Berrigan takes refuge. The Washington tunnel plan, still the golden fleece watched by dragon Boyd, is seen as a "disruption.")

> . . . then grab the Brain Child—this would be escallation enough. (New Paragraph) This comes off the top of my head. Why not grab the Brain Child, treat him decently, but tell him nothing of his fate—or tell him his fate hinges on release of pol. people or cessation of air strikes in Laos. Then have batteries of movement people—Brain Child blindfolded—engage him on policy. After he has been taught (the consideration of his safety will make him more and more human in his answers) . . .

That is a strange definition of how you make someone more human. It echoes Tricia Nixon's "Never underestimate the power of fear."

195

get it filmed and recorded. One thing should be im-
planted in that pea brain—that respectable murderers
like himself are no longer inviolable. (This should be
done just before release.) And that if he doesn't work
to humanize policy, the likes of him will be killed by
less scrupulous people. Finally, that political prisoners
are the best guarantee of his sweet skin's safety, and
that he better get them out of jail. (New Par.)
Taken along these lines, you have both a material
and personal confrontation with the warmakers. The
trick to pull off is to hit them very, very hard without
giving them violence to react to. . . .

Which is the rationale behind draft-board raids.

. . . or to justify themselves with. (New Par.)
He can be kept blindfolded, and participants can
wear stocking masks & disguise their voices. It can be
done and done brilliantly. (New Par.) I would
sic Eq on it immediately, but tie it in with the *D.C.*
fiasco, and keep his imagination under ropes. If the
investment in our best people is excessive, and if
they're caught—there'd be a massive manhunt—it
would be life. And this is a factor to be considered.
Grabbing our angel would involve 2 or 3 months dis-
creet work. I would imagine that he would have devices in his car to call for police assistance at the
slightest danger. The thing to do is find out where he
goes for weekends, or where he shacks up—if he
shacks up. (New Par.) I don't think E. can
build his own team on his—he'll probably need help.
But a rein of both ideas and modesty should be kept
on him. Furthermore, I don't think he'd be the easiest
guy to work with. Mind you, the criticism comes with
love for the guy, with gratitude for the past months,
and with a recognition of his intelligence and talent.
Davidon is good—a few wrinkles there—but perhaps
these have already been ironed out.

It must have been exhilarating for Berrigan to let his imagination fly along with Elizabeth's, out of his cell, over the walls of
the penitentiary.

After Lynch finished reading the two kidnap letters his voice was
the last car barely moving at a demolition derby. A recess was
called. Eqbal came over to Berrigan and embraced him. The

difference in their heights made Eqbal leave the ground to hug the tall priest around the neck. He hung there for a moment, on the broad beam of Father Berrigan's shoulders.

Amid all the adjectives of dismay that cover the "kidnap plot" —unimaginable, insane, impossible, ludicrous—one thing remains unnoticed. It worked. It was successful. It happened. Though not quite as planned. Some elements of modesty did get woven into it. By the Madame Defarge of the FBI: J. Edgar Hoover. As I listened to the letters finally being read in court, after having gone over them many times before, I was struck by their strangely prophetic note. They sounded like a report of something that had occurred.

Part of the plan was just left untold, it seemed. As Boyd related, they were concerned that it could not be done nonviolently. According to Lynch's indictment, the object of the conspiracy was, in part, to "obtain publicity . . . in the course of which they would express anti-war and anti-government statements . . ." How to kidnap Kissinger in order to hold "a trial or grand jury affair," to assemble "big wigs of the liberal ilk," to do something that is largely "drama," to have it filmed, to make an "impact" that would be "phenomenal"? How to do it nonviolently? This grandiose plan. Simple. Make J. Edgar Hoover believe you are bombers and kidnappers and have him manufacture the trial of the Harrisburg Seven. Hoover should be listed as an unindicted coconspirator. It was his elements of immodesty that were woven into the plan; he was the secret triggering apparatus. Nobody saw it that way though; the plan had, unbeknownst to all concerned, worked. They—foiled Pragmatists—then discovered that just because something can be made to happen doesn't mean it should.

On 6 March 1971 a few unindicted coconspirators of the first indictment had a meeting with Henry Kissinger in the "Situation Room" of the White House. They have a seventy-five-minute discussion. They report it as having been "civilized and amicable." So much for kidnapping Kissinger; they had him for seventy-five civilized and amicable minutes. They didn't get him on film, but they did get William S. Lynch.

During the lunch recess the day the kidnap letters were read, the press convened to pick up complete sets of Xeroxes of the letters. It cost each one five dollars. The Xerox machine at Bucknell University cost Boyd five cents a page, so it originally cost him the same amount. Boyd was reimbursed. For a five-dollar investment the government has admitted to paying him something over $9,200. Boyd has the Midas touch.

A two-and-a-half foot stack of Xeroxing is placed on a long table; it is then divided up into smaller stacks for collation. The press corps does a circular dance around the table, picking up a page at a time till each has his own set. They look like the centurions dicing for Christ's seamless garment. A woman journalist, appearing at the trial just for a day, comes into the press room and joins the game. The reporter who had organized the billing did not recognize her and says, "Hey, did you pay for those?"

"No," she replies, "I thought they were free."

"Free, hell; they'll cost you five dollars if you want a set. You do want a set, don't you?"

"I want them," the lady replies, an astronomer viewing another galaxy shrunk into a telescope's perspective, "But I don't want them five dollars' worth."

vii

Before the defense began its cross-examination of Boyd, Ramsey Clark and Father Berrigan went up to sidebar to talk with Herman. Berrigan still considered himself to be in a lawyerless limbo, able to defend himself. Clark told the judge that Father Berrigan wanted to begin the cross-examination of Boyd himself. Herman denied this; then Berrigan did his one and only imitation of Bobby Seale:

> FATHER BERRIGAN: Don't I have any judgment on what is proper or improper?
> THE COURT: I have ruled. I don't think you have any right to do it and I have ruled against it.
> FATHER BERRIGAN: What about constitutional rights? What about the Sixth Amendment?

THE COURT: Go back and sit down. I have ruled and that is all I want to hear. I have ruled and I think that is proper.

Not a word has been exchanged between Boyd and the defendants since January 1971; nor are any words exchanged here.

Boyd had been arrested in Acapulco, Mexico, where he had gone to spend the spoils of a year's worth of defrauding banks of close to sixty thousand dollars. Previous to this, while in the army in 1962, he was tried in Japan by a civil court for petty theft. Lynch objected to Clark's calling it "larceny."

MR. LYNCH: Well, the records that I have seen talk about some paltry amount in Hong Kong or Kowloon or some place like that.

MR. CLARK: Well, that would make fifty or sixty thousand plus thirty I guess.

Because of that Boyd received a less-than-honorable discharge from the army. Boyd admitted to having defrauded the Fountainebleau Hotel in Miami Beach, passing bad checks in Reno, Nevada. Boyd's bilking of America's gaudy tourist meccas gave his exploits a slightly Robin Hoodish tone. Captured in Acapulco, he was deported to the United States, handed over to the FBI on a footbridge in the border town of Loredo, Texas. At that time he gave a statement to the press, expressing surprise that it took the FBI so long to find him since they had been looking for him three years. One way to feel wanted, is to be wanted by the FBI.

He was tried in San Antonio, Texas, and received his original six-year sentence that he began to serve in Lewisburg in 1964. Clark then went through a list of Boyd's escapes and attempts. Boyd objected to the word "escape" in some instances; it was not accurate, there were extenuating circumstances. He had "eloped" from the National Institute of Health on 24 July 1966. He had volunteered for the experiments there while at Lewisburg. Boyd was looking for a way out, one reason why he volunteered for NIH experimentation: it increased the odds, gave him more elbow room, leverage. He worked to get on study-release for the same reason. It was a different type of experiment; it, too, left scars. Clark asked: "Now, was your civil suit actually settled

199

after the government told you that you had yourself induced the abscesses you were suing over?" Boyd's lawyer had mentioned something like that to him, but Boyd didn't think that was why it was settled.

Boyd admits to taking out "contraband" a "day or two" before meeting Philip Berrigan. It was a "memo," Boyd says, "something about a breakdown of black, white, Puerto Ricans, etc., in the population at Lewisburg penitentiary."

"You *stole* it," Clark says, indignantly, "and smuggled it out before you ever met Philip Berrigan. Did the FBI give it to you?" No. "Did the Federal Bureau of Prisons give it to you?" No. "Isn't it highly sensitive information; weren't you taking a great risk?" Clark asks, referring to a sheet of information about when Berrigan was to arrive at Lewisburg. "I knew I wasn't supposed to take it out . . ."

Clark points out discrepancies in Boyd's direct testimony and his previous grand jury testimony. Boyd settles them blithely: "If I said that I was mistaken. . . . The prosecutor asked me a pretty leading question . . ."

When Clark nettled him with the inconsistencies ("The grand jury is wrong for the third time today"), Boyd would strike back in his own fashion. Asked about giving Joseph Wenderoth the ROTC explosive-manuals the FBI had supplied him with, Clark says sardonically, "You just happened to have them on you?"

Boyd replies, "Yes, in my attaché [he pronounces it "apache"] case where I carry most of my things, *where I carried the notes Philip Berrigan asked me to go over with them at that meeting.*" To get back, Boyd would add what he considered to be incriminating things the question did not cover. He was referring to the "agenda" that he said Berrigan had given him the last time they talked, that Sunday before the Wisconsin bombing, an agenda to go over with Joseph Wenderoth and Neil McLaughlin, containing such matters as: Find out the size of the tunnels, etc. Boyd hadn't supplied to the FBI this piece of paper he says *he* made out at Berrigan's instructions that August Sunday, till after Hoover's statement in November.

Clark ended his cross with questions about the tunnels and the "generator plants" that Boyd had said were two of the things Berrigan wanted Wenderoth to find out about, how many there were and what their locations were. When were these first mentioned? he had asked Boyd. In May of 1970, Boyd supplied. He brought it up again, Boyd said, in his August "agenda." Clark went to the defense table for Defense Exhibit 16. He walked up to Boyd.

"You made all this up—the secrecy, the search for the number of generator plants—didn't you?"

"No, I did not."

"Look at this pictorial guide of Washington, D.C." Clark unfolds an Esso gas station "Happy Motoring" map.

"Read aloud what you see located by New Jersey and E streets."

"Power House for Capitol."

"And at C street and D street by twelfth and thirteenth."

"Central Heating Plant."

"Did it take them four months to find a gas station? I have no further questions, Your Honor."

A recess follows and prosecutor Lynch walks out of the courtroom, his mouth fixed into a *risus sardonicus,* repeating cynically, "Devastating. Just devastating."

Boyd was cross-examined by six defense attorneys: Clark, Paul O'Dwyer, Terry Lenzner, J. Thomas Menaker, William Cunningham, S.J., and Leonard Boudin. Everyone waited for Boyd to crack, to reach into his pocket and flourish his famous Beretta semi-automatic that was so much discussed. Herman took special interest in Boyd's Beretta, knew how it worked, one shell sliding into the chamber at a time, the necessity for it to be cocked before it could be fired: two steps. Herman knows how a Beretta works, but not what guerilla theater is, or what "Shalom" means.

O'Dwyer took Boyd through a series of reports: the telephone reports Boyd made almost daily to Molly Mayfield; the Danville report Boyd made in December with the FBI; the Phoenix, Arizona, report made months later when Boyd lived there, the grand jury testimony and his own testimony here. It did not all jibe. O'Dwyer took him through the list of monies the FBI paid him.

"He's taking a lot of blows to the body, but none to the head," was a reporter's estimation.

On the tunnel project, Boyd said that Tom Davidson's farm

would be used as the place to train people in the use of explosives. Davidson's farm, Boyd said, was near the Second White House, Camp David, Maryland. O'Dwyer asked, "What did you say when you heard that? Did you think it was a good place to fool around with explosives, near the Second White House?" Boyd replied, "I don't recall that I said anything. I did a lot of listening. I didn't do too much talking." And according to people who knew Boyd at Bucknell and were with him at parties and picnics and dinners that were later than the meetings and rap sessions of the overt acts, Boyd didn't do much talking.

Barely two months after Boyd left the Lewisburg area and began his honeymoon with the FBI, he was married in Phoenix, Arizona. It must have been love at first sight. Boyd went from doing a lot of listening to doing a lot of talking. When he was on the Bucknell campus the fact that he was Philip Berrigan's "friend" was his letter of introduction to whomever he met. He wrote to a man whom he had never seen, but he had heard of, who was connected with the American Friends Service Committee in Philadelphia, when he thought he might be getting up that way: "The people I know in Philly are movement." Armed with the names of his "movement" friends, he inquired, "possibly you could introduce me to a sharp, politically motivated chick . . ." Boyd cast Philip Berrigan into another strange role. Father Berrigan became a pimp.

Boyd spent the decade of the sixties either in custody or "eloping" from it; he was a sponge, though, and the social change he soaked up came from the people he met at Bucknell and the special home-tutoring he got through the McAlister-Berrigan correspondence course. He also wrote letters—to whomever he thought he would chance to meet, or want to meet: William Kunstler, for instance—and to "sharp, politically motivated chicks." A visitor to the planet of Resistance, he took his vocabulary and "right" ideas from the odd montage he was exposed to; his letters read like wild parodies of the McAlister-Berrigan letters.

> Dear —————,
> I am really sorry if at times I seem distant to you, but I have been that way since someone close to me testified for the F.B.I.

You know what I am about and I am totally committed to that movement. There is a possibility that I will return to prison and at the least, I will be under government surveillance as long as I live. That also means anyone near me. Anyone who talks about change in the system, faces the possibility of losing his freedom. But that doesn't paralyse me because I don't see my individual life as being so important. I have given my life to the struggle. If I lose my freedom or life in the struggle, well, then, that's the way it will have to be. I want no mysticism in regards to me.

As for you working with the movement, no problem. However, I get warm vibrations from you and I feel we can tune in on the same wavelength. You are a very strong and human woman. Possibly we can work together.

I know most of the people in the Midwest and East. They are very real people and they trust me. That is why I am always sensitive to certain elements.

My function in the movement is organization after people are definitely committed to some type of civil disobedience. That means after February, my official supervision ends, I will be on the road constantly. From California to New York City.

I want our relationship to be real for both of us. There can be no half-way point, and you have to support what I am about. Need I say more? No strings though.

Peace & Love,/s/Boyd

Boyd's complimentary closes grew with each letter till they included: Peace, Love, Right on, Z, He lives. Asked what "Z" meant, he said he didn't know (it refers to a foreign film about a Greeklike police state) but had taken it from a letter of McAlister's. Asked to guess, he said the only "Z" he knew was Zorro (a caped adventurer in a television show that ran in the fifties). The new film-culture was not a ready reference for Boyd; he had been in suspended animation courtesy of the Federal Bureau of Prisons. Boyd continually overestimated the talk he heard; for, in his experience, talk, like most things, was not plentiful; not having much, people said what they meant; he was used to people acting upon their words.

When Terry Lenzner questioned Boyd a certain parity was

reached; Lenzner was only a year older than Boyd; up to now Boyd had been confronted by elders, but here he faced a contemporary. Lenzner questions aggressively; during the *voir dire* he would grill a prospective juror as if he or she were a hostile witness. Lenzner has most always been a prosecutor; he was director of legal services for the Office of Economic Opportunity in 1969. There is some question whether he was fired or resigned under the Nixon Administration.

Lenzner could easily be one of the brighter colors of Boyd's fantasy spectrum. Lenzner and Lynch had squared off once during a recess called after their exchange became heated. Lynch, the aged pug, looked about to strike Lenzner, knowing it would not go beyond the first blow. Herman had left the courtroom. The marshals looked like they'd enjoy making side bets. Other lawyers took them from the middle of the courtroom back to their respective tables, like seconds separating boxers still slugging it out after the bell had rung.

Lenzner had been captain of the Harvard football team, vice president of the National Legal Aid and Defender Association, and is currently chairman of the Committee of Rights of the Accused, ABA. He is associated with the same prestigious law firm as Ramsey Clark. Lenzner had been leading Boyd through a maze of lies, to which Douglas admitted. He answered, "possibly," when Lenzner asked if he had told girls that he had gone to Ohio State on a football scholarship. There is Terry Lenzner, former captain of the Harvard football team, and there is Boyd F. Douglas, former phantom Ohio State football scholarship winner. Substance and shell. Earlier Douglas had been asked by Paul O'Dwyer whether or not he had proposed to one of the young women who had copied letters for him. It had been the first time Douglas smiled on the stand; his face went crimson and he answered, "Possibility," and began to laugh behind his hand at his own private absurdity.

Again, Lenzner asked if he had proposed, this time to the other young woman who copied letters. Boyd could reply about a proposal scoffingly to an old man, but he could not do so to Lenzner. There was a matter of competition here. Lenzner's unvoiced opinion after most of Boyd's answers was: "Don't hand me any of that shit." Asked further about the young woman, Douglas said—in answer to all those questions summoned up in him by Lenzner's person—"She went where I went." Now you know where I stand, buddy.

At the end of Lenzner's cross a reporter said, composing an imaginary lead sentence, "Harvard beat Ohio State yesterday . . ."

"I can sympathize with him to one extent," Daniel Ellsberg was saying. "I don't think I could remember all those dates and times either; oh, boy, when they start asking me those kinds of things . . ."

There had been discussion about Lynch's orchestration of Boyd's testimony. He was compared to Leonard Bernstein. If Boyd would pause two beats Lynch would object, point out where Boyd should pick up a phrase. A different tempo please. Leonard Bernstein had visited Daniel Berrigan at Danbury prison. Berrigan had come into the visiting room to find Bernstein sitting surrounded by musical scores. He had wanted Dan Berrigan to do the libretto for his Mass commissioned for the opening of the John F. Kennedy Center for the Performing Arts in Washington. Berrigan came into the room and Bernstein inquired where the piano was. "Maybe next time," Berrigan said, surprised by the expectation. Berrigan did not do the libretto, thinking it inappropriate for a man jailed by the federal government to share in the glory of the opening of the government's culture temple.

"Some do it with a ballpoint pen," Ellsberg was saying. "They click it. A signal system has been set up." Ellsberg's attorney for the upcoming Pentagon Papers trial was Leonard Boudin; Boudin came up and asks, "Do you think I'm being too hard on Douglas?"

Boudin had been asking Douglas about the circumstances under which he pulled out his Beretta before he had been apprehended outside a Wisconsin bank. The interplay of Lynch and Douglas, Douglas and Herman (THE COURT), and Boudin to them all, is readily seen in the following unedited, verbatim transcript:

> BY MR. BOUDIN:
> Q: Now, is it also your testimony that you pulled the gun out of your—was it carried on your body or in a satchel or an attaché case?
> A: I had the gun out.

Q: I beg your pardon?

A: I had the gun out in my hand.

Q: And did you point it at anybody?

A: Not that I recall, no.

Q: You might have?

A: I was scared. I don't recall. I don't think that I did. If I would have, I would have been shot.

Q: We understand that. What was the purpose of the gun? Why did you have it in your hand?

A: I was afraid.

Q: I understand you were afraid.

A: I testified. I can't give you a psychological answer.

Q: Yes, I know. Mr. Lynch made that observation.

A: You have already tried that.

Q: You just stick with your testimony please.

MR. LYNCH: Objection to his arguing with the witness, Your Honor. He has asked this question again and again, and he has gotten the same answer again and again.

MR. BOUDIN: All the witness has done is repeat Mr. Lynch's observation.

THE COURT: Well, you have gotten into this a number of times, Mr. Boudin.

MR. BOUDIN: The point I am now making has been gone into a number of times, yes, Your Honor.

THE COURT: The question was, did he point the gun. It was testified to just a few minutes ago.

MR. BOUDIN: Yes. Now my question to the witness —I won't repeat that, Your Honor. Your Honor is, of course, correct.

BY MR. BOUDIN:

Q: What did you intend to do with the gun if you were scared?

MR. LYNCH: Objection, Your Honor.

THE COURT: I think he answered that one a number of times.

THE WITNESS: I do not know.

BY MR. BOUDIN:

Q: You do not know?

A: I do not know.

Q: Were you attempting to avoid apprehension when you had the gun in your hand? Just tell us any way you want.

A: I have answered it.

Q: Yes.

A: I have answered it.

Q: What was that?

A: I don't know why I had the gun in my hand. I had the gun in my hand. I was scared.

Q: Fine, you were scared. Were you attempting to cause fear in the banking officials?

MR. LYNCH: Objection, Your Honor.

MR. BOUDIN: This is cross.

THE COURT: I think he answered that.

MR. LYNCH: Just because it is cross-examination doesn't mean you can ask the question thirty times.

THE COURT: I think he answered that one.

MR. BOUDIN: I don't remember.

MR. LYNCH: I object to the repetitive cross-examination.

MR. BOUDIN: I don't think anybody got into that.

THE COURT: Well, let us just stop a minute and we will get the reporter to go back.

MR. BOUDIN: Fine.

MR. LYNCH: I think it is a totally collateral matter.

THE COURT: It has been gone into a number of times. He answered it.

MR. BOUDIN: What was the answer?

THE COURT: I don't know. Whatever it was, he answered it. He was asked that same question. He said he was scared.

MR. BOUDIN: Well, I don't remember it, and I don't think anybody else does.

MR. LYNCH: I remember the answer, Your Honor.

MR. BOUDIN: I want the Court.

THE COURT: I don't remember what the answer was, and I am sure it was asked a number of times.

MR. BOUDIN: Well, if it was asked and answered and nobody remembers, Your Honor—

THE COURT: Well, we will go back and get it. Were you here or was Mrs. DePanfilis here at that time?

THE REPORTER: For which question, Your Honor?

THE COURT: Well, go back and see those questions about why he pulled the gun out.

THE REPORTER: Mrs. DePanfilis was here during that time.

THE COURT: Mrs. DePanfilis?

THE REPORTER: Yes.

MR. LYNCH: He has been asked that question about four times, and he has repeatedly answered it.

MR. BOUDIN: Well, he could answer it now.

THE COURT: Answer it one more time if you can. We will be all day on that one question if we get Mrs. DePanfilis in to hunt that.

You said you were scared. You said you didn't point it at anybody, to your knowledge?

THE WITNESS: At that time I was scared, yes. That is why I pulled the gun.

THE COURT: He asked if you were trying to avoid arrest.

THE WITNESS: I said I was scared. I also said I was trying to scare anyone that was trying to apprehend me.

THE COURT: Yes.

MR. BOUDIN: That is right. That is all I wanted to know.

THE WITNESS: I said it before.

BY MR. BOUDIN:

Q: Now, I want to call your attention to the fact that when you appeared upon sentence in Wisconsin with respect to this incident, the following statement was made by you. And I will be glad to show it to Mr. Lynch if he doesn't have it.

(Document handed to Mr. Lynch)

MR. BOUDIN: I will let Mr. Lynch look at it for a moment, then perhaps I can ask questions as to what you told the Court on sentence.

THE WITNESS: Well, I think I already know what you are going to ask. I know what I told the Court.

BY MR. BOUDIN:

Q: Well, don't anticipate me. Let me ask the questions please.

(Document handed to Mr. Boudin)

BY MR. BOUDIN:

Q: Did you say the following—

MR. LYNCH: Objection unless the entire document is put into evidence.

MR. BOUDIN: Oh, I would be glad to. Let me mark it for identification.

THE COURT: Yes, mark it for identification.

MR. BOUDIN: And I may say there is no such rule as Mr. Lynch has indicated.

MR. LYNCH: There is most certainly such a rule as Mr. Lynch has indicated.

MR. BOUDIN: Well, I am not going to argue with you.

THE CLERK: Defendants' 37.

BY MR. BOUDIN:

Q: Did I hear you say, Mr. Douglas—don't give us the answer—that you had anticipated what I was about to ask you, is that right.

A: Just anticipated it.

Q: Yes.

A: That is correct.

Q: Was your anticipation created by my reference to the official report.

A: No.

Q: All right.

A: After—

Q: No.

A: Let me answer.

Q: No.

A: You let me answer the other question.

THE COURT: Let him answer it. I am going to let him answer it. Go ahead, Mr. Douglas.

THE WITNESS: Yes. After I was apprehended I knew I had a very heavy sentence I might possibly receive. I told the Court at that time that I was carrying the hand gun on me so that in the case I was apprehended, I would shoot myself to gain leniency from the Court.

BY MR. BOUDIN:

Q: Shoot yourself to gain leniency from the Court?

A: Well, with that statement I could get a lenient sentence.

Q: Of course.

Now, my question—and you really anticipated my reading it and very well.

A: That is exactly what I thought.

Q: Now, let me read it, and then I will ask you some questions.

A: O.K.

MR. O'DWYER: Mr. Boudin, would you please pause for a moment. I didn't get the last answer.

BY MR. BOUDIN:

Q: All right, would you tell the Court again—

THE COURT: No. Read the question and answer, Mr. Reporter.

MR. O'DWYER: The last question and answer.

(The following was read back by the reporter:

"QUESTION: Now, my question—and you really anticipated my reading it and very well.

"ANSWER: That is exactly what I thought.")

MR. O'DWYER: No, the one before that. Just the answer.

THE COURT: Read the previous answer.

(The following was read back by the reporter:

"ANSWER: After I was apprehended I knew I had a very heavy sentence I might possibly receive. I told the Court at that time that I was carrying the hand gun on me so that in the case I was apprehended, I would shoot myself to gain leniency from the Court.")

BY MR. BOUDIN:

Q: Now, counsel suggested I read the entire statement.

The Court asked you, did it not—"Boyd Frederick Douglas, Jr., the Court invites you as a person about to be sentenced to make any statement you care to." Do you remember that?

A: I recall I made a statement, yes.

Q: And then you answered. It is called the defendant. And I assume it is you from the caption—"I think Mr. Padden . . ."—that was your lawyer, was it not?—". . . has covered everything very well. And I want to—and I would like to add that at the time I was at the hospital at the National Institute of Health and when I was given a parole from the hospital and they sent me home and I got to Chicago and overnight I had recurrence of the same ailment, which I had to be shipped back to the National Institute of Health for surgery again, and at this time is when I forged the checks in the hospital bank itself underneath my own name . . ."—that is the way it is written—". . . and this is when I took off on this spree."

Just for the moment—the spree, I take it, is going into that bank with the Beretta, right?

A: That is correct.

Q: "This is when I took off on this spree. And since that time I would like to add, as far as the gun was concerned, I did not have the gun in my possession with intent to hurt anybody, but to hurt myself if I was apprehended."

And I will read the rest since Mr. Lynch may want me to—"And also, Your Honor, I have been in the county jail out here since Christmas Eve with the ailment I have at the present time, which was initiated by this experiment. I was given shots in both arms and both legs. And I have an abscess—or the doctors here anyway say they don't know what it is. But I know there is, because I have fifteen of them, which is in my leg at the present time."

And that was all of the colloquy between you and the Court.

Now, I take it this is a correct statement, that you did say, "I would like to add as far as the gun was concerned, I did not have the gun in my possession with intent to hurt anybody, but to hurt myself if I was apprehended." Is that a correct statement of what you said?

A: That is correct.

Q: Now, in this Court, you remember what your testimony was—namely, you had the gun because you wanted to scare people, right?

MR. LYNCH: Objection—because he was scared and wanted to avoid apprehension.

MR. BOUDIN: I haven't finished yet, Mr. Lynch.

THE COURT: Yes, he said he tried to scare anyone who apprehended him.

MR. BOUDIN: Exactly.

BY MR. BOUDIN:

Q: And you, of course, did not tell the Court in Wisconsin that that was the reason you had the gun, did you?

A: I did not.

Q: Now, which statement is true, the one you gave to the Court in Wisconsin for the purpose of getting leniency, or the one you have made here in Court today with respect to the reasons why you carried the gun—namely, to scare people?

MR. LYNCH: Or both, Your Honor.

MR. BOUDIN: Let the witness answer. That is his prerogative.

THE COURT: Well, he could certainly have both of them.

THE WITNESS: At the time of the events they were both in my mind.

MR. BOUDIN: I will introduce in evidence Defendants' Exhibit 37.

"Well, am I being too hard on him?" Boudin asks again.

He is the last attorney to cross-examine Boyd, and the defendants thought Boyd had been put through enough. They wanted to curtail the long cross Boudin planned. The previous ten days of Boyd's vermiculated testimony was thought to be sufficient. To the defendants it was the continuous rerunning of an atrocity film. Even Herman, at a sidebar, admitted, ". . . you have attacked his credibility well . . ." There was one thing yet that Boudin wanted to show the jury, an aspect of Boyd which would make things clear beyond doubt, beyond simple credibility. Ellsberg did not answer Boudin, but suggested that Boyd might be on drugs: "He looks tanked up." Boudin told Ellsberg, "I still think he was a plant from the start, either FBI or CIA; but we're not going to be able to prove that. We're not getting to see all their records . . ."

I do not believe Boyd was a plant; Boyd knew that Philip Berrigan possessed a modicum of fame, which is currency in the market place. A contemporary Boswell, he copied the letters knowing that he could eventually turn them into something.

No one works harder than Leonard Boudin. He would regularly leave the offices the lawyers used in Harrisburg in the early morning hours, to return again at 7:00 A.M. "I do not lose cases," he has said. Perhaps that is why he didn't take the Rosenbergs' case when asked. The morning before his last day of cross-examination he had fainted; during a long argument on one of the many motions he filed during the trial he reached for the pills that he needed because of his injured heart. He would miss the glass invariably while pouring the water. Once, he said while doing so, "I just want to let my wife," who sat each day in the front row of spectators, "know that I am taking Valium, not nitroglycerin." He did not let up at any time during the trial; he once remarked on Ramsey Clark's less intense methods: "I don't know if I care for Ramsey's Protestant Work Ethic that calls for total relaxation at all times."

When he had the attack that wounded his heart, he lay on the floor of a Long Island dance hall, turning blue, where he had collapsed after dancing with four different women. A doctor was finally persuaded that he wasn't a drunk and began pounding on his chest. After he recovered, a pacemaker was inserted next to his heart.

Boudin saw Douglas differently from the defendants; he did not
see Boyd as a victim of oppression, or even ill-starred. Boudin is
acquainted with corruption, and not from the perch of a priest's
confessional. He is used to the FBI's and others' lying unceasingly;
they had lied in the Coplon case he handled. Judge Learned Hand,
in reversing her conviction, said she was undoubtedly guilty,
but that the prosecution had falsified—needlessly. Boudin does
not believe, as do the priests and nuns of the Catholic Left, that
man is redeemable, a being capable of salvation, sainthood. Boudin is a "man of the world," not of other worlds.

And Boudin treated Boyd in a way no other defense attorney
did: He treated him as an equal. Clark had treated Douglas as a
child gone totally wrong, a bad seed, a parcel of pathology.
O'Dwyer—more of the stern cleric than any he defended—
treated him as a sinner who would not repent. Boudin just took
him as he came, man to man. Boudin kept calling Boyd
"Mr. Witness." It soon began to sound like "witless." Later, he
said to the jury, "Boyd Douglas, also known as 'Z.' "

"Look at me, Mr. Witness," Boudin would say when Boyd's
eyes would scan for Lynch's signal. "I don't have to look at him,
do I judge?" Boyd would whine, the peevish child. Boudin became the tyrant father, dragging him from one squalid place to
another, to whom he sent home his .38. Boudin became the
physician holding up the hypodermic full of experiments for NIH.
Boudin became the warden of all his cellblocks; he was the elusive
target at which he pointed his Beretta.

Boudin led Boyd through another recitation about the two
phone calls Eqbal Ahmad was supposed to have made to Boyd,
the only thing that resembled evidence against Ahmad.

Eqbal was to have called Boyd a couple of hours after Boyd
had talked to Sister Elizabeth by her prearrangement. The conversation, culled from various versions given by Boyd, is as
follows:

Hello, Frank or Gary [Boyd's aliases]?
This is Egg or Eggbal. I am with Liz. Heard you received the letter about kidnapping Kissinger. I want
to discuss it with you. I want Phil's reactions. We'll

213

> plan the kidnapping depending on either your sched-
> ule or mine around Christmas. Goodbye.

The second phone call from Eqbal consisted of this:

> This is Egg. I'm calling you because Liz is tied up.
> She'll get in contact with you later. Goodbye.

The defense and Ahmad say these calls were never made. Two calls *were* made to the Lewisburg laundromat to Boyd from Sister Elizabeth. After testimony earlier about Eqbal's "calls," Defense Committee people would telephone each other and say, "Hello. This is Egg. I want to talk to you about kidnapping Kissinger. Goodbye."

Boudin takes Douglas through the sequence of calls once more, and elicits that Douglas was not surprised to get two calls, one earlier from Liz and another one later from Eqbal asking the same thing, for Phil's reactions to the kidnap plot. Douglas also says he is not surprised that Eqbal Ahmad would talk to a stranger. That if he was with Liz that he wouldn't put her on the phone. Boyd says that nothing would surprise him, after a plan to blow up tunnels and kidnap. "Don't smile," Boudin instructs. "This is serious."

Boudin goes on to list Douglas's aliases that he has used in the past and Boyd acknowledges them: Robert Hall, Meredith Dickinson, Charles Gray, Frederick Gordon, David Summerfield, Robert Blake, Donald Rogers, Carl Strand, James Scranton. The recitation of names is the stoning of Boyd Douglas. He breaks apart; little pieces of him and his past fly around the courtroom, torn batwing names flap against the ceiling. "Boyd," the cave they issued from, calls out "Boyd, who are you?" Boudin turns his whole life back on him with this recitation. Boyd squirms; the sores linger. The past year he has been living as Robert Dunn.

"How would you spell Dunn?" a reporter asks.

"Donne."

"No man is an alias."

Douglas had been denied parole at the same time his civil suit with the government was being settled; Douglas thought that the government denied him parole because he won the suit. Boudin concludes his cross-examination with the reading of a 1967 parole report on Boyd to the jury.

But first he gives it to Boyd to read, who, so he says, has never never read it. Douglas bends his head over the letter. It takes a minute or 365 days, or a mere week, and then Boyd's hands drop. The paper and his arms make a craft not fit for flight. Boudin pulls the report out smoothly from between Boyd's fingers. Arthur retrieving Excalibur.

Douglas lifts his drooped head back up slowly. His eyes come up two black suns. They beat down on Boudin. There it is: that terrible dawn.

Boudin steps out of the glare of Douglas's pure hate. He has just shown to the jury what he desired. Boyd expands and contracts; a malevolent glow hovers around him; it has silenced the courtroom. Hate that could fuel endless deceits.

Boudin reads, "The defendant thus far has made poor social adjustment after going AWOL from the military service [in 1962]. He has maintained himself with bad checks and certainly has many of the attributes of a confidence man . . ."

"Your witness," he says, concluding, to Lynch, handing him back for redirect. The pronoun was one, not of indication, but possession.

After Boyd

The war . . . rose above all from a monstrous lack of imagination.
— FRANZ KAFKA, *Conversations with Kafka*

i

Boyd returned the following morning for redirect. It was very brief. Lynch inquired of Boyd if he had a corrupt economic motive for doing what he did. Boyd replied, "I did not." He gave the same answer when asked if he did it all with an extortionist's intent. Then Lynch asked if had been employed during the time he lived in Phoenix. Boyd said that he had been gainfully employed at the Motorola Company there; he quit, though, "because of my marriage." When he moved to Des Moines, where he had stayed till coming to Harrisburg for the trial, he had worked as a men's clothing salesman for a large department store.

Lynch, earlier, inquired about a Master Charge card the FBI had supplied him with: How long had he had it? When did he return it? Who paid the bill? "The bill was sent from Omaha to the special agent in charge in Phoenix, a check was issued to cover that, rent-a-car, plane fares; to my knowledge it was included in that list of payments [admitted $9,200]." It had been returned "some time in March; I have [my own] cards now," Boyd added proudly. The FBI vouched for his credit rating?

Lynch took a few dainty steps back to his table and picked up a

sheet of paper that he held up high over his head like a proclama-
tion. It was, he explained, a letter of commendation Boyd had received from the manager of the Des Moines department store
where Boyd had toiled as a salesman. It would, Lynch said,
counter all the defense's slurs on Mr. Douglas's character. Lynch
tried to assemble his features into a sincere expression, but it
would not remain fixed on his face any longer than a stone could
hang in midair. This letter would show, Lynch said, that the
reason the defense had not questioned him about his recent life
was that he had been "hardworking and dependable." This letter,
he said, waving it triumphantly as if it were the ineluctable piece
of evidence that would settle every doubt, will attest to the
"sterling character of Mr. Douglas." When he said "sterling character," his face broke into a grin so hypocritical that he abruptly
turned away from judge and jury, and looked towards the
spectators, they being the only ones who could look upon him and
not act upon what they saw. The defense objected to the reading
of the letter of commendation; Herman sustained them.

Douglas looked shocked as Lynch pranced around the courtroom with the letter held high as if he were keeping it from someone who was trying to snatch it from him; and that shocked expression was the one that we were left with, hovering above the
empty witness chair, after Boyd stepped down from it after fourteen days.

"A great salesman! Was there ever any doubt?" William Cunningham says, in the recess that follows. "Boyd could sell ice-
boxes to Eskimos, buggy whips in Detroit . . ."

The government's case continued for six more days. More
Gauleiter FBI agents took the stand, to testify that Delaware
draft boards had been raided. A large outline map of the state of
Delaware was brought into court as Government Exhibit 73. J.
Phillip Krajewski, a very young U.S. attorney, who had sat silently
at the prosecution table through the trial, got to examine the witness about the map. "Does this map accurately depict the state of
Delaware?" Krajewski wears narrow, rectangular mod eyeglasses, blind to fashion.

On St. Patrick's Day each of the twelve jurors and six alternates
sported dyed Day-Glo green carnations. They looked like an

217

excursion group touring Atlantic City. A network TV commentator had asked his office if they'd like a St. Patrick's Day feature from the trial. The reply had been: "Only if you can get a black school-bus driver busing Irish kids."

"See him," Tony Scoblick said, indicating an alternate juror who was massively crippled. His legs totally braced, he would fold himself into his chair each day. "For our defense, we're going to cure him."

Paul J. Killion, the fourth U.S. attorney, who acted as their "go-fer," was a young corpulent man, who aped all of Lynch's mannerisms till he appeared to be mocking him, though he wasn't; he wandered about the hall outside the courtroom carrying a large blue government manual under his arm that was titled *How to Prove Federal Crimes*.

Handwriting exemplars were introduced. Father McLaughlin's was a letter about his will sent to the bishop of the archdiocese of Baltimore. Father Wenderoth's was a letter requesting from the bishop permission to be a godfather. The government seemed deaf to the innocence of the entreaties they rattled in front of the jury.

The Rochester draft-board raids were testified to; though tipped off by Boyd, the raid was allowed to occur. The Flower City Conspiracy, including the severed defendant Ted Glick, was caught in the building. "Unbeknownst to the raiders," an agent testified, "the 102s containing the names of all registrants were put in a walk-in safe."

A year after Boyd's summer and fall of informing, the Catholic Left found itself with another, Robert W. Hardy. The "Camden 28" were caught on 22 August 1971 in the Camden, New Jersey, post office building; Guy Goodwin, the original prosecutor of the Harrisburg case, the man Lynch replaced, was there in person to greet them all by their nicknames. While Boyd was on the stand, an affidavit by Hardy was appended to a pretrial motion in Camden. One of the Twenty-eight attending the Harrisburg trial said that Boyd's performance on the stand had partly prompted Hardy's affidavit; Hardy was said to have been disgusted by Boyd. Hardy's statement reads, in part, "Throughout I actually wanted to stop the action, but I think I became, unknowingly, a

218

provocateur. I provided 90 percent of the tools necessary for the action. They couldn't afford them, so I paid and the FBI reimbursed me. I rented trucks for dry runs and provided about $20 to $40 worth of groceries per week." Hardy had been an informer ("with twelve successful missions behind him") in other petty instances for the FBI; Hardy, too, was enthralled by the FBI's ethic of power, spirit, and courage. Hardy resembles Douglas in his identification with the men of the FBI. Hardy had run for a local political office and lost; he was an unsuccessful contractor, doing odd jobs and in need of money. It was loaned to him by members of the Camden Twenty-eight. His pastor, the man who converted him to Catholicism, was one of those caught and indicted. Hardy could slough his patchwork history while working with special agents, men who have never made a mistake in life, who have unblemished records. In the affidavit, he wrote that immediately after he was informed of the demise of the original draft-board raid plan, he went to the FBI office in Philadelphia. "I knew some of the agents, as I had given them tips before (but I was not a regular agent)." He could fancy himself an irregular one, though; like Boyd, Hardy has affection for guns, though the Catholic Left of the Camden Twenty-eight "were wholly opposed to the use of any force or any action that chanced someone getting hurt. At one point I tested [———] by offering him the use of my gun, and he flatly rejected it." Previous to Hardy's coming in, the draft-board raiders had been uncovered by the FBI, and *they knew they had been,* but with the same willed blindness of Berrigan and McAlister they resurrected their plans when Hardy assured them he could make it happen. Not so difficult, since, like Boyd, he had the FBI's assistance.

Hardy has the same pride in action as does Boyd. He felt he put some spine in the wishy-washy conspirators: "I had a leadership role from the first night I was in it. Many of them knew me and my abilities. It was difficult for me, because of my nature, not to assume leadership. After a short time, I was in command or at least equal to John Grady (we competed for leadership of the group), *and this is a matter of record with the FBI."* Hardy exhibits the dwarf megalomania of the neighborhood bullyboy. John Grady had been cochairman of the Catonsville Defense Committee.

After Hardy's testimony before a Camden grand jury, some macabre events occurred, the stuff of a Catholic's nightmares, which led to his recantation and affidavit. Hardy welcomed the press, gave interviews, enjoyed, as did Boyd (who had said on the stand, "All the press in the country were looking for me"), the notoriety. During an interview with a man from the Philadelphia *Inquirer,* Hardy's young son fell from a tree and impaled himself, mortally wounded. The same priest who converted Hardy and whom Hardy turned in officiated at his son's funeral. The months after the arrests were a dark night for Hardy; he swung on a Manichaean pendulum from the shadows of troubled conscience into the light of a clear conscience that this affidavit served to affect. The turnabout is a pathological one; Hardy was paid by the FBI sixty dollars a day, plus expenses. Boyd was never an Iscariot. The psychology of a Judas requires an anguish that leads to suicide. Hardy's affidavit, though, is the gnarled elder branch that held Judas's desperate rope.

Agents who surveilled Elizabeth McAlister previous to the capture of Daniel Berrigan take the stand. They report following her on the New Jersey turnpike, and being unable to keep up with her, contacting the state police, who stopped her on the pretense of checking out a stolen-car report, so they could catch up. The defense wanted to look at the surveillance reports that are filled out by agents and the prosecution objected. Boudin elicited from an agent that they contained nothing on Eqbal Ahmad: "Nothing on Ahmad since, as I've pointed out, he is a peripheral figure in this case." Lynch rose and said to Boudin, "It's regrettable the FBI wasn't following Mr. Ahmad, *a central figure in this case.*" Herman set his lips in his representation of a smile.

The black ex-seminarian who had been mentioned during the trip to Washington took the stand. He had met Tony Scoblick while at St. Joseph's Seminary in Washington; Tony gave him a chalice to sell to one of his fellow seminarians. A chalice, he explained to the court, "was a cup used by a Roman Catholic priest." On that occasion—the handing over of the chalice—they (Tony, Mary, and "a short fellow with a Boston accent") tried to solicit his participation in the peace movement. They talked about certain tactics, that Tony had been involved in draft-board actions. Lynch asked, "Did he talk about something ongoing, an action planned in D.C.?" Terry Lenzner rose: "Objection, Your Honor, leading the witness." Lynch pushes on: "Did they call it the 'D.C. Action'?" O'Dwyer leaps up: "That's not leading, that's atrocious."

The ex-seminarian said, "I thought it was a draft-board action because that's what they were involved in." In early May, he related, the night President Nixon made his speech announcing the sending of troops into Cambodia, "I was asked by Tony—though I can't swear it was Tony who asked—to drive a van and park it in a certain place." Asked to describe the van, he said it had "a makeshift back on it." Tony laughed. His panel truck was navy surplus; it is a distinctive wreck.

Lynch tries to place the surveillance at the Forrestal Building, where an entrance to the heating tunnels is located. Unfortunately for Lynch, that is some blocks away from where the van had been parked. Across the street, though, there was a building that housed Selective Service records. Asked why Tony had given him the chalice to sell, he explained that Tony was leaving the priesthood and was planning to marry. The chalice was returned unsold. It had been the chalice Tony received from his parents at the time of his ordination. Parents of a Catholic boy who becomes a priest spare no expense when buying the ornate chalice that is traditionally given as a present. They consider it to be a holy dowry. The chalice is selected, and often designed, by the young priest-to-be himself. They are one-of-a-kinds, and are difficult to sell secondhand, for each priest wants his "own," unused, chalice with which to commemorate his ordination. At a recess Tony was upset, realizing it would have made a fine exhibit. "Is this the chalice that Tony wanted you to sell?" It could have sat on the clerk's desk, golden and glowing.

GSA engineers testified about the tunnels; what they were made of, their dimensions (seven by seven), what buildings they served, where the generator plants were, from what points you could gain access, what kind of damage would be done if

221

they were blown up, and more. A reporter wondered aloud, "Do you think it's possible the defendants are learning more about the tunnels now than they ever knew?"

Two Catholic University students testified about conversations they had with Father Wenderoth: "He and Philip Berrigan had been in some buildings dressed in overalls."

"Now we know what we knew the first day of jury selection," a reporter says.

Wenderoth is reported as saying, "Danger to life; that is our primary concern," and, "Protest should show what is wrong with the war and not be alienating." The witness explains that at Catholic University in Washington, he was a member of the "Catholic Peace Fellowship," and he was an officer of the Biafra Relief Committee. "Yeah," a reporter from the Catholic University student paper said, attending for this one day, "he was the vice-chairman and the chairman left school and ran off with all the Biafra money collected."

The Catholic Peace Fellowship had meetings every Sunday that were open to "everyone." On even Catholic university campuses, such organizations are avoided by the student body and have the sodden pall of AA meetings. Out of these lethargic beds some sprouts of activism are forced up by frustration.

Lynch was getting so little from these witnesses that he didn't call the third and last Catholic University student, even after he had been the focus of a long battle over transactional immunity.

Boudin argues (without the jury present) that there are more FBI files that he is entitled to see. Lynch counters, "Mr. Boudin knows not whereof he speaks. This is a pointless and baseless motion; we have now reached the nadir." Lynch covers other ground, the possibility of a defense of entrapment, one reason the files are being demanded. "We have heard a great deal about moral witness; higher law they and no one else is privy to. These academics, Ph.D.s, have been manipulated," Lynch says, "by Boyd F. Douglas, who got his Graduate Equivalency Degree in prison. Raising the issue of entrapment is a usual procedure in criminal cases," he says belittlingly. "The Delaware raids have been proved, the Philadelphia raids have been proved; initiated by themselves and not Boyd F. Douglas. Entrapment is a common criminal defense," he says, stressing "common," and "they will have to prove facts; I detect here a slight shift of moral position on the part of the defendants now that they have taken up a more traditional line of defense, entrapment." Lynch is the practitioner of moral voodoo and the defendants feel the pins he is sticking into their images.

Menaker rises to object to a "surprise" witness. The prosecution replies that they only knew about her since yesterday. She is brought in—a young blonde, escorted by Connelly. They stand in front of the bench, a young couple about to be confirmed in Holy Wedlock by Herman.

The defense wants to question her before she takes the stand; she leans towards Connelly for protection. Lenzner makes some brusque demands. Herman says she doesn't have to talk to the defense if she doesn't wish to. Boudin comes up to the agitated crowd with its quiet blonde center. Connelly restates the judge's opinion to the young woman, but in more absolute tones. Boudin snaps at him, "Mr. Connelly, you are not in charge of these matters"—and in the next breath, as the young woman has stepped back away from the verbal swipe he took at Connelly, he resumes a mellow countenance and says sweetly to her, "Do you have any objection to talking to us?" He asks in the suave-sly manner of the negative form that allows the simple "No" to be one of affirmation. And that is what she says.

Later, on the stand, this is her story. She works in a local bank and has been reading about the trial. Some untold estimation of its progress prompted her to call the FBI yesterday with a bit of information she possessed. On Memorial Day weekend of 1970 she had been vacationing in Connecticut and had gone with a friend (who belonged to the League of Women Voters) to the annual luncheon of the Westchester Women for Peace held at a Schrafft's located in the Eastchester Shopping Center. Two hundred women were there. Bella Abzug was there campaigning for Congress. And Sister Elizabeth. McAlister gave a speech in which the blonde—whose dye-shade is called "ash"—says Elizabeth said that "she had been in contact with Daniel Berrigan; I couldn't understand how she could have been in contact with him when everybody at that time was looking for him . . ."

"It's good to see such innocence remains at large in the world," a reporter says, chuckling.

"She said they were working on something substantial, something criminal, for which they would receive substantial sentences."

"Was it a draft-board action?" Lynch asked.

"She made it clear it was not; she was evasive, but I was astounded she said that much."

Did Lynch want to counter all those blameless-faced nuns with a wholesome young lady of his own? This girl was the victim violated in every sadist's dreams. What pink ozone filled her head? What made her recall it so vividly, was that Sister Elizabeth "belonged to the same order that taught me in school; they were semicloistered then; and here she was, not even in habit, and *talking!*"

An alumna of the Religious of the Sacred Heart of Mary; little sweet ash-blonde Miss Bread Upon the Waters. Later, Sister Jogues Egan, past president of one of the RSHM schools, said as someone balefully tries to explain away a tragedy that started out as a prank, "We just taught her too well."

Father Neil McLaughlin said that she had come from Rent-a-Witness, thirty dollars a day, five cents a word.

ii

"Would it be appropriate to say that Boyd had been Molly-coddled?" a reporter queries another.

Molly Mayfield, Boyd's self-professed "handler," was testifying. "Molly" was a nickname Delmar Mayfield has had for a long time, since he was a lad. He has the body and face that attracts nicknames; he would have been an amusing-looking kid. Tall, gangly, ears sticking straight out of the side of his head; a whimsical country face.

Mayfield answers in loophole language: I can't *specifically* recall; to the *best* of my knowledge, I do not know that *of my own knowledge*. Clark asks about the explosive-manuals the FBI gave to Boyd. Molly says another special agent "borrowed them from the ROTC at Bucknell and brought them to the office in August of 1970."

Clark wanted to know why they got them from Bucknell: "Was it the only source you knew?" He showed Mayfield that they had been printed at the Government Printing Office.

He says, "You didn't doubt the ability of the Federal Bureau of Investigation to obtain these manuals for you?" Molly replied that he didn't. But, "You instructed [an agent] to get them from Bucknell?"

"I don't recall specifically if I asked him to get them from Bucknell." Clark left implied the reasons for obtaining the manuals from the ROTC at Bucknell. That would readily explain where Boyd got them and at the same time show his resourcefulness at being able to liberate explosive-manuals from the ROTC. Obtaining them at the local level would spare the special agents in charge any embarrassing explanations, if any are required, for why they wanted explosive-manuals.

The FBI, Mayfield stated, supplied Boyd with a cassette equipped with a device to record phone conversations; he was instructed how to use it. Clark questions him further on his knowledge of Boyd's criminal record. Mayfield indicated only a hazy familiarity with it. He said he could not recall specifically when he reviewed Boyd's file, and he claimed not to remember specific documents from it when he was shown them. Clark again appeared highly exasperated by this show of either incompetence or dissembling, as he had when questioning the associate warden. Lynch even addressed Mayfield by the associate warden's name. Boudin said, when Lynch corrected himself, "It's understandable."

Clark asked, "Did you prepare a report describing Boyd Douglas as an 'accomplished confidence man'?"

"No, I did not," Molly replies. He is shown a document. It is a letter to the director of the FBI. Molly says, "That *letter* does say that . . ."

"Molly is antisemantic," a reporter says. It is not a report, it is a "letter" to the director.

O'Dwyer questions him about the monies the FBI paid Boyd. What was the standard of payment? Did he know what he was getting paid for? Did he know, for instance, what the fifteen

225

hundred dollar payment he received was for? Not specifically, Molly says. O'Dwyer returned, deadpan, "He never knew how he came by this bonanza?"

"He knew he was getting paid for information received." Boyd received fifteen hundred dollars for information on the Rochester raid, but only two hundred for the capture of Daniel Berrigan, the equivalent sum of a one-dollar donation for every agent who had worked on it. Mayfield answered in explanation of this, "Boyd didn't say Daniel Berrigan was on Block Island at a specific time; he just helped.

In the case of Rochester, he told us specifically." Boyd had said he was never told that it was he who initiated, through Elizabeth's letter, the capture of Daniel Berrigan, or that one two hundred dollar payment was a reward.

In asking Mayfield why he wasn't told, O'Dwyer speculated, "Would you be expecting an argument [about the paucity of the amount]?"

Mayfield replied: "Not particularly." But what generally, then?

"Did there come a time when you recommended that Boyd get regular money for expenses and services?" Mayfield is asked. He testifies that he arranged for Boyd to receive up to one thousand dollars a month in payments and expenses for a six-month period after his parole on 16 December 1970. Douglas was to "penetrate the movement." The arrangement was approved on the same day Hoover testified before the Senate subcommittee. Under a subsequent order from J. Edgar, "all Mr. Douglas's obligations should be completed so he'd come to trial under no obligations." Boyd's contract was made and broken on the same day.

O'Dwyer asked Mayfield what monetary recommendations for payment was he prepared to make for Boyd at this time, for his services at this trial. Mayfield replies, "Sitting here in court right now I don't know the answer to that question." But, Mayfield tags on, Boyd has not been promised "one cent."

O'Dwyer questions him, voice laced with fervor: "You came through for Rochester, you came through for Daniel Berrigan, so will you come through for this?!"

Mayfield replies meekly, "He didn't know he was getting money for Rochester; he didn't know he was to be paid for Daniel Berrigan."

226

After a recess O'Dwyer asks Mayfield, "Was there a step up in activity [in your investigations] after Hoover's statement?"

"Not to the best of my knowledge," Molly says, while a grin bends his answer.

"Did you instruct him to record with his pickpack cassette after that?" O'Dwyer asks.

"What?" interrupts Lynch, "fluctuations of the moon?"

"To record whatever is to be recorded," O'Dwyer replies flatly. To Mayfield: "Did you instruct him to record any phone calls of the defendants?"

"My instructions *may have been* before that date [27 November]," Mayfield answers evasively. Mayfield is handed what he describes as a rough itemization of Boyd's expenses. Asked to refer to it, he is asked at what point Boyd asked for an increase of two hundred dollars a month.

Lynch rises to object: "He's plowing the same ground they covered with Boyd Douglas, ad nauseam."

O'Dwyer responds, "The nauseam is on your table, Mr. Lynch."

"Your Honor," Lynch squeals, "Please instruct Mr. O'Dwyer to refrain from his idea of comical remarks."

O'Dwyer continues, "In dealing with the money . . . did Boyd say . . . the increase would be justified by the additional information he would give you in regard to the case?"

"Yes, that's what the statement said."

Boudin questions Molly about his knowledge of Boyd's enthusiasms.

"Did he ask you for information about primer cord?"

"He did tell me he suggested the idea of using primer cord, rather than plastics [explosives], or TNT."

"Did he tell you that he told Philip Berrigan that a gun would be needed for the Washington affair?"

"Not that I recall."

"If you had known, would you have had the same confidence in Boyd?"

Lynch objects to what Mayfield would have thought.

Earlier, Molly had said he had "complete faith" in Douglas. Herman sustained Lynch's objection, and Boudin complained that far from being irrelevant, what Mayfield would have thought was

227

pertinent since he "is vouching for the credibility and character of an instrument called Boyd Douglas."

Boudin asked Mayfield if he authorized, or was aware of, the letter Boyd had included along with Philip Berrigan's reply to her kidnap letter. In his letter, Boyd said he could easily obtain a gun to use in the kidnapping. Mayfield said he "first heard of that letter via the news media," and that he had asked Douglas "had he written the letter and he said it was true."

When Boudin had questioned Boyd about the letter he held a piece of paper in his hand. Lynch rose, unwittingly aiding Boudin, and said, "Is he [Boudin] reading from something?"

Douglas admitted to the letter and to its contents as repeated by Boudin. What Boudin held in his hand, and appeared to be reading from, was not Douglas's letter. It does not exist.

Elizabeth McAlister destroyed it. She had told an intimate, "It was like holding something hot and horrible. I could hardly even bare to look at it [Boyd's letter]." Had she ever held something hot and horrible? What would it be? It is a description brewed in a carnal vat.

Boudin asks about the tape from which Boyd had identified Eqbal's voice; where did Mayfield get the tape? Molly replies, "It was being maintained . . ."

Boudin stops him, irritated: "I don't know words like 'maintained.' "

"Kept," Mayfield corrected. The tape had been kept in the FBI's office on the floor above. Earlier in the trial there had been this colloquy, prompted by Boudin's requests to see files:

> MR. BOUDIN: I am glad you mentioned that. I have not gotten the Berrigan files.
> MR. LYNCH: You are examining them upstairs now.
> MR. BOUDIN: I am not.
> MR. LYNCH: Your girls.

Another change in his world that Lynch could not reconcile was that two women were lawyers working with the defense; one of whom, Dee Dee Donovan, was upstairs examining the files. What he found to soothe his uneasiness and to salve the insecurities that the intrusion of women brought into his men's-bar world of the law, was the balm of contempt: "Girls."

Boudin swirled around and said sharply to Lynch, "I don't have any girls. I don't know what that expression means. I have lawyers working with me."

Boudin knows that every foul deed ever done can be sweetened by words; and this case was built on the perverting of sense, the written word of the letters. Language is corrupted only long after the heart has been.

Asked by another attorney if he had any other informers working with him other than Boyd, Mayfield replied that he did. Here is a report—unconnected with this trial—from the Media FBI internal documents, of another kind of Pennsylvania informer operating at the same time as Douglas.

> Date: November 15, 1970
> Time: 10:00 A.M.–1:00 P.M.
> Place: Chelsea Hill Farm, Upper Chichester Township
>
> Alan arrived at George's farm at approximately 10:00 P.M. George told Alan there would be a klavern meeting of Klavern #10 on Thursday, November 19, 1970, at Keystone Hall, Upper Darby, Pa. George told Alan he would show the new klan movie he bought in New York City for $300 in which it shows a "nigger with KKK carved in his chest and another nigger who was castrated by the klan" . . . this concludes this report.

"Snuff" films, it appears, aren't the sole province of an avant-gardist like Charlie Manson and his kin; the informant does not provide a review of the movie.

Boudin inquires about one of the FBI men taking quotidian notes in the courtroom. Mayfield explains he has been sent down from the "seat of government."

"Seat of government?" Boudin says, puzzled.

"That's our term for FBI headquarters in Washington," Mayfield supplies.

"Are you serious?" Boudin asks.

iii

Bringing up the rear of the government's case are handwriting and fingerprint experts from the "seat of government," FBI headquarters. They are to testify that the letters of Philip Berrigan and Elizabeth McAlister were indeed written by Philip Berrigan and Elizabeth McAlister.

"Save it for the *Late Show*," Paul O'Dwyer says, objecting. "You're beating a dead horse. We'll stipulate as to the authenticity of the letters."

It is not enough for Lynch. "I'll present my case, you can present yours." He passes out charts prepared by the handwriting experts to the jury, as efficiently as a maître d'hôtel dispensing menus.

Intermittently during the technical testimony, O'Dwyer rises. "If we're interested in facts, not histrionics, Mr. Lynch will accept the stipulation."

A letter is passed among the press, titled in the same manner as the Berrigan-McAlister correspondence; their studious sounding headings were to give the letters, transcribed by the two women students at Bucknell into Boyd's notebook, the look of schoolwork: THOUGHTS ON THE STIPULATION THAT STIPULATIONS SHOULD BE STIPULATED TO.

It reads, in part:

> . . . it is up to us to carry out the plans of the inner circles. We, fine conspirators all [here, a list of prominent members of the press corps] should contact Jill St. John to lure our angel, "Brian child," "K", also known as "someone like," to our farm near the Second White House where we can carry out our plan to blow up Henry Kissinger with primer cord, and to kidnap the Washington heating tunnels. Peace Love Boyd Z He lives Right On!

And in the lower lefthand corner: "cc: Molly."

Fingerprint experts take the stand. An easel is set up, and a ten-minute lecture on methods of fingerprint detection is given to the jury. O'Dwyer is up again: "This is all for show, a charade; to establish that his fingerprints are on a letter he wrote and sent is grossly unnecessary." It also confirms that Wenderoth's prints are on the ROTC explosive-manuals Boyd, via the FBI, gave him.

A cadaverous fingerprint expert slaps a huge blowup of a

fingerprint as he describes "friction ridges" in a training-film voice. "This arrow indicates Point A, and this arrow indicates Point B." The greatly enlarged fingerprint is a gray nebula.

Lynch, following the weeks of airy testimony, wants to leave the jury with the concrete. They have placed aside their menu-exhibits; they are ready to order.

Another piece of paper circulates through the press section. A drawing of a fingerprint, redolent with arrows, aiming at "Point A," "Point B," "Lewisburg," "Route 83."

The witness stand is vacated and Lynch says, "Your Honor, subject to the availability of [the librarian jailed for contempt] the government rests." The restoration of J. Edgar Hoover is finished; Lynch has just finished unveiling a million-dollar white elephant: this case. Look what Hoover has wrought.

iv

"Your Honor, these defendants shall always seek peace, and they proclaim their innocence of these charges. The defense rests."

Ramsey Clark sits back down, and so does William Lynch, who was halfway out of his chair, starting to protest what he thought was a continuation of Clark's "when I was attorney general" speech he had just given before the jury was brought in. In midair, Lynch looked as foolish as a floozy burst too soon from her conventioner's display cake.

Each attorney then rises and solemnly rests, each for a different defendant. Philip Berrigan rises, and the jury hears his voice for the first time, a startlingly diffident one from such an imposing man: "Since I discharged my lawyers, I'll rest my own defense."

Herman had spent the day denying motions; he considered striking the testimony of one government witness, a bomb-squad chief who said that a flashlight that had been discovered in the attic of a Delaware draft-board was indeed a flashlight. Herman also considered removing Eqbal Ahmad from Counts II and IX, the threatening-letter count and the contraband charge that accompanied it. Boudin, in a long argument for judgment of acquittal, pointed out from the transcript that during questioning about the

231

laundromat phone calls from Eqbal, Boyd gave this version of the conversation that was supposed to have ensued: "I understand that you have received *the letter of Liz's* . . ." Boudin had made Boyd repeat over and over the contents of the alleged phone-calls, and Boyd, trying to hammer another nail into McAlister's coffin, unintentionally pried open the lid of Ahmad's. Herman would not take Eqbal out of Count I, the conspiracy count, even after a detailed argument of Boudin's, and a rebuttal by Lynch, that caused one member of the press to shake his head and repeat, "Lynch, have you no shame?" Herman, in the tradition of Pilate, wants to send all the dirty laundry out for the jury to wash.

Near the end of the day, after other defense attorneys had argued motions for judgments of acquittal, Clark had risen and said, "I am shocked that the U.S. government produces such flimsy evidence on such grave charges. If this had been presented to me when I was attorney general I would never have had it presented to a grand jury. I move for judgment of acquittal."

One spectator clapped. Lynch rose and said, "I would remind the court that Mr. Clark handed down the Spock indictment."

Clark returned, "And Your Honor knows what happened to that." Leonard Boudin (who won the Spock case on appeal) rises and appears to bow to the prosecution and the judge.

Lynch continues, "Two of them were returned for retrial."

And Clark: "And the U.S. attorney had the good sense not to proceed."

Lynch: "When a man stands in court and leans on the weight of his former office to make an argument with no analysis of testimony, I think it is fair to observe that argument is less than rational."

The entire day had been spent on analysis of testimony by five defense attorneys. Lynch gave a brief rebuttal to their arguments. "What we have on trial is a cadre . . . people taking the law into their own hands . . . the draft actions were training grounds for subterranean actions . . . there was one overall conspiracy to disrupt government agencies . . . they said they wanted peace trying to sanitize the illegal means they use to obtain their good quote unquote objective." Lynch had been actually shaking. Coming to the unique laundromat phone calls, he says, "How many Eqbal Ahmad's does Elizabeth McAlister know?" And then, in the next sentence, he reveals the strange kind of logic that his apprentice Boyd had become the master of, "the circumstantial evidence allows the phone calls as additional circumstantial evidence." He goes on to praise the Delaware draft-board raids, calling them "ingenious." He can admire a crime well done, though not good intentions. "Rather impressive from a technical point of view."

There had been a recess. Herman denied the motion to introduce a defense of discriminatory prosecution. He said it could have been raised pretrial, perhaps posttrial. What motions he didn't deny, he reserved decision on.

Eqbal Ahmad had put aside his casual outfits for the first time during the trial, and he was wearing a staid black pin-striped suit, complete with a vest. He looked like a character populating the colonial world of E. M. Forster. A Pakistani immigrant ready to begin at Oxford. He was about the only clue that something special was being planned; after the recess all the defendants returned to the courtroom wearing pink carnations.

After the defense rested without presenting a defense, Lynch said, "I must say I'm somewhat surprised, Your Honor."

V

F. and I sit on the velvet couch of the mayor of Harrisburg, looking at our faces, shrunk to the size of coins, that are reflected on the many angles of the chrome spider legs of glass-topped furniture. We are wrapped in a package of pop-art graphics wallpaper. "Isn't this the kind of décor," F. says, "one usually associates with group sex?"

The weekend that the defense rested, there were two parties. One, given by the Defense Committee, is a songfest romp at Augsburg Lutheran Church, and the other is given by the mayor of Harrisburg for members of the press corps covering the trial.

233

The defendants had announced three principal reasons for not conducting a defense: The first was that they realized—but only after it was concluded—what a thin case the government had. Their early fears had generated costly overruns of estimation; they also contended that they didn't want to legitimize the charges and the entire courtroom proceedings by offering a rebuttal. And they were concerned about the FBI man taking his daily notes (though the FBI also received weekly transcripts of the trial); and if the defense presented other draft-board raiders as witnesses they feared the substrata of Resistance would be opened to still more investigation. These considerations, in the main, were eleventh-hour rationalizations. In the hall, after the defense rested, Lynch said, "If you have no defense, you have no defense."

How do you protest calumny? Tacitus has advised that it will expire if neglected. The defendants, caught in the six-pronged trap of Count I, were put in an untenable position. They could deny the whole, but not one of its parts. The draft-board raids are difficult to disown.

Later, talking with defense attorney Terry Lenzner in a bar, he outlined what the defense would have been like, had one been presented: Ex-convicts who knew Boyd would take the stand and testify that he had brought heroin and LSD inside the penitentiary.

After the cross-examination interment, the corpse of Boyd's testimony would be exhumed. An autopsy would be performed: The tissues would be examined for traces of poison.

There would be testimony about the frequency of letter-smuggling. People connected with the Rochester draft-board raid would testify that (excepting the severed Glick) they had nothing to do with the other defendants. "In fact," Lenzner said, "Liz did go up there; but they avoided her, didn't want anything to do with her. The Catholic Left, by that time, had gotten a reputation for terrible inefficiency and loose security." Philip Berrigan would not have taken the stand. "We couldn't let him do it; Phil keeps referring to 'our people,' meaning anyone he sympathized or agrees with; we couldn't let him take the stand, continually saying, 'our people' did this and 'our people' did that."

234

Tony Scoblick had said, before they rested, that he would take the stand *if* he could get it out of the building.

"The defense rests," is how it is put, but here it was more a case of the defense resting. They had put forth a defense. It was called jury selection. And, during the government's case, they introduced over sixty defense exhibits. Including a witness. Boyd, in cross-examination, was asked about a conversation he had with a young woman on the Bucknell campus, where he had regaled her with tales of his life as a young revolutionary—this before he had met Philip Berrigan. Boyd did not recollect such a conversation. A young woman was brought into the courtroom, asked to stand up, and Boyd, presented with living flesh, did then recollect her, but not the conversation. It could only be presumed that when she was called to testify she would substantiate what the defense said: that Boyd was posing as a "revolutionary" before Berrigan arrived at Lewisburg. When it had been suggested by the defense that Boyd began to copy letters, not to help the FBI, but to use in some future blackmail scheme, the judge admonished them that they better have witnesses, and Boudin assured Herman they did, that subpoenas had been sent out already. During cross-examination of government witnesses, the defense used the time for a presentation of its case so often that it prompted Herman to say more than once at sidebar, "But here again you are attempting to put your case in through cross-examination of a government witness."

"Do you know how I got elected?" the mayor of Harrisburg asks rhetorically. "Well, I'll tell you; I went door-to-door campaigning, but not when the hubby was at home. I went from ten till four; and when each of those wives went into the voting booth they remembered that nice man who called on them, and not the oaf their husbands told them to vote for. I'm sure they never even mentioned I had come by; they just voted for me."

F. puts a cigarette to her lips, and the mayor's hand, holding a blazing lighter, materializes instantaneously. "He has the reputation as the fastest cigarette-lighter in Democratic politics."

"That's how he got elected."

Some members of the press are elated, since they will be leaving Harrisburg sooner than they expected.

The mayor has sprinkled the party with his friends who would best mix with a national press corps. One woman explains the fastest route out of town is through "the ghetto." "I just roll up my windows, put the air conditioning on, lock all the doors, and drive as fast as I can. I just wish," she says, gesturing towards her husband, who has something to do with the department of transportation, "he would get the bypass finished."

"What would you think," a network sketch artist asks, "if a federal marshal came up and said a juror would like to have the sketch I did of her that appeared on the news the other night; they're not supposed to be watching the news."

"Don't tell the defense, or you'll turn into an affidavit."

"If they asked me about it, I wouldn't tell them; I'd lie."

"Well, there's one legitimate explanation—perhaps a husband on visiting day told her how nice she looked on TV."

"Well, they're not even supposed to talk about the case."

A black maid keeps replenishing the canapes. The liquor does not run dry. One journalist keeps referring to Sister Elizabeth McAlister as a "*nun*compoop."

"You know how I fixed it so I don't owe anybody anything?" the mayor asks, again rhetorically. "Well, I'll tell you: I declared myself to be a one-term mayor—that way I can't owe anybody any favors. And if they want anything out of me, I can just show 'em the door, because I don't have to be concerned about getting reelected."

A defense had been awaited with perverse expectation. And if in presenting no "formal" defense deprived those who desired that kind of spectacle, that, in itself, was reason enough. Philip Berrigan and Elizabeth McAlister at first were against resting; they felt it was their "duty" to explain their actions (i.e., the letters). They realized along with the others that the best decision was to rest; it was decided only the night before.

What was there to explain? Answers, these days, even correct answers, are no longer solutions. Elizabeth and Philip felt they should set the contents of the letters in a "context." The letters mean what they mean; people didn't desire explanations; they wanted more spectacle, more pathetic revelations, *more of the same.*

vi

Sheaves of palm blades under their arms, black-robed, faces chalked white, the first of the protesters marched by the gleaming char-glass Federal Building. Holy Week had begun. Prosecutor Lynch had said earlier in the trial that he didn't care about the planned Holy Week demonstrations, as long as the case didn't go to the jury on Good Friday and a verdict wasn't returned Easter Sunday. His fears were realized.

Summations to the jury were to begin the Monday after Palm Sunday. The Susquehanna had not been long freed of ice when the marchers crossed over it from City Island, a lozenge of earth that lies in the center of the river directly across from Harrisburg, to a rally held on the grounds of the capitol. It is a brilliant but cold day. Palms are distributed to the few citizens who watch the procession of three hundred. One man, a veteran of a foreign war, now gone to seed, heckled the marchers, until a number of them began to hand him palms. A speechless rage built as he curtly refused the proffered fronds that were then dropped at his feet. A tinder-pyre of palms soon formed; he was rigid as a saint tied to a stake for immolation. A young girl of seven was the last to try to hand him a palm, and she became the unlikely antagonist for his vented anger: "You little bastard; you dirty little cock-sucker!" Wide-eyed, the child hurried back into the line of march.

Lynch watched the march and rally from the Federal Building's front steps. During the business week, Lynch's hair has the "wet look," but on the weekend when he wears the natty plaid pants of a Sunday golfer, it has the "dry look."

Lynch would not deliver the government's closing argument; he would not have the wind for it; the younger man, Connelly, will do it; after the defense's summations, Lynch would have rebuttal, the last word would be his, since the prosecution is burdened with the burden of proof.

The two young crisis-managers from GSA have returned to shepherd the press through the final days of the trial. After they and a federal marshal explain what the procedures will be during the jury's deliberations, they congratulate the press for being so cooperative during the long ordeal.

"That's the vaseline before the screwing," a TV cameraman says. He is correct; new security measures have been instituted; pockets are emptied, the body is combed with a metal-detecting device, two poles are passed through. This had been done all along to the spectators, but the press received the treatment as a going-away present.

Connelly gives a four-hour summation. Referring to the letters, Connelly says, "It has been suggested [in Clark's opening] that these were letters sent to a child at camp; I trust that must affront your good common sense."

One evening two reporters found themselves dining at a table near the four prosecutors and they sent them over a bottle of cheap champagne. A note was returned on the back of a business card: "To the summer camp of '70: We just wrote to keep our spirits up. Abelard & Heloise."

Connelly characterized Philip Berrigan's "charitable view" of the difference between a liberal and a radical as between those who do and those who do not "violate federal laws."

His summation's unifying theme is: Boyd Douglas, more sinned against than sinner.

"For the first time," Connelly says, "on June 3 [1970], long after Philadelphia draft-raids, long after Delaware [draft-raids], long after the tunnel had been entered, the FBI first heard of the situation." Connelly reads portions of the letters; his is a more effective reading than Lynch's. He reaches the "kidnap letters" and he hopes that subjected to the heat of repetition he can forge the words around a conviction. He refers to Elizabeth's "cover letter" to Boyd that came with her letter: "*The enclosed is dynamite*—that is her own characterization—biased, hah!"

The only surprise is Connelly's continuous references to Eqbal Ahmad as "the man behind the scenes." The fact that Ahmad has been dropped from Counts II and IX seems to have increased the government's zeal to get him convicted under Count I. The reasoning behind the designation, "man behind the scenes," that is presented to the jury is this: Why we don't have any evidence against Ahmad is because he is the cleverest one of them all, this slippery camel-driver (as one of the marshals likes to refer to Eqbal) is the man behind the scenes, so far behind, so deeply involved, that there is nothing we can show to prove it. Eqbal is made out to be a one-man yellow peril. Ahmad—who never even favored draft-board raiding!

Connelly, as is his wont, blackens every patch of white he sees. He quotes from a letter of Joseph Wenderoth's to Boyd, after the first mention of the "kidnap plot" appeared in newspapers following Hoover's leaks. "Boyd," Wenderoth wrote, "I feel responsible for you." Connelly reads it again, as if it is an acknowledgment of Dr. Frankenstein's. "Two weeks to go!" Meaning, two weeks before Boyd's upcoming parole. Wenderoth did feel responsible; he just didn't know to what dire portals it led him. "The leak?" Connelly asks. "The leak of what? The charges in this indictment!" His end is his beginning: Boyd.

He tells us Boyd has been in no trouble since his release. Considering Boyd has been in the protective custody of the FBI, that is not much of a feat, unless, perhaps, Connelly, equipped with proximity, has a dim view of their ability to contain him. "Well, I say to you, we didn't pick the witness, Phil Berrigan picked the witness. I don't mean to abandon Boyd Douglas," he says, abandoning the lectern for the first time. He approaches the defendants. Can one truth stain a falsehood till it too has a shade of truth? Does it dilute the first till they both share the same weak hue? Connelly finishes with this mix. "Boyd Douglas had no real home. He had a high-school equivalency degree obtained in the penitentiary. He didn't have the association with the intellectual community (as these defendants had); instead he had seven years in the pen." Connelly names each defendant, beginning with Ahmad, and lists their credentials. "A scholar, a Ph.D., an educator, teacher . . . and," he says, ominously, ". . . a planner." To each one he does this, not humbly washing their feet, but stopping nonetheless. He points at each of them, the finger of shame. "And then, finally, there's Philip Berrigan, the priest of peace, whose most famous letter is his kidnap letter—a disparagement of true peace, an obliteration of the distinction between violence and nonviolence."

Connelly is in the center of the courtroom, his arms folded against his chest in the gesture of a maiden proclaiming her disputed virtue. Connelly, the volunteer for this prosecution, has his moment of triumph over the nuns and priests of his youth. "These people found good in Boyd Douglas; they didn't try to bring out the good in him," he says, tripping in the dark over the fact that only the divine can be guilty of divine disobedience, "but they didn't use the good in him. They wanted to use his criminal background." Connelly's voice is rapt with indignation: smite, smite, smite, it echoes off the lizard-green walls. "And now they come before you and say, 'Oh, find us innocent. *Damn* Boyd Douglas.' I say to you, don't be a part of it."

He makes a tragedian's exit immediately out the courtroom's front doors, though not pursued by a bear.

Later, William Cunningham, the Jesuit defense attorney, says, "Not since the time of Solomon have so many been slain by the jawbone of an ass."

vii

"The war has destroyed us and our children; yes, us and our children."

Leonard Boudin's is the penultimate summation of the five the defense will present to the Harrisburg jury; none of them know just how intimately Boudin is speaking. "Let me show you a picture of a wonderful girl," he said to a friend at another time, whereupon he pulled from his wallet a picture of his young daughter, Kathy. It was a composite of mug shots taken by the Chicago police department. The same pictures that are on the FBI's poster; Hoover placed her on the Most Wanted list shortly after her father became involved in the Harrisburg defense.

American parents have orphaned so many of their children to the war that now nears a decade in length. This war has entailed harder sacrifices than any that has come before it—not in physical deprivations, surely—but because it has never been seen so clearly just how much is being sacrificed for so little. The evening at the suburban church for the performance of the play of the trial of the Catonsville Nine, a man, agitated by the remarks of William Kunstler during a question-and-answer period, yelled out, "The war is immoral only because we haven't won it." A man quizzed for jury duty here had said that he didn't favor total pullout from Vietnam because that would imply that it "all had been a terrible mistake." It is between those two manacles our hands are chained. Paul O'Dwyer had preceded Boudin and he gave a long summation that included reading from the over-ten-thousand-word correspondence all the parts that had nothing to do with draft-board raiding or kidnap plots. No one has escaped this war. There is no avoiding the injury of war made so personal as Vietnam; at best you are left with choosing not the wound but the scar.

"The war has destroyed us and our children." When O'Dwyer finished the long, racking recitation and returned to the defense table, Boudin said to him, "If my daughter ever comes before a court of law in this country, I want you to be her lawyer." O'Dwyer also had the distinction of being the only lawyer threatened during this long trial with a contempt citation.

Boudin continues, "My words are supposed to have some effect on you. I came to Harrisburg with a terrible sense of trepidation. I did not feel the people of Harrisburg, very frankly, would appreciate the issues in the case, no matter how educated they were . . . we spent an arduous month selecting a jury that we hoped had an understanding of human beings, a knowledge of technical problems, of complexity—if not of law—life, who could tell the difference between ideas, aspirations, discussions, protest, and entering an agreement to commit a crime. The reason the case is so complicated is Count I of the indictment. The rest is peripheral."

Indeed, Connelly in his long summation, never moved from the mare's nest of Count I.

Boudin stressed that the six offenses charge under Count I must be considered as a single conspiracy ("Entered into a single conspiracy to commit six offenses against the U.S.") and so considered, the jury should examine the relationships of the three different types of crimes—"three basic categories, three different kinds of things"—draft-board raiding, blowing up heating tunnels, and kidnapping Henry Kissinger.

"Now I come to my point. Where that is done [establishing a conspiracy] A., they have entered into an agreement, and secondly, there is a relationship between the overall agreement." He questions whether Eqbal Ahmad would have anything to do with draft-board raids, and then he says, that is why "I adopted Joseph Wenderoth, since he seemed to be on opposite poles . . . to raid draft boards is a very different kind of agreement than to blow up heating plants, which cause injury, and to kidnap Henry Kissinger . . . excuse me for a moment," he says, and goes to the table and takes a pill. What a thing to watch, a man literally dying while he tries to save the freedom of others; later, in a melancholic mood, Boudin says to a few associates, "You have witnessed the last year of my life."

Boudin continues with his complicated and subtle argument. Throughout the trial the prosecution talked down to the jury while the defense tried to educate them. Boudin makes it clear that taken together the three basic categories make a triad impossible to hear. Boudin moves on to Boyd.

"My clients still have charity, I have none . . . if you took him literally, what an arid field of human life! The only thing Boyd F. Douglas talked to these defendants about was bombings, tunnels, kidnapping. Philip Berrigan never talked to Boyd F. Douglas about peace, the world, life. After the sacrifices Philip Berrigan has made? It is incredible! Even if that man had no criminal record, even if he did not talk like a machine . . . he added names that he did not give before the grand jury, he just spilled them out; he will also elaborate on the conversations he had with Father Philip Berrigan.

"There was a man of violence in this case; they never used a gun," he says, indicating the defendants. "These were the people Boyd F. Douglas handed manuals, offered a gun, his admission by letter."

Lynch's carefully made indictment had begun to crumble earlier.

242

One of the charges under Count I did not become a law until October 1970. Boudin points this out and says, "Is it conceivable that they entered into a conspiracy on January first to break a law passed on October fifteenth?

"Let us assume these people went into the tunnels, let us assume there were discussions. At worst it is preparation, *investigation.* They are charged not with attempt, but with agreement.

"I thought this was an area where a lot of ideas were in the air; international incidents, terrible things were happening; everyone of us were talking about these problems and what should be done."

He describes a lunch at the Harvard Law School where Boudin had been a visiting professor the previous year; he and colleagues discussed various felonious ways to protest. "When we left that table do you think I felt guilty no matter how hare-brained some of my colleagues' schemes were. We all spin these fantasies, these hopes; the realities of the world made us look for ideas. These people [the defendants] have commitments; I have no right to talk about the area of religion. How is somebody moved? How is somebody from this proposed idea, plan—how are they moved into action? It required Boyd F. Douglas to try—he failed—to move them to action, to a firm commitment." Boudin talks about telephone calls that Boyd Douglas originated which had been brought out in cross-examination.

"Came these incessant calls to action, even though he never moved them to agreement. They were the acts of a provocateur who also deceives his masters." Boudin mentions the fifty thousand dollar Molly letter. What will Boyd receive for his services at this trial? "That remains to be seen."

"Now I want to come to the kidnapping; I thought it was ludicrous; the last of the six objectives."

He focuses on the calls Boyd was supposed to have made to his client, Eqbal Ahmad. " 'Dr. Ahmad will call you in two hours.' " (He quotes Elizabeth to Boyd from Boyd.) "What kind of mad world is this? Why would Dr. Ahmad call a man he never met? He knows something about police agencies and so do I. Again the answer is simple. This man [Boyd] saw his quarry, thought he might be worth more than fifty thousand dollars. What gossamer. Incredible."

Lynch had, after Boyd left the stand, tried to place Ahmad's second supposed call on the twenty-first of August, not the twenty-second. Boudin asks the jury, "Why was an effort made to have the date swing to the twenty-first?" In a pretrial motion for a bill of particulars and a subsequent court order, some of the overt acts listed in the indictment were elaborated. The two rara avis Boyd-calls of Ahmad's were listed as two overt acts. The bill of particulars reads, "The Government shall specify the telephone that Eqbal Ahmad called at Lewisburg on August 20th and the person he called at that number. Answer: The telephone number believed called was 717-524-0038 [the laundromat]. The person called was Boyd F. Douglas, Jr."

Boudin answers his own question for the jury, of why Lynch tried to move the date of the second call to the twenty-first. "Boyd F. Douglas hadn't decided when the call was made, if it was made, and where it was made. Now I come to the killer," Boudin says, and reads from the bill of particulars the government's answer to the same question asked of the August twenty-second call, Overt Act No. 26. " 'Answer: The telephone number called is unknown to the Government. The person called was Boyd F. Douglas, Jr.' The telephone number called is unknown to the Government; I accept this as coming from reputable members of the bar." When the bill of particulars was filed, well after the indictments, and many months into Boyd's protective custody with the FBI, Douglas had not yet sorted-out his skein of testimony.

A lunch recess interrupted Boudin's summation. Outside demonstrators surged around the Federal Building. A liturgical service was being held on the Walnut Street entrance. A gallon bottle of wine was being passed through the crowd; the throng knew nothing of the summations that were being given inside. Large, colorful felt banners were hoisted over the heads of the sidewalk congregation. One proclaimed: IF WE KEEP QUIET THE STONES THEMSELVES WILL SHOUT HOSANNAH.

244

viii

"As the last lawyer to sum up I want to give you some overview," Ramsey Clark says. Boudin had concluded his summation centering on Eqbal Ahmad. "Why is he charged with being the 'man behind the scenes'?" Boudin says this was necessary to establish "a foreign international influence; a foreign-devil theory that can be passed on to judges and juries. He is the object, or he can infect the people." Boudin cites cases from the past, and then the Ellsberg case where the government added, as an unindicted coconspirator, a Vietnamese, a former South Vietnam official. "Here," Boudin says, "it is Eqbal Ahmad, of Pakistan."

Clark continues: "Sixty-four witnesses have spoken to you from that witness stand. Twenty-one were agents of the FBI . . . nine policemen . . . sixteen officials of various sorts . . . seventeen ordinary people. Sixty-three witnesses, and what do you know? Nothing. There is no way you can torture out of those sixty-three witnesses, that will support this indictment. Not that it wasn't fun. But the case is built on Boyd Douglas and the letters. A man you can't believe and letters that don't say what they were tortured or twisted to say." He refers to Paul O'Dwyer's reading from the missives. "If you weren't moved you're harder than I am. The letters were noble. This is the first time and I hope the last that the U.S. government tries to prove a case by dramatic readings, instead of evidence . . . then the indictment, never doubt the importance of the five to ten counts. Ten years for taking out a letter, if that's the law. Five years for conspiracy. *That's* dynamite. What does it mean? Why all these months? The FBI was reading the letters before. If you cannot control a prison situation, what can you control? Count Four," Clark says (announcing the only contraband count that could be said to have happened "without knowledge and consent of the Warden"), "happened before June 3, 1970. That magical day they say that Boyd Douglas became an informer. They say about May 24th [the date the letter was taken out]. The carrier. That's the offense. The U.S.

attorney declined prosecution [of Boyd, at the time the FBI stepped in]. No—it was put in the Daniel Berrigan file. 'We opened an informer file on Boyd Douglas.' Took them to April 30th to think of that [the inclusion of that particular letter came in the superseding indictment]. Because of entrapment. Somehow let's get one before June third. I don't believe that date. On the study-release, one prisoner out of eighteen hundred? Ten years out of school. I say there is no evidence by which you can find beyond a reasonable doubt. You have a U.S. attorney behind you [the one who declined to prosecute Boyd when he admitted to the FBI he took out the letter]. Declined the Prosecution of the man who did it.

"These threatening letters weren't in the first indictment [Counts II and III of the superseding indictment]. The draft board raid happened; beyond a doubt. Five hundred people knew, she [Elizabeth, in a letter] said. If it's true as Boyd Douglas says, that Joseph Wenderoth told him [about a specific raid] why [was there] a hundred agents to look for Daniel Berrigan, but not one to stop a crime? You'll just have to muddle through it yourself. Where is it? The agreement. If there is a conspiracy it must be in the mind of Boyd Douglas, but I couldn't even find it there.

"History will never remember those board actions. This is a kidnapping and bombing case. That is how history will remember it.

"If individuals can't grow and change, all is lost." As an example, he describes himself when he was a "young lawyer in Texas," hearing about Martin Luther King, Jr., and the first freedom rides and boycotts and thinking to himself, "that's silly"; and when he heard of the draft-board raid at Catonsville, asking himself, "What are they doing?"

"Now I think I know," he says, and "I say, 'God bless them.'

"Big kidnapping plot. Two letters. That's it.

"Why does Philip Berrigan have to be made the keystone? Reflect on where Boyd Douglas was. They say he [Berrigan] was directing this from prison. Who was his line of communication? Boyd Douglas. The Count of Monte Cristo couldn't do it. He [Berrigan] could care. He could suffer through Cambodia and Kent

State. Spend a big chunk of his life in prison since he put his life on the line.

"The only thing worse to believe than that he could direct people on the outside is that the government let him. And the only way Philip Berrigan could do it was to believe that the government just stood there and watched him do it and provided the agent, Boyd Douglas. It can't be.

"More distressing is the government's effort to paint these people with a passion for peace, violent. There's enough violence in the world." Clark brings up Boyd's University of Wisconsin bombing statement. "The animus that shows. Philip Berrigan never saw Boyd Douglas after the explosion. 'What's one life in Wisconsin when so many are killed in Vietnam'—he just volunteered that, it just came out.

"Warmakers cannot stand those who seek [peace]," Clark says unmoralistically, just stating a fact. "What will happen if we are afraid of peace and freedom? You have power. Look for the truth. Find it. Grapple with it, and hold it with all your strength.

"The truth is, that these charges are false. And these defend-ants—driven as they are—have only a passion for peace."

Two of the women on the jury openly cry. Later, an ac-quaintance gushed to Clark's wife, Georgia, "Ramsey didn't seem to do very much during the trial, but when he did do something, he was very effective." And Georgia Clark, her high Southern accent tuned to its most acerbic, replied, "My dear, perhaps that's just what he intended."

Lynch followed immediately with his rebuttal. It had been his task from the inception of his involvement in this case to put on it a presentable face. Now he had to wipe the tears from the faces of the jurors and try to return their features to a grave countenance.

"When the law is against you, you argue the facts; when the facts are against you, argue the law; when both are against you, attack the prosecution."

Lynch has bared his teeth; after the long interval of Clark's sonorous voice, Lynch's is all static and scratchings; juror no. four, her white hair a smooth turban, who had sat through the trial with the dignity of a suburban Nefertiti, winced at the sound of his voice.

"Please don't take seriously the law you've heard the past one and a half days.

"I wish the chart was still here," he says, referring to the blackboard Terry Lenzner had filled up with the names of people mentioned associated with draft-board raids. The names of the defendants were the ones least mentioned. "But it's been taken and erased. The chart says: Prosecute the Donkeys, don't prosecute the leaders. This indictment says: Prosecute the leaders in the conspiracy they were engaged. There are the gurus sitting behind counsel."

An enlargement of a telephone "mark sense" card is carried into the courtroom. F. says, "Is that Lynch's wife's rhythm chart?" Lynch points out a number of long phone calls from Elizabeth McAlister's phone to the Weston, Connecticut, phone where Eqbal Ahmad had been staying for summer vacation. One call is for twenty-six minutes. Lynch implies that such a lengthy long-distance phone-call could have only been spent on kidnap-conspiracy plans. He refers to Boyd's Wisconsin statement: "It wasn't such a big lie . . ." There is laughter; he realizes what he has said. "It wasn't a lie; even so," he stumbles, flustered; he rambles on that men have faults, can we condemn "lesser mortals." Realizing he is running in the wrong direction, he says, recovering, that the defense attorneys "never, never turned him from the basic thrust of what he testified to—the letters that corroborate Boyd Douglas to a T." He reads again from the kidnap letters and Berrigan's remark: " '. . . the first time opens the door to murder. . . . when I refer to murder it is not to prohibit it absolutely . . .' That really sticks in the craw of the defense; we have his words. You will look through the Bible until your eyes go blind and never find anything that says: This is not to prohibit murder absolutely."

Red-faced, angry, puffing, Lynch, in this strange emotional case has violated, even more than the defense attorneys, that old lawyer's chestnut: Never become emotionally involved. Lynch's emotions are engaged second to none; he truly believes them guilty, though not of just what is charged in the indictment.

"When you talk of betrayal," he says, referring to Boyd, "let's talk of the betrayal of leadership. Student raps. What kind of betrayal is that? Students should be led to 'zap' Selective Service boards on campuses? What are they doing? Playing handball with the consciences and ideas of these students?"

And, needing so much to personalize his attack, to square off with an opponent, a rival he can meet on a dirt lot, he says, "Who gave him"—meaning Father Berrigan—"the mandate? Who elected him?" And, from a case tried in ancient Athens, he pulls: "If you were a parent of a child at that school, wouldn't you shudder?"

Most of his rebuttal has been extemporaneous and therefore hit and miss, a brawler's wild punches. But the end has been prepared. It is on index cards which he consults. It is an address to the fears that feed repression: "A society bent on destruction could find no better way to do it than to let each person decide what law he will obey in response to his higher motivation, for law of necessity must bind us all." Law of necessity? Law of the jungle. Who penned that, I wonder. Spiro Agnew's ghostwriter? But William Sebastian Lynch knows the law of necessity; it has regulated his life. I had been trying to think of something nice to say about him, after being in his company so long. I have often wondered about the banter between victim and executioner. It happens here often. It is the acknowledgment that they are both acceding to higher laws. I come up with a compliment. William Lynch went through Harvard Law without acquiring any affectations. Quite the contrary, Lynch saw there and elsewhere the mess slick, pampered men can make, that waits for someone like William Lynch to come in and straighten out. He has the insight of a valet who knows his master's disgusting habits. All his life he has gotten nothing without a great deal of work; nothing has come too easy, been delivered up to him, in payment for an especially pleasant face of a Paul O'Dwyer, or the entertaining wit and intellect of Leonard Boudin, or a family with a former attorney general in it like Ramsey Clark. No, Lynch prospers by doing what no one else particularly wants to do; and by fixing what his nominal betters have screwed up. He buries skeletons; someone was required to clean up the fetid mess of J. Edgar

249

Hoover's aged incontinence. William Lynch, I salute you. It is those who are willing to be meek that will continue to inherit some of the world.

"There is only one conclusion you can rationally draw," he tells the jury now. "These defendants are guilty."

And perhaps, since he is a practicing Catholic, Lynch might find some merit in the notion that one day in a future untold he might awaken and find supernaturally impressed upon his body, a strange blessing: Boyd Douglas's scars, a modern stigmata.

Verdict

I may not understand good and evil, but I know what pains me and, I pray, others.
—EDWARD DAHLBERG, *The Confessions*

i

Islanded, they rest on a raised back of earth, while the river flows in two strands around them. They might as well cling to a dead rock cleaving space since they hail a corpse's rising. The sky at dawn is preternaturally pink. Gathered at the water's edge, they appear to be a sect which practices baptism by submergence. Glum exiles, they sing hymns, the grateful and perplexed survivors of an unseen deluge. Harrisburg's skyline, viewed from City Island, is substantial; a black chunk of the Federal Building can be distinguished. Easter Sunday daybreak service; a group of younger celebrants have broken off from this group and moved into a wooded area where they have begun their own service around a campfire. Theirs is a more fundamental worship. Awed by the elements, they stare transfixed by the flames. They wrap themselves in gypsy blankets and softly chant rock lyrics.

Across the river, in the city, the traditional observance of Easter Sunday, of hats and frocks, will take place; but not yet. Harrisburg sleeps; spirits still walk. They dance in a circle, pass to one another crescents of oranges. It is the feast of the Resurrection.

Holy Week concludes. The eyes of the stragglers that are left behind here are glazed with the look of those who endure

251

marathons. Holy Thursday, the day of the Last Supper, the jury took the case. After Judge Herman's charge a woman from UPI composed her lead sentence: It won't be a Good Friday for the Harrisburg Seven if Judge R. Dixon Herman has his way. Herman had to settle one question with his charge to the jury. Whether to be found guilty on Count I the defendants, or any one of them, must have conspired to do all the six offenses, or only one. S. John Cottone, the U.S. attorney from Scranton, held the view that the jury could return a guilty verdict and no one would know for which of the six offenses they were condemned. The defense held that to be found guilty all six offenses must be proved. In his charge Herman told the jury both things, letting them settle it.

The press realized that they might have been forever reporting the charges wrong; instead of conspiring to raid draft boards and blow up tunnels . . . it should have been to raid draft boards and/or blow up tunnels, and/or kidnap Kissinger. It was now all in the hands of the jury.

Good Friday found five hundred demonstrators in front of the rear entrance of the New Cumberland army depot, which, among other things, repairs the large troop helicopters damaged in Vietnam. The object of the demonstration is to plant a "tree of life" on the grounds of the base. Permission to enter the base and plant the seedling was requested.

"The gate is locked and will remain locked."

"Then would the guards plant the trees?"

"The answer is negative."

A handful of VVAW and one young woman scale the ten-foot hurricane fence topped with barbed wire and run towards a likely plot. FBI agents run after them, armed with cameras, snapping their pictures like humane hunters on a photographic expedition. One veteran holds aloft a tiny seedling, its roots wrapped in clear plastic, as if it is a fire bomb ready to be tossed.

Others in the crowd debate whether they too should commit "CD," as they call civil disobedience. An olive-drab bus comes up from the far reaches of the concrete runway that the cyclone fence traverses and debouches a contingent of MPs. They are a stern, healthy lot, uniform in height. The tall fence, subjected to a storming by members of the crowd, begins the queasy undulations of a suspension bridge just before it crumples. A medley of tormented "Nos" wells up out of the crowd. The fence settles back to its rigid shape.

The MPs have lined up on a flatbed truck right in front of the fence. They are exposed to a bit of psychological warfare from the handful of Vietnam Veterans Against the War who are present. "Join us. Join us," they yell. "We won't court-martial you. We've got a lot of good dope." A young woman takes a turn at the bullhorn and says, while her voice breaks with sobs, "Does it make you feel good to kill women and children?" Does it make her feel good to ask? Receiving no response from the MPs, she says ambiguously, "Fuck 'em."

Those who scaled the fence with the trees have returned; now others, one by one, go over and offer themselves to the fiery furnace, the olive-drab bus which serves as a detention center. Each does it in his own form of somnambulance, entranced by the unreality of arrest. They go over singularly, with a polite space of time between each, so each can have the stage for a moment, while they receive their award. A young blond boy of around ten has gone over and planted a tree. The MPs will not move to arrest him—he is made invisible by his age— he runs around and plops a tree in front of a second group of MPs who stand in formation, at parade rest.

"If that was a Vietnamese kid, you know what would happen to him," a Vet yells out, "He'd have a can of peas in his head by now."

One young man who has been working for the Defense Committee for the last three months goes over; today is graduation day for him, he gets his diploma in Resistance. He is an awkward youth and has trouble getting across the fence. He lacerates the palms of his hands on the barbed wire; he falls to the flatbed truck on his knees, rests there a minute crying, the tears are a sluiceway that are meant to wash out the gold of his courage. He fears arrest but will court it. On his knees shaking with woe, it is the posture of a man, not in valor, but remorse. A soldier weeping at the carnage he has caused.

From a nearby hilltop three gold-braided officers watch behind sunglasses.

It is three o'clock, the hour of Christ's last words: Consummatum Est. The curtain in the temple is rent; the earth quakes; the dead walk. The demonstration breaks up. The olive drab bus speeds off with its passengers. The demonstrators wander away from the gate like the crowds dispersing from the top of Golgatha. New Cumberland Army Depot: the place of the skull.

At this hour the jury has sent a note to Herman: "There is considerable confusion and difference of opinion among the jurors with reference to the meaning of conspiracy as it relates to the indictment."

Those who have risked arrest have been taken to another entrance of the base and released without being charged.

And those here on City Island this Easter morning have the exhaustion of miners who have not been able to rescue their buried comrades.

Christ has risen. Philip Berrigan does not rise from his seat when the jury, later this day, finds him guilty on Count IV, the contraband letter sent out before Boyd teamed with the FBI. The jury had sent Herman another note: " . . . after long, serious, and conscientious deliberation . . . [we] are unable to arrive at a unanimous verdict on nine counts of the indictment." Herman returns them to their deliberations on the remaining nine counts, citing the length of the trial and the expense involved, and the unlikelihood that "a retrial would get a better trial."

ii

The press waited through the seven days of the jury's deliberations like men and women made homeless by a freak of nature. No one strayed too far from the Federal Building. There would be less than fifteen minutes in which to get into courtroom no. one after the jury announced it was ready. The attendance of the press at the trial was like a barbell: It swelled at both ends. The TV networks had sent down tape machines that would speed

254

transmission of the outcome. They ran continually, test patterns fixed on their monitors. A bored technician draped a foldout nude from *Playboy* magazine over the test pattern. A taut papilla filled the tiny screen.

Filled with expectation, reporters pace, maternity-room fashion. Some, exhausted by anticipation, just sit along the halls. Card games start; betting becomes fatalistic. Doom leaks into the sealed building like carbon monoxide. Since the guilty verdict on Count IV came in, the press assumed that the continued deliberation is focused against those holding out for acquittal. It is expected that the others are trying to break their conviction. Frozen in time, guided by the hand they have shaped themselves around for the last three months, the press forms its own tribunal and tries one of its company. A young reporter had come in the middle of the trial, who had told a few reporters conflicting stories about his background. He was patronized by the prosecution, allowed into their rooms on the tenth floor, and given their copies of daily transcript to read. He told stories of being up there; one of a time Lynch came in at the end of court, told a subordinate to get Mardian on the phone. In the other room, there was an extension phone; the intrepid young reporter lifted the phone and overheard the conversation. "How'd it go?" he said Mardian asked Lynch. "A toughie," Lynch is said to have replied. The dialogue which followed seemed authentic; Lynch would say, "a toughie." But the tales he told about the prosecution, learned through his privileged access, were just tidbits. Boyd-bait. What was he? a few members of the press wondered. The press room, with its telephones and wire machines linked to every media connection throughout the world, was a space station of orbiting information. Calls were made. It was quickly learned his credentials were bogus.

Had the press for the past month harbored its own Douglas? He had said he was filing daily stories; in his typewriter there was a sheet of paper, on which was typed, over and over, in the manner of Sirhan Sirhan: HARRISBURG, HARRISBURG, HARRISBURG.

He was summarily expelled by GSA, who removed his typewriter and tape recorder from the building. He was up on the

255

tenth floor at the time and was not seen again by anyone. Immediately after the purge a marshal announced that the jury was coming into the courtroom.

iii

"Most certainly the system works," a drunk tells me, referring to the spate of editorials that have appeared immediately upon the results of the hung jury on Counts I, II, III; Philip Berrigan and Sister Elizabeth McAlister have each been found guilty of four and three crimes of passion, respectively, on the contraband Counts, IV–X. "It works all right. If, first of all, you are charged with an indictment that is essentially false, you spend a half-million dollars in your defense, you have a cause that rallies thousands of people around you, you have over a dozen of the best lawyers in the country, one of whom is a famous constitutional lawyer, another one of whom is a former attorney general of this fair land, you have also an unhostile press covering it, you spend four weeks handpicking twelve individuals—and if all this is part of the system, you stand a fifty-fifty chance of getting a hung jury." My interlocutor refills his glass. "Just between you and me, the FBI is such a lame-assed organization that they wouldn't know what time the film starts at the Senate [the local movie theater] if they didn't have an informer in the ticket booth."

Holy Week pilgrims added up to a little more than three thousand souls the day of the climactic Saturday rally. A separate and unconnected event billed as "the Seventeenth Annual Christ's Ambassadors Youth Convention," arrived in Harrisburg the same time, and it brought six thousand whey-faced Jesus advocates, none of whom were aware that there was a trial of Christian radicals going on. On Wednesday of Holy Week the Federal Building had been rung by a human and metal chain. Arrests were made; young seminarians predominated and served out five-day sentences. Fort Lauderdale, Florida, the perennial resort for senile spring-vacationing college youths, reported their largest crowds ever this past week.

Twice, the jury had read to them the judge's charge on conspiracy; on the fifth of April they sent in their next-to-the-last note: "Do we find some of the defendants guilty, if we have evidence that they have conspired to commit a, b, c, and f, and *if* we cannot find enough evidence that anyone conspired to commit d and e in Count I." D and E refer to the explosives and tunnel charges.

Herman had received another note, the day before, the anniversary of Martin Luther King's assassination, the wording of which indicated that he had sent them an oral message through a marshal. Herman saw this and he emitted his little nervous laugh, followed by interior dyspeptic explosions which often pouched his cheeks. He had not told the defense attorneys about the oral message. Boudin questioned him then about its contents, since all messages to the jury were to have been in writing. Herman said it was only to inform them that they would be called in when the defendants and attorneys were assembled. "Could it have been more than that," Boudin pressed, regarding any messages at this critical time as highly suggestive and sensitive. "Could Your Honor have told them they would receive further instructions, as the note from the foreman suggests?"

"Possibly. Maybe," Herman replied. Possibly. Maybe. Herman was imitating Boyd.

Wishing to halt this questioning, Herman said impatiently, reaching for the first available cliché to indicate he didn't want to keep the jury waiting any longer: "Nothing further you want to say; good, we just can't leave the jury hanging . . ."

Realizing he just said what the defense thought was his true desire, he appended, after an abashed silence, ". . . in midair."

With the jury present, he reversed what he had said the first time they indicated they were hung; you are "not to be concerned with the cost or length of time of the trial. If you were hopelessly deadlocked, the court would have no choice but declare the jury deadlocked."

The foreman replied ominously that "during the past two hours progress had been made."

The jury, it was later learned, did not compromise on the convicting of defendants, but on Counts. At the end, they were

257

10–2 for acquittal on the conspiracy and threatening-letter counts, but chose to convict Berrigan-McAlister on the seven contraband counts.

Over the defense's objections Herman answered Yes to the abcfde question. The jury retired once more; the defendants and attorneys, as well as press and spectators, rose in obeisance, indicating a perhaps-never-realized homage to the power that the jury now had. Sister Elizabeth had gotten a severe Jeanne d'Arc haircut, a drear going-to-jail style.

I had long since grown disconsolate over the fact that I could tell from twenty feet whether or not she had tears in her eyes; they would brighten, filling with fluid, become a pond dazzled with sunlight. Her eyes at such times would be pierced with a dozen sharp needles of light.

Dear Reader: Be sure that I realize I am dancing on these people's graves.

Eqbal, on a previous evening during the week of deliberations, gave an enraged speech, in which he listed six different kinds of trials he saw possible. The first was a confessional trial in the style of Catonsville and Socrates; the second is an attempt to prove innocence; the third a confrontation trial like the Chicago Seven where you say, basically, Fuck you! The fourth, a political-legal trial; the fifth a noncooperative trial in the spirit of Gandhi, and the sixth, a revolutionary trial in the manner of the Reichstag fire and Castro. "The tragedy of this trial," Eqbal said, was "we started with no. four, good, hard legal defense, maximum concentration on the issues, then we shifted to no. five." Leaving the church, it was heard said, "The tragedy of this trial is that it shifted from two-to-six to one-to-three to four-to-five."

After the jury was dismissed, deadlocked on Counts I, II, III, Lynch's first comment was, "No comment." A few reporters went out to the Penn Harris Motor Inn and watched the jurors depart from their home of ten weeks. The van that brought them to and fro had the paper that covered the inside windows ripped down; they were finally given a view on their last ride back. Juror No. Four, who appeared so aloof and stately, now looked humbled by an impatient husband leading her quickly to their car. A newsman asked, "Could you spare us a couple of minutes?" Her husband replied angrily, "No, *we* can't."

When the defendants left the Federal Building that final day, a small group of supporters applauded as they came through the doors. The hollow clapping might have been the diminished echo come thousands of miles of the bombs from the B-52s that had begun to fall that day on North Vietnam.

iv

It did not take long for Harrisburg to grow back over the paths cut by the trial. A week after the trial ended, this notice appeared in the local paper, buried in the middle of an AP dispatch devoted to different subjects:

> —A lifetime pension of $22,409 was approved for U.S. District Judge R. Dixon Herman, who presided over the conspiracy trial of the Rev. Philip Berrigan and six other antiwar activists, which recently ended with a deadlocked jury on the main conspiracy charges. The award was based on Herman's prior service as a state judge and legislator and supplements his current $40,000 annual salary.

In an uncertain world Herman is secure; his daughter had said that he had worried that the length of the trial might curtail his hunting and fishing weekends.

Shortly thereafter this information appeared in the New York *Times:*

> Robert C. Mardian, a conservative who has directed the Justice Department's internal security division for the last two years, resigned to work in President Nixon's reelection campaign. He is said to have decided to quit because he was not named Deputy Attorney General after Richard G. Kleindienst was named to replace John N. Mitchell in the top spot in Justice. While in his post, Mr. Mardian increased the size and aggressiveness of the internal security division, but many of his initiatives—such

as the attempt to stop publication of the Pentagon Papers, the conspiracy trial of the Rev. Philip Berrigan and his antiwar followers and the wiretapping of domestic radicals without court approval—did not fare well in the courts.

As Lynch might have said, they were all "toughies." It is good that men like Mardian have a place to go—back into advertising and the challenges of reelection campaigns.

And what of the defendants? Fathers Joseph Wenderoth and Neil McLaughlin return to Baltimore and their duties as diocesan priests. Eqbal Ahmad and his wife and newborn child were contemplating a vacation on a plantation in the southern hemisphere. Elizabeth McAlister along with Sister Jogues Egan went back to their apartment in New York and business with the order of the Religious of the Sacred Heart of Mary. What would her sentence be? One year suspended?

The last sight of Elizabeth in Harrisburg was her backing a rent-a-truck, big enough to contain the contents of a hundred draft boards, into a "No Parking" sign. It twanged like a struck tuning fork. Tony and Mary Scoblick, the only defendants without an institution to return to, went back to Baltimore to visit Mary's gravely ill mother. Since they had been awarded pauper status by the court for the trial, they had been living better than ever before, Tony had said. The Reverend Philip Berrigan, S.S.J., was returned to Dauphin County Prison, eventually to be transferred back to Danbury Federal Correctional Institute to continue to serve the six year sentence he received for pouring blood on a cabinet full of 1-A draft records.

And Boyd F. Douglas, Jr.? The FBI hadn't, at the time Molly Mayfield was on the stand, decided what Boyd would get for his services at the trial. Boyd, on his own initiative, and through intermediaries, tried to interest *Life* magazine with his story; *Life,* just then emerging from their dealings with a more hightoned specimen of Boyd's brotherhood of con men, Clifford Irving, did not want anything more to do with dubious memoirs. It is fitting that the real gods, in this case the plutocrat Howard Hughes, ground Boyd's hopes of lucre to dust.

The pilgrims had long departed the city; the Defense Committee had broken up and dispersed. The houses were returned to their landlords, except for Green Street, which is the last to go. There is a dinner and "liturgy" here tonight. The tenants of Green Street, all of the trial of the Harrisburg Seven that remains in the city, have invited over a Catholic family, the wife of which had showed the house some kindnesses by bringing over a few cooked meals during the trial. They were returning her consideration. Her husband was an obstetrician; they had two young boys and an adopted daughter. There are some Catholic mothers I know who feel impelled to haunt disaster with hospitality; this one, also shared the habit of other Catholic women, who, whenever the conversation should happen to swerve accidentally to a woman's sexuality, champions her own by saying, "Well, just look at all the children we have."

William Cunningham, the Jesuit defense attorney, was visiting with Philip Berrigan at Dauphin County Prison and when he returned he would perform a liturgy, or rather, mass, for that is what it was.

The day Leonard Boudin left we talked about the jury. The mother of four conscientious-objector sons was one of the two who wanted conviction; a sense of irony should have foretold that possibility. Because of their church affiliation their CO status was an authoritarian and not a conscientious choice. The other who desired conviction, Juror No. Six, the owner of supermarkets, wanted it for every defendant, on every count. He had wanted to stand up during his last minutes in court, he announced later, and say, "I voted guilty on every count and I want the world to know. And then turn and face the defendants and say, 'May God have mercy on your souls.'"

How did he get on the jury? Boudin mused. The defense had learned he was a "staunch reform Democrat." The government had counted on getting twelve just like him. "In that crowd of forty-six [from which the twelve were picked]," I said, "someone was bound to slip right past everyone; he was your Jack Ruby." Then I remembered why he did get on; he had made everyone in the courtroom laugh with his joke about golfing. The laughter bespoke a humanity that could be trusted.

The mother, here at Green Street, tells about shopping at Mary Sachs, a fashionable downtown department store, where a sales-girl told her that they were glad the trial was over, since most of their good customers had been afraid to come downtown during the trial. " 'But the kids that came here are so nice,' the salesgirl had said, 'they hold the door open for you and everything.' "

Father Cunningham returned; the liturgy began in Green Street's living room. Seated on the haphazard furniture of Green Street, the linoleum far from the gleaming marble of the Cathe-dral of Mary Our Queen, I attend my first mass in a decade. Songs are sung, one of the young women of the house plays her guitar, the antiphonal responses come forth, bits of poetry are recited.

James Joyce has said that he lived only to die a bad Catho-lic. Joyce was a victim of the Church; I, in many ways, am its victimizer. It had been a gray proctor, but had given me gold, frankincense, and myrrh. The Church is tenacious and even after you leave it, it still claims you, forever branded with a hyphen: ex-Catholic, lapsed-Catholic, renegade-Catholic.

"I wish," Father Cunningham says, as part of the introit, "in almost a felonious way, that Philip could be here with us now."

Father Philip Berrigan, S.S.J., mastermind, peace-plotter, con-vict, felon; a man whose qualities can lead you to heaven, but a man, who, with another inclination, you would just as glad to tag along with to hell. How far have we come that today a man of plain common goodness is a moral paragon?

One of the obstetrician's sons, a curly-headed eleven-year-old, irrepressibly trying to please, as I did when his age, says, "I think we should offer our prayers for the astronauts who are going to take off tomorrow for the moon."

Has time moved at all? There I sit fifteen years ago. Praying for the astronauts! When will he be shaken from a childhood as placid as mine—his family's station wagon parked in front of Green Street, his strict and god-fearing parents.

"And I think," he goes on, "we should also pray for vocations to the priesthood and sisterhood."

His parents beam proudly at him. What kind of priests and nuns will replace the bats in his belfry? So different are they now from mine, yet will it matter a cubit?

262

We go into the dining room. Loaves of freshly baked bread are on the table. A water glass full of red wine waits to be consecrated. Transubstantiation. The longest word we knew as children. The conversion of bread and wine into the body and blood of Christ, only the "accidents" of bread and wine remaining.

Pieces of the loaf are broken off and passed around. Why didn't the government withdraw from this trial? Why didn't they withdraw from Vietnam?

Father Cunningham says the words of consecration, holding a plate containing the tufts of bread. "This is my body. As this bread is broken so my body will be broken for you tomorrow. Remember me."

Does the country mind spending millions of dollars to conduct a sham trial? That waste, that excess speaks of tremendous resources, great stores, inexhaustible supplies. It—like the great sums lost on war—paradoxically whispers to them: life. The pinched amounts a welfare recipient receives are scorned and hated, for that shriveled dole speaks of death and want. The Death Empire worships life, too, though from another source.

Father Cunningham blesses the wine: "This is my blood, that will be spilt for you tomorrow. Remember me."

And the Catholic Left? Broken by the mortar and pestle of this trial, it now resembles the rest of the movement that gave it birth. Small groups of people without media leaders.

I swallow the bread and drink the wine and it does not go down easily; everyman's heart is his own Gethsemane. The months spent with these people have been enriching; it is not a boast that can be made too often.

The liturgy concluded, one of the radiant young women of Green Street asks, "Can we be dismissed in peace now?" The mass ends with the words, not yet spoken, "Go, the congregation is dismissed." Another amends it to, "We should be dismissed in hope."

Father Cunningham, attuned to three months of trial and more, patiently awaiting a resolution yet to come, gives to all surrounding the table an injunction—given regardless of all the evidence to the contrary. "Yes," he says, "you can go; but you are to be sentenced to hope."

Epilogue

At the end of the street the Federal Building is on, the good citizens of Harrisburg have erected a small monument in the narrow park that runs along the bank of the Susquehanna. It is a white, six-foot shaft of granite with bronze plaques at the base, which read, in part:

> TO THE BI-CENTENNIAL COMMITTEE
> Beneath this monument is a container of letters written by area residents to their descendants.
>
> It is our fervent hope that you will bring them to light during 2060, prior to your bi-centennial celebration, sort them out and again inter some of them along with your own for evaluation by future generations.
>
> May God guide your endeavors!

Buried there in that quiet earth would be the most fitting place for the letters of Philip Berrigan and Elizabeth McAlister. The sky is not benign and the earth above is not still, yet perhaps their brave and foolish letters could slumber peacefully in that ground.

O America, how little you have to fear from your sons and daughters, if your revolutionaries have to witness so much and agonize at such length, before they will strike out at you!

Harrisburg, Pennsylvania—West Barnstable, Massachusetts
January–June 1972

264

Afterword

Jonathan Swift (1667–1745), late in his life, leafing through an early work he had written (*A Tale of the Tub*), exclaimed, "What a wit I had then!" When I look back at my Harrisburg book forty years later I realize not that I was once so full of wit but how I was certainly the right author for the right subject. I was, in the early 1970s, a friend of Diane Schulder (now Abrams), who was one of the lawyers involved in the case. Diane is Jewish and I was raised Catholic, and she kept asking me about her Catholic clients and their motives. I would supply answers, and she kept saying, "You should write a book about them," and I did.

The book, as they say, was well received. I was only twenty-six when I wrote it, quite naive, though I didn't think so at the time, and its reception then didn't surprise me. You write a good book and people pay attention was my attitude. What could be strange about that? Well, at the time, the *New York Times Book Review* was edited by John Leonard, now, unfortunately, deceased. Leonard was interested in books concerning the Vietnam War, then being waged at high heat, including books about the antiwar movement that was trying to bring the war to a halt. So the *TBR* gave my book, and another volume on the trial, a substantial review by Garry Wills. And, eventually, the *Times* put my book on its "New and Recommended" list and in its notable books of the year compilation.

Garry and I had sat side by side for a number of weeks in the windowless courtroom in Harrisburg; we were in a small pool of writers who weren't writing on daily deadline. We were writing for so-called journals of opinion and were an eccentric bunch: Garry, myself, Francine du Plessix Gray, Paul Cowan (also, alas, deceased), and Ed Zuckerman, editor of the *Harrisburg Independent Press*, a creation of the Harrisburg defense committee.

I had never taken a journalism course, and for my first week in the courtroom, I just sat and listened. There was a long period of jury selection going on. It is often remarked that the Harrisburg case was the first time experts were employed by the defense to study the jury pool to help select a favorable panel. I don't recall a team of experts around, but there was Jay Shulman, a rumpled sociology professor, on the scene; nonetheless, he did spawn a lucrative new business, though Jay seemed to be working on his own (he may have shanghaied a few of his students), a large, bearded, bear of a guy, with an easy laugh and definite opinions. But the jury still ended up with some ringers. I knew I was there to do journalism, but I thought of myself coming out of the eighteenth-, nineteenth-century essay tradition, someone in the mode of, say, William Hazlitt. The Harrisburg trial, for the three months it went on, was the biggest thing happening in the States, so newspapers and magazines had sent their best people to cover it. Homer Bigart, the famous World War II reporter, Champ Clark, and other senior members of the country's press corps were there. It was quite an education for me, being a member of that distinguished corps of forty members of the national press.

Finally, I noticed that everyone else in our section of the courtroom seemed to be taking notes, so I found a stationery store and bought a number of stenographer's notebooks. Each had an ad for pantyhose as the first sheet of paper. That was a sign of the times. I filled over fifty of them.

Back in 1972 I was living on roughly $300 a month. That now seems fantastical (and it seemed fantastical then, too.) A $2,000 advance from my publisher, Thomas Y. Crowell, funded me. I had bought a trench coat before I left New York and wore it more or less every day, looking like my idea of a foreign correspondent; and I had found a hundred-dollar apartment downtown within walking distance of Harrisburg's federal building.

Those were the days. I was two years out of graduate school and had been living on a tiny fellowship at the newly begun Fine Arts Work Center in Provincetown, Massachusetts, from which I bolted in January and to which I returned after the trial was over (in April) to write the book, which I did in three months (July); the book itself appeared three months later (October). One eerie moment for me was seeing an ad for the book in *Publishers Weekly*, with a title, the present one, which the publisher had given it, embossed on a book cover, before I had actually written a word of the book. I intended to call it *Sentenced to Hope*.

After the book came out and the *Times* (as well as other outlets) had made a fuss about it, I was the toast of the town for a few months, though as I was going out to fancy literary parties at night, I spent my days doing a manual labor job in the South Bronx, working at Feller's Scenery Studio. Though the book was praised, there had been no great rush to the bookstore by buyers. That, too, did not surprise me. My book was, as it was put, a *succès d'estime*. The presumed audience wasn't Catholics but those interested in radicalism, primarily Jewish readers. Catholics weren't then the largest single religious group found in higher education—not yet, in any case—but soon they were, and the Catholic audience has grown over the decades. My joke back then was that I wouldn't have read the book had I not written it.

Though I labored in the South Bronx, I was occasionally offered other employment. A publisher, not Crowell, offered me $50,000 in 1974 to do a Patty Hearst book, shortly after she was kidnapped (they assumed she would be found and the perpetrators caught and tried). I, amazingly, turned it down. I didn't want to be typecast as a trial author. Had I known how that case would play out over the years, I might have been more interested. But I wanted to finish my first novel, since I never considered for myself the life of a nonfiction book writer. (My dream had been to become a novelist.) My first novel came out in 1974 (*The Meekness of Isaac*), and I fell, simultaneously, into teaching—teaching, ironically, journalism, plus creative writing. It's become obvious over the years that I have never been the best steward of my own career.

But what of the New Catholic Left?

Though the government "lost" the trial of the Harrisburg Seven—achieving only a hung jury on the major conspiracy counts (10–2 for acquittal) and convictions on the minor "contraband" counts, the smuggling of letters in and out of prison, for just two defendants (Philip Berrigan and Elizabeth McAlister)—the government actually won the trial, accomplishing what it wanted to do, by toppling the Catholic Left from its pillar of moral superiority.

Public opinion—whatever small part of the public that was paying attention—certainly noted that the trial had ended ambiguously, without vindication for either side, but the public also absorbed the message that the priests and nuns involved no longer seemed exactly like saints and had if not abandoned their commitment to nonviolence at least flirted with it, coming closer to the other protest movements of the time that had taken on violence as a tactic, such as the Weathermen.

The paradox made visible was this: by the end of the Vietnam War the most successful antiwar protest group still standing was the Vietnam Veterans against the War. It is a long, strange war that puts up the men who had fought it as the most effective protesters against it.

Originally, the Catholic Left had scored a substantial victory with the trial of the Catonsville Nine, the protest action itself, and the play and movie that resulted from it. There had been a number of draft board raids in the late 1960s, a clot of them that alarmed the government, but the ones that garnered the most publicity involved the Berrigan brothers, Phil and Dan. (The Boston Five draft card burning case of 1968 set the stage for further prosecutions, since it established a precedent for going after leaders rather than followers.) But even then, the seed of violence was planted in the draft board raids at Catonsville (and even earlier in the case of the Baltimore Four, another less-covered draft board action). In order for the Catonsville draft files to be burned, they had to be procured, and instead of breaking in at night and getting them, the group took them in the daylight (for better press coverage) and had to push aside the women who worked at the draft board. It was a puny amount of violence, but since the Catholic Church is tied to so much symbolism, doing symbolic protest almost always requires artifacts, something to work with. In Baltimore, blood had been poured on the files, but inside the draft board office itself. Blood, paper, fire. Catholics are used to having one thing turn into another. It's the basis for much of the church's rituals.

So, it seemed like a leap, but not that much of a leap, for Philip Berrigan and a couple of other defendants to contemplate more complicated actions, scaling up to violence against property, not people. Though people are hardly absent from property. So, heating tunnels in Washington were investigated, kidnapping Kissinger was discussed. One successful action prompted dreams of other, larger ones; it was hard to retain stasis. They wanted to "up the ante," as Daniel Berrigan has said more than once.

The civil rights movement already had a track record of nonviolent protest. The Reverend Martin Luther King, Jr., was the legitimate American heir to Gandhi; the example of the freedom riders bestirred the country in the early 1960s, and King and other groups who fought for civil rights, fought nonviolently and, ultimately, effectively.

Their vein of Protestantism eschewed a lot of the redolent symbolism of the Catholic Church. No mass, only services. No adoration of the Eucharist, no conversion of bread and wine into the body and blood. This led to a critical difference in behavior; it actually made embracing nonviolence easier. But Catholics revered their symbols, and the Catholic Left wasn't any different. Pouring blood, burning draft files, were all rituals they couldn't avoid or abandon.

Such actions all had their camel-nose-under-the-tent aspect when it came to violence. A little something physical was required to get things going. The Catholic Left wasn't necessarily in competition with the civil rights protest movement, but it took King a while to turn his attention away from his cause to the Vietnam War. And he began to address it publicly only the year before his death in 1968. But the Catholic Left was, like King's movement, religious at its core, with priests as prominent figures, as King and others in the civil rights movement were ministers. Again, they all gained moral authority from their professions, which often brought along skills at leadership. But the Catholic Left quickly became identified with the Berrigan brothers, and the mixture of the two brothers' temperaments made a powerful brew. Philip was forever the man of action, champing at the bit, whereas Daniel was more contemplative, though not chary of acting—his period underground post-Catonsville was proof enough of that—but in combination, they did set up, if not polar opposites, at least a demonstration of the tensions within the movement. Nonviolence or escalation? Symbolic acts, or bold acts?

The civil rights movement, too, had its contending sides, including those who wanted more than nonviolent protests, such as the Black Panthers, who took another stance. And, of course, there was Malcolm X, another religiously oriented figure, who had moved from violence toward nonviolence but was killed before any actual transformation showed itself.

It is difficult to do a thumbnail sketch of the evolution of the protest groups of the 1960s and 1970s, but not impossible—it is even harder to condense forty years into a few pages, but here goes. The civil rights movement coincidently shadowed the history of the Vietnam War, starting slowly in the mid-1950s and developing throughout the 1960s, ending with the fall of Saigon in 1975 and the fading of the black power movement. And that pivotal decade of the '60s was marked with individual and group violence, beginning with the assassination of a president, John F. Kennedy, by a former Marine, Lee Harvey Oswald. President Kennedy had to be dragged into the civil rights fight by the earliest protestors at the start of the '60s, culminating in the violence wrought upon the freedom riders of 1961. King, though not an instigator of the freedom riders (that was the Congress of Racial Equality [CORE]), lent his presence to them, since they professed his nonviolent tactics.

Though the Vietnam War, in the early '60s, still involved a mere handful of American advisers, Kennedy was already dealing with the botched CIA invasion of Cuba and the creation of the Berlin wall and the Cuban missile crisis that followed. Before Kennedy's assassination, Vietnam was on the back burner of the American consciousness, but there was plenty of violence to go around.

But the combining of the two movements, civil rights and anti–Vietnam War, came about with the coincidence of the two later assassinations, those of Martin Luther King, Jr., and Robert Kennedy in 1968. Lyndon Baines Johnson had undertaken both causes: civil rights legislation was passed in 1964, and the escalation of the number of troops in the Vietnam War began (thanks to the Gulf of Tonkin resolution) the same year.

It is hard to minimize the military atmosphere of the late sixties. The collapse of the Soviet Union had not yet occurred and the Cold War atmosphere was acute. As for the Berrigan brothers, I assume they thought that nonviolence, ultimately, would not necessarily end a war, though they must have seen it had resulted in victories for civil rights. Civil rights, unfortunately, seemed an easier sell to the American people. But war—as many have noticed (beginning with Randolph Bourne in

1918)—is the health of the state; it keeps the armaments industry humming and imposes a certain military discipline on the citizenry. It is difficult to remove that dark engine from any nation, or, at least, our nation, begun with armed revolution and the suppression of native peoples, and in its entire bloody history, now revered by our present-day tea party advocates. The idea of demilitarizing our country is one of the most laughable tasks on the face of the earth. Imagine what the unemployment rate would be if the United States got out of the arms business?

The Cold War did a lot for education in our country, the space-race part especially: the Sputnik moment made it seem we were behind the Soviet Union in technological know-how, and so generous amounts of money flowed into higher education. Kennedy wanted to go to the moon and back by the end of the decade, but his space-race challenge had more effects on earth than on the moon. And though the demographics may have forced the fact in any case, the 1960s saw the number of people in institutions of higher learning triple. (In the decades before it had never even doubled.) And the country got to see what you get when you educate so many of your young, so quickly.

You get protest movements, you get a high enough percentage of young people who will be altruistic and involved, courageous and stubborn. Off they went, to the civil rights movement, the antiwar movement, so men like King and the Berrigans had recruits for their causes, followers for their talents at leadership.

For a while, the rise of protest groups of the young mystified and then angered the powers that be. Demographics may be destiny, but those in authority certainly wanted to put a stop to the rebellious, activist youth. The Cold War ideology still alive then in the FBI and the CIA let them think of the protesters as spies in the heart of the country and they were dealt with as such, with wiretaps, surveillance, informers, agents provocateurs—the whole nine yards of Cold War techniques.

While a small proportion of America's youth went a'protesting, another portion (with some overlap) headed off in the direction of the summer of love and/or Woodstock. (This part of the youth culture did spawn some of its own trials, but of the Charlie Manson sort, when hippies began to haunt the imagination of the middle class, with youth cast as vagabond killers, as the members of the Manson family actually were in

1969.) All of this "rebellion" did not happen without notice. Members of the power elite decided they couldn't have succeeding generations get too much smarter, and have so much free time and life choices, so they set out slowly but surely to make education more expensive; they under-funded it and did their best to saddle college graduates with so much debt that they needed to get jobs immediately, if they could find one, to pay off their debts. It took nearly four decades, but they have more than suc-ceeded. The question is asked, Where are the young protestors? The tea partyers had to be invented to fill the vacuum in the streets, as geezers displaced the young. Two recent exceptions have brought out the young: the pro-union rallies in Madison, Wisconsin, and the fledgling Occupy Wall Street groups.

A melancholy gathering took place shortly after the Harrisburg trial ver-dicts, when Elizabeth McAlister came to talk to some of the defense com-mittee kids who had worked so hard during the trial, getting the word out, organizing events, and the like. I was the only journalist in the room. Elizabeth looked distracted, worried (she had been convicted on minor contraband counts), but she said a few words, and the strangest ones were when she said for the first time that she understood why women were starting to protest, what the grievances were that feminists felt. And that was about all she said, a nod to the nascent feminist movement, the one that would begin and then replace both the civil rights movement and the anti–Vietnam War movement, after the war in Indochina concluded in 1975. (And I certainly took some criticism from women friends for my reference to "the Avis girl," in the second line of my book's first chap-ter. Even I was behind the times.)

For the Catholic Left, the Berrigan circle part of it, their movement, because of the trial, would disperse in disarray. What seemed to announce that discombobulation most poignantly was Elizabeth's arrest for shoplift-ing, as *Time* reported it on September 10, 1973:

> Elizabeth McAlister, an ex-nun and the wife of Antiwar Activist Philip Berrigan, and Sister Judith Le Femina were shopping at the Sears, Roebuck store near Glen Burnie, Md. When they left, the store's detective said, they took with them, without paying, a $20.99 handheld electric power saw, a

$6.90 package of sandpaper and a $1.90 package of picture hangers. Charged with shoplifting, the pair gave their address as Jonah House, Baltimore, a commune established by Elizabeth and Philip Berrigan for members of the peace movement. . . .

The country as well was falling apart in any number of ways at the time. The Watergate caper had happened in the summer of 1972 after the trial was over—and I have always regretted not mentioning it toward the end of my book (p. 260, first edition), when I discussed Robert Mardian's resignation—but it was outside my time frame: the Watergate burglary appeared to be a typical Mitchell/Mardian bag job. Nixon had been re-elected in a landslide against the antiwar candidate, George Mc-Govern, in November of '72, but in short order, Nixon's hold on power began to unravel, as the White House's involvement was revealed with the break-ins at the Watergate complex and the doctor's office of Daniel Ellsberg, the provider of the Pentagon Papers. Fulfilling that awkward cliché, the White House was being hoist with its own petard. All the conspiracy prosecutions they had originated against the ranks of the antiwar protestors (scores of grand juries and nearly a dozen trials) had prepared the larger public for a conspiracy trial against themselves. It had been an education for the public, all those prosecutions.

By the time congressional impeachment proceedings against Nixon started in 1974, the Ellsberg trial had collapsed in scandal, after most of the mischief the White House engaged in had begun to come out. The boil had been lanced. The Camden Twenty-eight draft board raid trial of 1973 had ended in acquittal, a post-Harrisburg win for draft board raiders. The Camden Twenty-eight had a sympathetic judge, as well as their own informer, an agent provocateur named Robert W. Hardy, a fellow defendant, though at the time so much was going on it wasn't covered extensively. (But in 2007 a documentary film on the trial was released.) At the same time as these events, FBI offices in Media, Pennsylvania, were raided and FBI internal documents were released—a minor WikiLeaks event in a Xerox age, compared with the release of the Pentagon Papers in 1971. Congress finally shut off funding for the Vietnam War, and it came to an end in 1975, ignominiously, as our military fled the region, pushing helicopters off ships into the deep blue sea. (The draft, too, had ended by then, after switching in 1973 to an all-volunteer system.) But it wasn't the only thing that ended—the war, that is. The antiwar movement came to a screeching halt, too.

The end of the Vietnam War is what allowed the seventies' protest movements to shift almost entirely to the personal, the leftover business of various civil rights causes: the women's movement, the gay rights movement, issues that are still alive and not entirely resolved today. And those on the Left who were already committed to violence and stayed violent as the war wound down became ludicrous. The Weatherman faction had gone underground, occasionally blowing up a bathroom in a public building. A California group, the Symbionese Liberation Army, grabbed the heiress Patty Hearst in 1974, ostensibly to highlight the mistreatment of the poor by the rich (not an obscure thing, even then), and demanded the Hearst family feed the hungry. The SLA became a blueprint, unfortunately, for a number of fringe groups, offering an unstable amalgam of white college dropouts and black men with criminal records. The SLA looked like a cartoon version of the Weatherman faction, but eventually the remnants of the Weather group ended up looking like a cartoon version of the SLA. When the last hold-outs of the Weather people emerged to public view it was during a murderous rampage in Nyack, New York, in 1981, the robbery of a Brink's truck and the subsequent killing of policemen at a roadblock, which resulted in one of Leonard Boudin's last trial appearances, when he helped defend his daughter, Kathy, against charges of capital murder.

For as much as the Left was the dominant force in the world of protest movements from the end of World War II to mid 1970s (roughly, from the Rosenberg case of 1951 to the end of the Vietnam War), the Right has dominated the protest terrain since then. Civil rights and antiwar protestors were the story for three decades until 1975. (The "Left," pre–World War II, was largely the Communist Party–dominated Left, with more doctrinaire fights between Soviet-dominated party members and native socialists; after the greatest generation, it more or less became thoroughly Americanized.) The last three decades have witnessed a turnabout.

After the Harrisburg trial, the New Catholic Left became the New Catholic Right. Again, a lot of subtle things account for that change, but some are not so hard to see. The rise of Ronald Reagan heralded the switch, and Jimmy Carter's one-term presidency is instructive. Carter was a victim of the peace in Vietnam, insofar as the economy no longer ran smoothly on guns and butter. By 1975 the boom years were over. The economic restructuring left Carter with high inflation and limited oil supplies. Gas lines and the bottom line undid him. There is a parallel here with the situation of our current president, Barack Obama. Jimmy Carter suffered a backlash for being the president presiding over a country that had lost a war; a substantial portion of the country felt further victimized by the bad economy, stagnating wages, gas lines, and Carter's talk of wearing cardigan sweaters and lowering thermostat settings, and so forth. His handing over of the Panama Canal, the Iran hostage debacle, and his amnesty for draft resisters were all things that didn't endear him to the more martially inclined of the citizenry or to the corporate behemoths of the military-industrial complex that politicians are beholden to. The rise of Reagan and Bush (thanks to both inflation and interest rates under Carter hitting 18 percent) altered the landscape and paved the way for the American Right to gain power. A new sort of conservative American "exceptionalism" would rise from the ruins of the Vietnam War's end.

But the Carter administration did signal the global realignment of the post-Vietnam world. The Iran hostage crisis of 1979 was the harbinger of the geopolitical shift. Indochina would recede and the Middle East would step forward. Oil (which began to stand in for the industrial part of the military-industrial complex) and the economy became prominent in the public's consciousness and in the world's. Reagan's elderly cabinet of Cold War and CIA has-beens began a variety of illegal escapades that would outdo Richard Nixon's earlier schemes. Central America and the South American drug trade became entwined with the Middle East conflicts during the Iran-Contra period of the mid 1980s. And then the former head of the CIA, George H. W. Bush, became president for one term, following the old Soviet model, in which the head of state security became president, and our country got used to the spectacle of governmental lawlessness, followed by congressional hearings, spectacles that replaced trials for public entertainment. With so many heavy hitters and government officials testifying under oath, the minor law-breaking of antiwar Catholics demonstrating against nuclear weapons was hardly considered news.

Meanwhile, in reaction to the appearance of women's and gay liberation, all happening on the periphery of the public's attention, counter groups were established. Large right-wing foundations and like-minded CEOs began to fund all manner of right-wing think tanks and protest organizations. The anti-tax forces assembled themselves, as did foundations dedicated to ending Social Security and Medicare, such as the Cato Institute, begun in 1977 by one of the now notorious Koch brothers. And the legalization of abortion in 1973 (*Roe v. Wade*), gave fuel to the creation of the largest Catholic protest movement, the antiabortion, or prolife, movement, even though, at the beginning, it was largely an evangelical, white, male, Protestant movement. The Republican years of the presidency, the Reagan-Bush, then Bush-Quayle, of the 1980s and early '90s let all these movements take root. What derailed this Republican supremacy in the executive branch was the eccentric presidential run of H. Ross Perot, which allowed Bill Clinton to assume the presidency. There were two trials that occupied the public's consciousness during the Clinton years: O. J. Simpson's and Clinton's own impeachment. Trial reporting changed forever with the Simpson trial. Traditional trial reporting more or less stopped and was turned over to television, and the "reporters"—more commentators—on trials henceforth were lawyers, which always produced a conflict of interest, as a special kind of moral hazard informed their coverage. And for our recent wars, television networks have hired retired generals to report and comment, another blow to journalism as a whole. The cult of the expert, which had flourished in journalistic circles since the 1980s, had its downside. The Harrisburg trial was one of the last print-only trials.

Cable television was in its infancy in 1972, and few (or none) of the events I wrote about in Harrisburg were recorded for television. Once, I did see a man I took to be an agent of the FBI (or some branch of intelligence) filming a demonstration outside the federal courthouse with a small camera, an expensive object back then. He was tall, fit, and wearing a suit, but he also sported cowboy boots. Camcorders didn't come along till the 1980s, and in the early '70s, though parents might be filming children at home with 8 mm cameras, there wasn't much private use of them to cover public events. Court TV was begun on cable in 1991. CNN had televised a sensational New Bedford, Massachusetts, rape trial in 1984; since then television has co-opted trials as entertainment, and there have been fewer trial books like mine published. That absence is sometimes filled by the occasional decent documentary film.

The start of the Clinton administration was both inauspicious and prophetic. In February 1993 the World Trade Center was rocked by an explosion, and soot-blackened faces emerged on television screens from one of the Twin Towers. Two days later four federal agents were killed while raiding a religious compound, that of the Branch Davidians, outside of Waco, Texas, and by April 19 fire consumed the compound, killing men, women, and children. Some twenty years earlier there was a precedent: a good many members of the Symbionese Liberation Army were also consumed by fire, during a shoot-out with police at their "safe" house in 1974. Burning draft files had long ago receded as effective protest.

During 1993 two more predictive events happened. In Somalia, American soldiers were dragged through the dusty streets, and one captured soldier, Michael Durant, was videotaped by his captors and shown worldwide. In September 1994 a small plane was flown into the White House by Frank Corder. A suicide mission, it did little damage, but it did show how easy it was to fly a plane into the White House. Then, two years after the Branch Davidians' immolation, Timothy McVeigh's rental truck bomb destroyed the Murrah Federal Office Building in Oklahoma City. At first, Muslim terrorists were suspected, but then the disaffected Army veteran was apprehended.

So fierce was the determination of the right wing during the Clinton years that they discounted Clinton's abdication of the economy to the Wall Street barons, allowing the financiers to do almost everything they wanted, including wholesale deregulation of the industry. The radical Right still treated Clinton as an illegitimate president, managing to turn a cheap real estate deal into a sex scandal, and then finally actually impeaching him, though they did not succeed in having him drummed out of office.

But the impeachment did affect the voter's judgment of Clinton's vice president, and Al Gore managed to lose the presidential election in

2000, even though he won the popular vote. But Gore, it was clear, never had his heart in the postelection fight, as the forces of George W. Bush obviously did. Bill Clinton's true legacy is the George W. Bush administration. After two terms of that, we were able to elect the "anti-war" candidate in 2008, one who then continued his predecessor's two wars. And who would bother to ask, by that point, whither the Catholic Left?

As Carter dealt with an America wallowing in post-losing-war blues, President Barack Obama has had to deal with the collapse of Wall Street and two unpopular wars, as well as the prevailing atmosphere of vulnerability established by 9/11, and the legacy of fear fostered by the George W. Bush administration. Obama was, lest we forget, the antiwar candidate. During the last few months of the 2008 campaign, Obama unleashed a powerful nostalgia for the bygone sixties generation and its children. But the eventual right-wing backlash of 2010 was fueled largely by the same constituency that had hounded Carter: racists and anti-immigration forces, and the whole panoply of right-wing Astroturf protest groups spawned by the economic upheaval.

The religious antiabortion forces had more or less taken over the strategies of the Catholic Left shortly after *Roe v. Wade* was decided, bringing along the same mixture of symbolic protest that put them on the road to violence. Those on the Catholic Left watched with great dismay, if not horror, over the years, as the antiabortion movement adopted the protest tactics of the Catholic Left. Instead of draft boards, it was women's health clinics that were targeted, and eventually attacked. Pickets acting as roadblocks, harassment of women who sought the services of the clinics, "nonviolent" interventions with foul-smelling chemicals to render the clinics inoperable—all the variations that were developed during the draft board raiding period of the Catholic Left.

Men ran these protests, and the women of the Catholic Right didn't seem to chafe at this. Then abortion providers were attacked, and eventually killed, by other men, zealots who often claimed religious motivations.

The Catholic League for Religious and Civil Rights was founded in 1973 but was more or less moribund until the newer wave of right-wing groups and their funders emerged in the early 1990s. The earlier incarnation of the Catholic League was a supporter of school vouchers, and by the time William Donohue took over in 1993 (finding a high-paying job for himself), it began to champion conservative causes across the board. Seeing anti-Catholicism everywhere, its board of directors consisted of a gallery for the poster children of right-wing causes. The Supreme Court now boasts six Catholics, five of whom make up its conservative-bloc majority. Radical Protestant evangelicals would have trouble winning congressional approval for the court, but conservative Catholics became their acceptable stand-ins.

The Catholic Left, after a period of regrouping, returned to its first impulses, working primarily on social justice causes, forming Catholic Worker houses, doing "good works," mostly out of the public eye. Philip Berrigan and Elizabeth McAlister staffed Jonah House in Baltimore and by the start of the 1980s had reconstituted, not as the East Coast Conspiracy to Save Lives but as the Plowshares movement—beating swords into plowshares, and promoting pacifism. Championing pacifism has not been a popular political stance the last three decades, so much so that the *New York Times* published an article about the phenomenon on August 28, 2011, with this tongue-in-cheek headline: Give Pacifism a Chance.

From protesting the humble starting point of organized warfare—draft boards, the recruitment of soldiers as good ol' cannon fodder—the Berrigans jumped to the end of the process, protesting the technological height of the military-industrial complex, its most sacred and scary weapons, its nuclear stockpile. In some ways this could be seen as penance for their earlier work. If Gandhi could end the British Empire's colonial domination of a country, why couldn't the Berrigans end our reliance on nuclear weapons? They chose to go from the limited and symbolic to the purely symbolic and sorely limited. But some of the same draft board–raiding tactics were used in the various actions that the Plowshares group engaged in, beginning with the 1980 King of Prussia, Pennsylvania, GE Missile Re-entry Division episode (GE makes arms as well as medical machines). Daniel and Philip and the usual "six others" came a'calling with hammers to pound and blood to be poured. They couldn't abandon the ritual and symbols.

But there was limited reaction.

The "Catholic Left," more importantly, had been globalized in the 1980s, along with much else, and Central America had become a cynosure of Left political action. The New Catholic Left had moved south of our border. Four American nuns and a laywoman were killed in El Salvador in December 1980, where Archbishop Romero had been murdered earlier that year. "Liberation theology" had become the conservative world's bugaboo. The American Catholic Left did not come equipped with a coherent political economy analysis at the time it burned draft records, though in England during the same period, what was called there the Catholic "New Left," inspired by Vatican II, attempted to work out a humanistic socialist theory. What I called the New Catholic Left in 1972 placed the emphasis on the "New" Catholics, not the "New" New Left. A new American Left barely existed in 1972, except as an abstraction, a smattering of undercooked historic impulses. In 1983 Pope John Paul II, while touring Central America, told nuns and priests in El Salvador to cease their political work. So, back in the USA, the antinuclear actions of the Plowshares group, given their big target, seemed too easy to hit; the Plowshares group may have been David versus Goliath, but this Goliath did not fall when hit by a stone or hammer. Even the American government wanted to limit, eventually, the number of nuclear weapons worldwide. The fall of the Soviet Union in 1991 got the United States itself into the dismantle-nukes business. But the Plowshares group persisted, and after some fifty lesser actions went off with their hammers and blood in 1997 to the Bath, Maine, ironworks, where a nuclear weapon–equipped destroyer, *The Sullivans*, was moored before being commissioned. The Plowshares people (absent Daniel Berrigan) hammered missile hatches, and eventually blood got poured on guidance instruments of the destroyer. (In 2000 *The Sullivans* was the target of attack in Yemen by al-Qaeda, but the attacking boat itself was too full of explosives and sank before detonating.)

After the 1997 *The Sullivans* arrest, the case did make the news, though more for an exchange between the prosecution and the judge at the bail hearing. Denying the need for high bail or confinement for Philip Berrigan, Judge Joseph Field said, "Anyone of my generation [the judge was fifty] knows Philip Berrigan. He is a moral giant, the conscience of a generation."

But the trial judge, Gene Carter, thought differently, and after their convictions sentenced Berrigan and the others to two years in prison. But Berrigan's act remained inspirational. John Peck wrote a poem, "On the Sentencing of Philip Berrigan, Portland, Maine, 1997," which contains these lines:

> *A trained efficient killer*
> Berrigan's phrase for himself in the war,
> artillery then infantry. Then the collar
> on a Josephite teacher of black kids in D.C.,
> New Orleans, Baltimore—
> sentenced once more in old age
> for boarding a destroyer at the Bath Iron Works
> in Lenten daybreak.

Persistence pays off in this country and Philip Berrigan persisted till the end. When he died at age seventy-nine in 2002, I wrote the following about him in a column for the *Chicago Sun-Times* (December 17, 2002), which I reproduce in its entirety, so the context will be clear:

The bad old days have been much in the news recently: Trent Lott mourning the loss of segregation forever at Strom Thurmond's 100th birthday celebration, plus John Snow, President Bush's choice to replace Paul O'Neill as Treasury Secretary, reviving once again memories of the Ford administration, plus Snow's belated resignation from that other Southern institution of life as it used to be, The Augusta National Golf Club, with its female-free comforts. And, most sorrowfully, the death of Philip Berrigan, the anti-war former Catholic priest, who spent his life attempting to turn swords into ploughshares.

There is always a variety of pasts to choose from: Lott's and Snow's versions may still command the attention of the powerful, but Philip Berrigan's concerns were always aimed at benefitting the powerless.

Lott, the Senate Majority Leader to be, unless his paean to the Plantation era becomes his undoing, was doubtless infected by the occasion, Sen. Thurmond's centennial retirement party, which rendered the minds of many who should know better completely daffy. Thurmond has evolved over the years, from an out-and-out segregationist threat, to a dotty old freak show, though one dutifully reelected term after term by his state's all-too-accommodating electorate.

281

Treasury Secretary designate John Snow's chief virtue, allegedly, is that he will be a more effective PR spokesperson for the president's already-in-place economic policy (Cut taxes! Cut taxes!). Though, even the conservative Forbes magazine had already labeled Snow an inferior CEO of the heavily government-subsidized CSX railroad, giving Snow a grade of D for performance, noting he paid himself about $30 million, while overseeing a five-year annualized negative 1% percent return in his company. Doubtless, Forbes will find something nice to say about him now.

Philip Berrigan certainly could have been a CEO at a large company, if he had hankered for great wealth. He was tall, good looking, strong and uncompromisingly certain in his views. He became a CEO, of sorts, of the anti-Vietnam war protest movement. After the somewhat disastrous 1972 federal conspiracy trial of the Harrisburg 7, which the government lost, insofar as there was a hung jury on the major counts charging Father Berrigan and six others of conspiring to kidnap Henry Kissinger and blow up heating tunnels in Washington, D.C., but was won because the trial itself deflated the moral capital of Berrigan's group of Catholic Left anti-war protestors, leaving their movement somewhat splintered and dispirited.

Philip Berrigan was drummed out of the priesthood, married the former nun Elizabeth McAlister, and started Jonah House in Baltimore and carried on with a smaller group of like-minded individuals. Their focus of protest became nuclear weapons, since the Vietnam war, which they had fought effectively through many anti-war draft protests—enough so to have brought the wrath of J. Edgar Hoover down upon them—finally ended.

Today, an anti-war movement continues to exist, but, unfortunately, with no greater public profile than Sen. Lott's pro-segregationist movement—"if the rest of the country had followed our lead we wouldn't have had all these problems over all these years"—and the anti-women in golf clubs movement advocated by corporate chieftains of various kinds, who enjoy the good life at Augusta.

Strom Thurmond's remarkable longevity is further proof that the good die young. But, fortunately, some of the good still die at 79, like Philip Berrigan. Given the Catholic Church's current bad press, it is remarkable to think back to the late 60s and early 70s, when Berrigan and his Jesuit brother Dan, were seen by American bishops as "bad" priests, their dastardly anti-war deeds filling the pages of newspapers. Then they were the public face of the Catholic Church, not today's predatory pedophiles and weak-kneed bishops.

All those involved in the trial of the Harrisburg 7 have scattered, most drifting away from the issues and lives that brought them together. Philip Berrigan, though, stood the course, fought the good fight. Unlike the departure of Thurmond and Lott (if he forfeits his post), Berrigan's inspiring presence will be missed.

Unlike the liberation theologists of Central and South America, as well as those in Britain, the Catholic Left here at home might have had a hard time attaching itself to a coherent economic ideology, but the Catholic Right has had no trouble whatsoever. The Right goes with winners: the oligarchs, the plutocrats, and so forth. The Catholic Left, at its start, was pacifist and vaguely socialist—though more of the each according to his or her needs, each according to his or her abilities sort. They favored communes, not communism. But one reason such issues weren't much discussed (beyond the fact that our postindustrial society made a mockery of third world economic enthusiasms) was that priests and nuns were already living in a communal socialistic environment, used to if not a "vow of poverty" at least the idea of share and share alike, though the hierarchy of the church's share was a bit more grandiose than mere clergy enjoyed. Overall, it was a French sort of socialism.

But reverence for the rich returned with a vengeance during the Reagan years, stoked by the religious Right's fervor for all things conservative. The Catholic Left's heartfelt pursuit of peace had always been centered on stopping the mechanics of war. But at its heart it was never an economic movement, and during the height of the anti-war protests in 1970, following the killings at Kent State, it was most disheartening to see union workers attacking peace demonstrators in downtown Manhattan. And the history of Catholics' participation in the struggles of organized labor in the twentieth century shows their battles for workers' rights were simultaneously fused to a fierce anti-Communism, which created unresolvable tensions and contradictions. The rise of Reagan Democrats was also a phenomenon of class interests being betrayed, but was part and parcel of a group (the Reagan Dems) wanting to align itself with winners, rather than losers. In America there always has been a parallel outcropping of protests by populists; populism, too, has its own vacillating history, but in the main it has been more right-wing and racist and, not to put too fine a point on it, fascist.

Again, populist movements usually have a mistaken idea of where their economic interests are located. But if the variety of leftist groups during the antiwar period of the Vietnam War required an enemy, other than the government, to berate, they would choose "liberals" (new Democrat liberals of the Michael Harrington sort), a word uttered only with some derision. Even today the word is spurned, and *progressive* has been resurrected, though it still smacks of its radical roots. But reducing all these matters to two sides required only one standard: the distinction between those who acted and those who remained on the sidelines. Liberals, of whatever stripe, by and large remained spectators, and retreated to the sidelines and to, more or less, terminal superfluity.

Bernhard Schlink, the author of the international best seller *The Reader*, as well as a book of essays, *Guilt about the Past*, was asked recently here at Notre Dame if he had any analysis about the American protestors of the Vietnam War period, since he had such a full analysis of the German student movement of the same time. Schlink said he did not, which I thought strange, since he had talked about how the German student movement was influenced so much by the history of World War II, with the students not wanting to do what their parents had done, and how their reaction to the country's Nazi past had radicalized a generation. They wanted to do something, not sit back and do nothing. And some of that, of course, was full of violence, such as the Baader-Meinhof Group, which operated throughout the 1970s and into the '90s. But, it is often overlooked how that German World War II history affected the same generation of protestors in America. It was the Nazi atrocities, the films of concentration camps and victims, the Nuremberg trials, the convictions of war criminals, which influenced my cohort, as well as myself. Never again. But the difference was World War II itself accounted for the ambivalence shared by so many individuals in the antiwar movement. America had fought the "good war"; but in Vietnam it was fighting a bad war. Nonetheless, many protestors were lost in internal conflict, wanting their country to do right again, instead of wrong.

Leonard Boudin died in 1989. The Boudins provided for me a link to the pre–World War II Left, the internationalist Left, the Cold War Left, as well as trials that took place before I came along (such as the Boston Five, much less the Rosenbergs' trial). Through the Boudins, with whom I remained friends until the ends of their lives, I was exposed to a living history of America's radical past. They served as a family tree, linking many generations of left-wing movements. Jean Boudin's sister was married to I. F. Stone (1907–89), so he was often at their house, and I met, in no particular order, Judith Coplon, Alger Hiss, and other notorious figures of that period, as well as dozens of other less famous activists, both of the civil rights era and of the antiwar period. After the Harrisburg trial Leonard continued to represent Cuba, and then Iran, when the United States seized its assets during the Carter administration. "Fame is nice, but money is better," Leonard told me, during the time he was representing Iran. We shared a cynical humor with each other any chance we could, since we both knew we were less cynical than we seemed. Leonard had, nonetheless, grown quite fond of flying to and from Europe on the Concorde.

He represented Jimmy Hoffa in 1974 over Nixon's imposed ban on Hoffa's holding union office till 1980 (Nixon released Hoffa early from jail in exchange for the support of the Teamsters in Nixon's '72 re-election bid), and Hoffa fired Leonard when the suit's verdict went against him. Hoffa didn't understand—and Leonard couldn't get it through his thick skull—that Leonard expected to lose the first round but eventually to win the case on appeal. But Hoffa was distraught at not winning. And of course Hoffa doubtless knew it was a more important life-or-death issue than Leonard had considered, one that needed to be resolved quickly; for Hoffa disappeared forever in 1975, shortly after losing in federal district court in Washington, D.C.

Ramsey Clark, who had served as attorney general in the Johnson administration, underwent a remarkable metamorphosis (unlike Boudin, who had no such conversion), from orchestrating the Boston Five conspiracy case, full of East Coast luminaries, such as Benjamin Spock (Leonard's client) and William Sloane Coffin, Jr., and notable others, to serving as counsel for the Harrisburg Seven. Clark has argued (about his fashioning the Boston Five case of 1968) that he wanted to charge famous people who could afford the prosecution in order to air the issues around the draft. Be that as it may, Clark has since gone on to defend or be associated with less admirable defendants, including, but not limited to, Radovan Karadzic, the Bosnian Serb war criminal; and Slobodan Milosevic; Sheikh Omar Abdel Rahman; and Moammar Qaddafi. Back in the States, Clark also helped the Branch Davidians file for damages against the government, for, as Clark has called it, "the greatest failure of law enforcement in the domestic history of the U.S."

Like Leonard, Clark turned into an internationalist practitioner, even offering assistance to Saddam Hussein when he was on trial in Iraq. Having seen the rule of law abused during the Johnson administration, Clark didn't hesitate to shine a light on any place it is being abused again. Bill Moyers, also of the Johnson administration, has had a similar change of allegiance since his service as press secretary for LBJ. But Ramsey Clark's transformation has been more extreme, though it wasn't anything like the guilt-racked transformation undergone by the former secretary of defense during the Vietnam War, Robert McNamara (1916–2009).

The only defendant I stayed in contact with after the trial was Eqbal Ahmad, and that had more to do, I suppose, with the academic circles we both traveled in: Eqbal taught at Hampshire College in the early 1980s when I was teaching at Mount Holyoke College, a few miles away. Shortly after the trial, Eqbal had an idea for the next book I might do. He suggested I investigate the phenomenon of migrant Muslim labor going on throughout Europe and what the consequences of that might be for all the countries involved. He suggested this in 1973. Obviously, Eqbal was prescient. In one of the last essays he wrote before he died in 1999, titled "A Jihad against Time," he wrote, "Complexity and pluralism threaten most—hopefully not all—contemporary Islamists, because they seek an Islamic order reduced to a penal code, stripped of its humanism, aesthetics, intellectual quests, and spiritual devotion. . . . Neither Muslims nor Jews nor Hindus are unique in this respect. All variants of contemporary 'fundamentalism' reduce complex religious systems and civilisations to one or another version of modern fascism. They are concerned with power, not with the soul, with the mobilisation of people for political purposes rather than with sharing or alleviating their sufferings and aspirations." He had remained prescient. After he died I spent time correcting a variety of obituaries and tributes, where the writers invariably claimed the Harrisburg defendants had been "acquitted." No acquittals had occurred in Harrisburg.

Of the handful of "others" of the Harrisburg Seven, Tony Scoblick and Mary Cain Scoblick have stayed out of the public eye the most; they, seemingly, had been the most disaffected by the trial, not thinking well of Philip's various pronouncements and what they saw as his high-handedness and hypocrisy on the subject of priests marrying nuns. The Scoblicks eventually divorced. The Reverend Joe Wenderoth, though, has remained active. In 2008 he took part in a panel at St. Joseph Parish in Cockeysville, Maryland, speaking on the sacrament of reconciliation. Perhaps the Scoblicks should have attended. Neil McLaughlin, by now retired, was reported, by Charles Meconis, to be running an antique store in Maryland. In fact it was a successful bookstore.

Elizabeth McAlister and Jonah House still carry on lives of protest in Baltimore, protests that now include her and Philip Berrigan's daughter. Information about their actions can be found at the Jonah House website: www.jonahhouse.org. Seeing photos of Elizabeth and Philip Berrigan's daughter, Frida (named after Philip's mother), one is struck by how much she looks like her father.

The other major book on the trial, *The FBI and the Berrigans*, was co-written by Jack Nelson (1929–2009) and Ronald J. Ostrow. Jack was the former head of the Washington bureau of the *Los Angeles Times*. Jack covered the trial (I don't think I ever laid eyes on Ostrow) and was the consummate traditional-style reporter, the more or less mythical tradition of the *Dragnet* sort: Just the facts, ma'am. Jack was born in Alabama and had a distinguished career covering the FBI and the civil rights movement. Our two books were often reviewed together.

My book was never a favorite of the New Catholic Left itself or of the Berrigan group. Nor did I expect it to be. Philip Berrigan, I was told, had circulated a long, seven-page letter about my book (written while he was still in prison—he was released right before Christmas 1972), though I was never able to come upon a copy. And as the years went on, when the Harrisburg trial was mentioned in histories, such as *Disarmed and Dangerous: The Radical Lives and Times of Daniel and Philip Berrigan* (1997) and *Harder Than War: Catholic Peacemaking in Twentieth-Century America*

(1992), when my book is referred to it is usually dismissed as less "factual," whereas Jack's book is "the most thorough account of the Harrisburg trial." Nelson and Ostrow's book may be the most thorough account of the events previous to the trial (they wrote about what they knew, the FBI), but it certainly isn't the most thorough account of the trial itself. The original edition of my book had no index, which, doubtless, altered the facts equation. I had not wanted it weighed down with what I thought then to be scholarly apparatus. But I discovered that historians don't usually consult modern books without indexes, since that would require them to read the whole thing.

The animus toward my book of authors sympathetic to the Berrigans always strikes me as strange, since their analyses of the trial (all coming years later) consistently echo my own. In *Disarmed and Dangerous*, Jim Forest, a Catholic Left activist, is described as abandoning a publisher's contract for a book on the trial, because of his being "estranged" from the Berrigans. After my book came out, however, Forest told me that he abandoned his own book because mine had made the one he intended to write superfluous. But my position vis-à-vis activists was always clear to me. Shortly after the book appeared I was with some contemporaries who were connected to the case at McSorley's, the off-Bowery saloon. One young man, my age, asked me plaintively, How could I have exposed the defendants as I had, since they had befriended me? We had even gone sledding together on a snowy hill in Harrisburg. Long before Janet Malcolm—who had become famous because of her remarks about backstabbing journalists in her 1990 book, *The Journalist and the Murderer* (I had written my version of them in my third novel, *Criminal Tendencies*, in 1987)—I understood how journalists were guilty of "selling out" their subjects, as Joan Didion wrote in 1968. So, in response to my acquaintance's complaint (he was in law school at the time), I just reminded him of my line in the book about dancing on their graves. And though I liked them, I never thought the defendants were my friends.

I wasn't invited, but I attended the celebration of the Berrigan/McAlister earlier wedding (which supposedly happened in 1969, the self-marriage, officiated by Philip himself) held in Montclair, New Jersey, in June 1973. Diane Schulder had been invited and asked me to come along. Paul O'Dwyer, in attendance, was also unhappy with me, since I had alluded to some facts about his brother, William O'Dwyer (1890–1964), the former mayor of New York City, in my book. Paul was the youngest of eleven children; he died in 1998, at age ninety. Irish Americans often take offense at the truth, if it happens to be uncomplimentary. So, I lost my chance to be part of the Irish American mafia in NYC back then, while I was still doing manual labor in the South Bronx. The most memorable thing about the party, except for the good weather, was that a couple of male members of the McAlister/Berrigan extended family got in a fistfight in the backyard during it. Daniel Berrigan, SJ, has been threatening to die the last twenty years, but amazingly he still is alive at this writing. He published books in 2007, 2008, and 2009, and had been working with hospice patients for a decade or more. His 2008 book is called *The Kings and Their Gods: The Pathology of Power*.

Of the small group of writers I was in the "pool" with, all have continued their trade in admirable fashion, with, of course, the unfortunate exception of Paul Cowan, who died of leukemia at the age of forty-eight in 1988. Garry Wills has written at least a couple dozen books (including a novel!) since 1972; Francine du Plessix Gray has turned her pen toward fiction (*Lovers & Tyrants*), memoir (*Them*), and biographies of famous women. Ed Zuckerman went into writing and producing for television. His script was used in the first episode of *Law & Order* ever aired, and he wrote for that show on and off for its entire existence. One of the best episodes of *L&O* was about an underground radical being caught late in life (ripped from the headlines!), notable for the cops' lines joking about J. Edgar Hoover wearing a feathered boa. When it first aired, Hoover was of course long dead, but what he had always feared had finally come true. Hoover had controlled and manipulated the image of the FBI and himself in television and radio, and a couple of decades later, there he was, being treated as a figure of fun.

Unfortunately, that other cause of the trial of the Harrisburg Seven, Henry Kissinger, is not being treated as a figure of fun. His mischief continues to be legion. From his shop, Kissinger and Associates, came L. Paul Bremer, its former managing director, who had been an assistant to Kissinger from 1972 to 1976, the years the Vietnam War was "winding down." From K and A he moved to the Coalition Provisional Authority in Iraq, where he became the U.S. administrator and managed to bungle everything there was to bungle, besides setting in motion most of the privatized corruption and ethnic cleansing that cropped up during the first few years after George W. Bush's invasion. Most of Hoover's mistakes were buried back in 1972 when he died, but Kissinger's are ongoing. Publicizing his most recent book, *On China*, Kissinger told *Time* (June 6, 2011), "It may turn out that Iraq will be the only country in the region with a representative government. But would I have recommended fighting for 10 years in order to achieve this? I would have said no." Yet another of Kissinger's self-aggrandizing pronouncements, while simultaneously claiming blamelessness.

The FBI continues to be busy, conducting its business with the same level of competence it displayed during the Harrisburg case; and since 9/11 and the creation of Homeland Security, the country and its citizens are hardly without daily internal scrutiny. The Office of the Inspector General, in September 2010, published a lengthy document, *A Review of the FBI's Investigations of Certain Domestic Advocacy Groups* (I love that new coinage, "domestic advocacy groups"; the review itself is redacted in parts), defending the bureau's aggressive tactics. The groups in question were: The Thomas Merton Center of Pittsburgh, Pennsylvania; People for the Ethical Treatment of Animals (PETA); Greenpeace USA; the Catholic Worker; Glen Mill (an individual); and the Religious Society of Friends (the "Quakers"). Sound familiar? So, don't worry, the FBI, if no one else, is keeping track of the remnants of the religious and do-good Left. A footnote in the 191-page report tells us that "PETA was the only one of the groups we reviewed that the FBI had investigated during our review period as a terrorism enterprise."

The FBI still behaves in its traditional way, especially with potential protest groups, exploiting informers and agents provocateurs. One such case involved antiwar protestors at the 2008 Republican National Convention in Minneapolis–St. Paul, two of whom (Bradley Crowder and David McKay) eventually pleaded guilty to lesser offences and served time. Their case received little national attention and what notice they did get was hostile to them. There was no defense committee, crowds supporting their actions, and so forth. One oddity, though, was that they had documentary filmmakers contemporaneously on the scene filming and interviewing them as their case wound down to a conclusion. The "documentary" aired on PBS's *POV* series on September 6, 2011, titled "Better This World." Precious little journalism infiltrates this particular genre of filmmaking; for the viewer, it's a kind of make-up-your-own-mind experience. The FBI had an unstable volunteer informer (Brandon Darby) who continually provoked the two young men to consider acts of violence, which then never actually occurred. But they did make old-fashioned Molotov cocktails (the limit of their weapons sophistication), the offense that resulted in their convictions. But their informer was reminiscent of, and even more egregious than, Boyd Douglas in creating the case, but, from the amounts of money mentioned, he appeared to have been paid less than Boyd was paid back in 1972. *Plus ça change, plus c'est la même chose.*

And Boyd Douglas, the other preeminent cause of the trial? Taken up in the federal witness protection program, he is lost to history, but not to some records somewhere. I used to wonder if Boyd would ever pop up again in my life, but like most Americans he may never have read my book and felt no need. In any case, Boyd Douglas has now, too, reached geezer status, and he is no doubt collecting Medicare and Social Security benefits.

And the Catholic Church? John Paul II let his native anti-Communism run roughshod over liberation theology and progressive clergy, and the current pope, Benedict XVI, has in his biography the unfortunate facts of once having been a member of the Hitler Youth, a conscript in the German army, and an inmate of a POW camp; he has been a later-in-life supporter of the most right-wing aspects of the Catholic Church, which has resulted in the gentle handling of such archconservative organizations as the Legion of Christ and Opus Dei, as well as the defective oversight of the molestation crisis of the John Paul II era.

The solace one usually attempts to draw from the deeds of good men and women that largely go unrewarded at the time is that, without their "brave and foolish" acts (to quote myself), the world would be a worse place today if they hadn't done what they did. It's difficult, though, to think the world has turned out better today because of the New Catholic Left, though they did certainly affect the fortunes of the past.

We are engaged in a number of wars, fought by 1 percent of our countrymen, the result of the "volunteer" army; if one is cynical enough, that

291

can be seen as the triumph of all that youthful protesting. America's young can choose not to participate in the killing, if they wish. And what has changed from the Vietnam era, because of the volunteer military, is the average age of the dead; we are no longer killing teenagers but young men and women in their early twenties who have lived a bit of life, had jobs and marriages, and so forth. And beyond that fact, we now wage preemptive wars, though the Vietnam War was largely that too, though never advertised as such.

And where is the Catholic Left? Nowhere, it seems, except for the remnants of the original groups that are now slowly dying off. Protest went global in the decades following the trial: civil rights turned into human rights and went back to basics, health, survival, the most basic freedoms. NGOs have replaced the SDS, or the SLA, in the protest alphabet wars. There are now protest groups of the Green, eco sort, marked by sporadic anarchistic blowups around G-20 meetings. Yet the religious Right is everywhere, throughout the world. We now have a Department of Homeland Security (the Bush family and administration rekindling its alliances with its German past and its love of homeland; see Kevin Phillips's *American Dynasty*), and the public has gone along with the disregard of a number of our civil rights, as well as condoning torture. America's prisons are so full that courts are ordering the release of more prisoners than protest groups ever managed to set free. Secularism wanes and religion waxes everywhere. Religious conflicts and political conflicts are now so intertwined throughout the globe it is fruitless to try to disentangle them. Abroad the major religions fight each other for survival, and back home, sectarian splinter groups, evangelicals, charismatics, both Protestant and Catholic, vie for control over how people live, what laws they will follow. Meanwhile, as our ninth president, William H. Harrison, said, while a candidate, in 1840, "I believe and I say it is a true Democratic feeling, that all the measures of the government are directed to the purpose of making the rich richer and poor poorer." One depressing fact: forty years ago, when the Harrisburg trial concluded, marked the peak of the rise of male earnings. Then the slide began, and a widening gap opened up between the rich and poor, resulting in the present concentration of so much wealth at the very top. President Harrison's characterization of government has never been more true.

When I concluded the Harrisburg book by crying out, "O America," I never thought the country would be worse forty years hence. But it is hard to conclude otherwise. The trial was thrust upon its defendants in 1972. It was nothing they wanted. Perhaps it is just their fate that they were among the last, best, hopeful protestors, wanting only for the country to do right. They were living through an actual golden age of protest. Let me repeat: it was a golden age of protest. Whereas, protests in the decades that followed were clothed mainly in self-interest and megalomania springing from a variety of twisted motives: for notoriety, for economic advancement, for exhibiting private pathologies. And at the most extreme, from Timothy McVeigh ripping the face off the Murrah Federal Building, to the men who brought down the Twin Towers, they no longer came in relative peace to protest wrongs; they came with fire and brimstone to punish.

October 2011

Selected Bibliography

Below are books and articles I have found useful and informative, while writing the afterword. For matters concerning the Catholic Left a number of cited books have bibliographies, and one such substantial bibliography, up to 1997, can be found in *Disarmed and Dangerous*. Luckily for the baby boom generation, just as our memories have faded, Google has come on the scene to refresh them, and I have made use of a number of the Internet's search systems. Caveat emptor!

Books

Alpert, Jane. *Growing Up Underground*. New York: William Morrow, 1981.

Ayers, Bill. *Fugitive Days: Memoirs of an Antiwar Activist*. Boston: Beacon Press, 2009.

Baker, Kimball. *"Go to the Worker": America's Labor Apostles*. Milwaukee: Marquette University Press, 2010.

Baker, Peter. *The Breach: Inside the Impeachment and Trial of William Jefferson Clinton*. New York: Scribner, 2000.

Bates, Tom. *Rads: The 1970 Bombing of the Army Math Research Center at the University of Wisconsin and Its Aftermath*. New York: HarperCollins, 1992.

Berger, Dan. *Outlaws of America: The Weather Underground and the Politics of Solidarity*. Oakland, CA: AK Press, 2006.

Berrigan, Daniel. *The Kings and Their Gods: The Pathology of Power*. Grand Rapids, MI: Eerdmans, 2008

Berrigan, Philip, with Fred A. Wilcox. *Fighting the Lamb's War: Skirmishes with the American Empire: The Autobiography of Philip Berrigan*. Monroe, ME: Common Courage Press, 1996.

Branch, Taylor. *Pillar of Fire: America in the King Years 1963–65*. New York: Simon & Schuster, 1998.

Braudy, Susan. *Family Circle: The Boudins and the Aristocracy of the Left.* New York: Knopf, 2003.

Caute, David. *The Year of the Barricades: A Journey through 1968.* New York: Harper & Row, 1988.

Cowan, Paul, and Nick Egleson, and Nat Hentoff, with Barbara Herbert and Robert Wall. *State Secrets: Police Surveillance in America.* New York: Holt, Rinehart and Winston, 1974.

Cowie, Jefferson. *Stayin' Alive: The 1970s and the Last Days of the Working Class.* New York: New Press, 2010.

Frankfort, Ellen. *Kathy Boudin and the Dance of Death.* New York: Stein and Day, 1983.

Garfinkle, Adam. *Telltale Hearts: The Origins and Impact of the Vietnam Antiwar Movement.* New York: St. Martin's Press, 1995.

Gettleman, Marvin E., Jane Franklin, Marilyn Young, and H. Bruce Franklin, eds. *Vietnam and America: A Documented History.* New York: Grove Press, 1985.

Gray, Francine du Plessix. *Adam & Eve and the City: Selected Nonfiction.* New York: Simon & Schuster, 1987.

Guttenplan, D. D. *American Radical: The Life and Times of I. F. Stone.* New York: Farrar, Straus and Giroux, 2009.

Harris, David. *Dreams Die Hard.* New York: St. Martin's/Marek, 1982.

Harrington, Michael. *Socialism.* New York: Saturday Review Press, 1972.

Hedges, Chris. *Death of the Liberal Class.* New York: Nation Books, 2010.

Karnow, Stanley. *Vietnam: A History.* New York: Viking, 1993.

Kissinger, Henry. *Years of Renewal.* New York: Simon & Schuster, 1999.

Lukas, J. Anthony. *Nightmare: The Underside of the Nixon Years.* New York: Viking, 1976.

McNeal, Patricia. *Harder Than War: Catholic Peacemaking in Twentieth-Century America.* New Brunswick, NJ: Rutgers University Press, 1992.

Meconis, Charles. *With Clumsy Grace: The American Catholic Left 1961–1975.* New York: Seabury, 1979.

Michel, Lou, and Dan Herbeck. *American Terrorist: Timothy McVeigh & the Oklahoma City Bombing.* New York: ReganBooks, 2001.

Miller, James. *"Democracy Is in the Streets": From Port Huron to the Siege of Chicago.* New York: Simon & Schuster, 1987.

Morris, Charles R. *A Time of Passion: America 1960–1980.* New York: Harper & Row, 1984.

Nelson, Jack, and Ronald J. Ostrow. *The FBI and the Berrigans: The Making of a Conspiracy.* New York: Coward, McCann & Geoghegan, 1972.

Newman, Michael. *Socialism*. New York: Sterling, 2005.

O'Rourke, William. *Signs of the Literary Times: Essays, Reviews, Profiles 1970–1992*. Albany, NY: State University of New York Press, 1993.

Phillips, Kevin. *American Dynasty: Aristocracy, Fortune, and the Politics of Deceit in the House of Bush*. New York: Viking, 2004.

Polner, Murray, and Jim O'Grady. *Disarmed and Dangerous: The Radical Lives and Times of Daniel and Philip Berrigan*. New York: Basic Books, 1997.

Ricks, Thomas E. *Fiasco: The American Military Adventure in Iraq*. New York: Penguin Press, 2006.

Rumsfeld, Donald. *Known and Unknown: A Memoir*. New York: Sentinel, 2011.

Sandbrook, Dominic. *Mad as Hell: The Crisis of the 1970s and the Rise of the Populist Right*. New York: Knopf, 2011.

Schlink, Bernhard. *Guilt about the Past*. Toronto, ON: Anansi Press, 2009.

Sloane, Arthur A. *Hoffa*. Cambridge, MA: MIT Press, 1991.

Stern, Kenneth S. *A Force upon the Plain: The American Militia Movement and the Politics of Hate*. New York: Simon & Schuster, 1996.

Wills, Garry. *Outside Looking In: Adventures of an Observer*. New York: Viking, 2010.

Wittner, Lawrence S. *Rebels against War: The American Peace Movement, 1933–1983*. Philadelphia: Temple University Press, 1984.

Wright, Lawrence. *In the New World: Growing Up with America from the Sixties to the Eighties*. New York: Vintage Books, 1989.

Articles and Other Media

Ahmad, Eqbal. "A Jihad against Time." *Al-Ahram Weekly*, no. 415, February 4–10, 1999, 1–2.

Berry, Jason. "The Shame of John Paul II: How the Sex Abuse Scandal Stained His Papacy." *The Nation* 292, no. 20, May 16, 2011, 11–15.

Galloway, Katie, and Kelly Duane de la Vega. "Better This World." Loteria Films. POV. Corporation for Public Broadcasting. September 6, 2011.

Giacchino, Anthony. "The Camden 28." ECC Media, LLC. POV. Corporation for Public Broadcasting. September 11, 2007

Luscombe, Belinda. "10 Questions." *Time*, June 6, 2011, 64.

Peck, John. "On the Sentencing of Philip Berrigan, Portland, Maine, 1997." *Notre Dame Review* 33 (forthcoming).

Radin, Charles A. "Warriors for Peace." *Boston Globe Magazine*, July 27, 1997, 12–26.

Saunders, Josh. "Ramsey Clark's Prosecution Complex." *Legal Affairs* (November/December 2003): 1–7.

Thomas, Louisa. "Give Pacifism a Chance." *New York Times*, August 28, 2011, 7.

U.S. Department of Justice. *A Review of the FBI's Investigations of Certain Advocacy Groups.* Oversight and Review Division, Office of the Inspector General. September 2010.

Annotated Errata

1.   p. 2.   "rough" should be "rouge". Doubtless, the brick was rough, but I meant the color.

2.   p. 5.   The bailiff recited "Oyez, oyez, oyez." It only sounded like "Oh yea."

3.   p. 30.   "RAND study" should be "Department of Defense study". Ellsberg procured the study from RAND, which employed people involved in its creation.

4.   p. 32.   GSA is the General Services Administration, not the Government Services Administration, although, of course, it is run by the government.

5.   p. 49.   "exericse" should be "exercise"

6.   p. 50.   "Clergy and Laymen" should be "Clergy and Laity"

7.   p. 54.   "*tabularasa*" should be "*tabula rasa*"

8.   p. 82.   "Boyd Douglas" should be preceded by quotation marks, for the start of a quote.

9.   p. 109.   "Cattone" should be "Cottone"

10. p. 119.   "Origeons" should be "Origens" (of Origen of Alexandria fame)

11. p. 129.   "in Time magazine" should be "in a news magazine"; the magazine wasn't identified.

12. p. 150.   "Augsburn" should be "Augsburg"

13. p. 150.   "1949" should be "1940". The start of prosecutions of Communist Party USA members under the Smith Act of 1940 was in 1949.

14. p. 156.   "three black girls"; it was four girls (Addie Mae Collins, Denise McNair, Carole Robertson, and Cynthia Wesley) who were killed in

the 1963 16th St. Baptist Church bombing in Birmingham, Alabama; there was a large funeral held for three of them, which caused my confusion.

15. p. 162. "Camel cigarettes" should be "True cigarettes". Lynch smoked True during the trial, though I had imagined him as a younger man smoking Camels.

16. p. 182. "much to-do" should be "much ado"

17. p. 188. "Loose talk sinks ships" should be "Loose lips sink ships"

18. p. 189. "half jokingly" should be "½ jokingly". I am quoting a letter, and that's how it was written.

19. p. 191. "and so-called" should be "and the so-called"

20. p. 195. In "interdiction, etc.," the closing quotation marks should follow "interdiction" rather than "etc."

21. p. 212. "tanked up" should be "tranqed up". In 1972, use of sedatives or mood-altering drugs had not been common. Ellsberg was using a new piece of slang.

22. p. 220. "*Inquirer*" should be "*Bulletin*"

23. p. 226. "In the case" should be preceded by quotation marks, for the start of a quote.

24. p. 239. "(as these defendants had)" should be "[as these defendants had]". The interjection was mine, not Connelly's.

25. p. 239. "stopping" should be "stooping"

26. p. 264. "six-foot" should be "ten-foot"

Index

319

WILLIAM O'ROURKE
is professor of English at the University of Notre Dame and the
founding director of the graduate creative writing program. He is the
author of four novels and five works of nonfiction, and the editor of
two anthologies. His most recent books include *Notre Dame Review:
The First Ten Years*, coedited with John Matthias (2009), and
On Having a Heart Attack: A Medical Memoir (2006), both published
by the University of Notre Dame Press. A new book, *Confessions of a
Guilty Freelancer*, is forthcoming.

Lightning Source UK Ltd.
Milton Keynes UK
UKHW011224040922
408256UK00002B/54